# SCHOOL GOVERNMENT:

## A PRACTICAL TREATISE,

PRESENTING A THOROUGH DISCUSSION OF ITS FACTS PRINCIPLES, AND THEIR APPLICATIONS;

WITH

CRITIQUES

UPON CURRENT THEORIES OF PUNISHMENT, AND SCHEMES OF ADMINISTRATION.



FOR THE

USE OF NORMAL SCHOOLS, PRACTICAL TEACHERS, AND PARENTS.

BY FREDERICK S. JEWELL, A.M.

The government of the child should be kingly.—ARISTOTLE.

A. S. BARNES & COMPANY,
NEW YORK AND CHICAGO.
1875.

# PREFACE.

The work here presented to the public was undertaken under the deep conviction that a thorough and practical examination of the field of thought involved, was pressingly demanded by the wants of teachers and the interests of our public schools.

It has, therefore, been expressly prepared with a view to meet that particular demand, and, hence, has taken upon itself some features which otherwise the writer would have chosen to avoid, as unfavorable to logical exactness in order and execution.

Thus, knowing the difficulties in the way of mastering an extended discussion, likely to be encountered by the great body of public school teachers, and growing inevitably out of the close employment of their time, the wide diversion of their attention, the exhausting nature of their duties, and their lack of philosophical familiarity with the topics suggested, the following general method has been adopted as both just and necessary.

The introductory topics have been considered more in detail than might otherwise have been proper; a comparatively discursive method in discussion has been, though somewhat reluctantly, adopted; objections have been particularly considered, and, as naturally suggested, instead of being left to the necessary inferences of individual reflection; at the risk of some criticism, principles have been repeated in different connections, that their relations may always be immediately apparent, and that their nature may be more clearly apprehended in the light of the relations thus evinced; and studied excellence in style has been steadily made to give place to a diction chiefly intent on simplicity, earnestness, and force.

It is hoped that the practical advantages sought to be secured for the less favored class of readers, by the pursuit of this method, will so far approve it to the good sense of those endowed with higher learning and leisure, as rather to add to their interest in the work, instead of detracting from it. Let us sow, that the many may reap rather than the few.

Prosecuted under the pressure of peculiar perplexities, and discussing a subject of peculiar difficulties, it is not for one moment fancied that the work is without its defects. Doubtless, here and there, the individual teacher will look for a minute elucidation of some specific difficulty,—some question of casuistry, case of discipline, or particular method,—with reference to which his own mind has been exercised, but which has not here been fully discussed. It would not be strange if the cottager should look in vain in the artist's best transfiguration in color of the overshadowing Alp, for the distinct delineation of the particular cleft or crag which, as hovering around, or hanging over his own dwelling place, seems to him the object of especial mark.

It will, however, occur to such teachers, upon proper reflection, that it must be impossible within the brief practical compass to which this work has, for obvious reasons, been restricted, to discuss in detail an entire field so mazy and manifold in its particulars, as must be that of school government. The only consistent effort must be that of establishing broad principles, and indicating clear lines of inference and application, leaving still something to be done by the teacher in his own thought and experiment.

It is proper to remark here, that while the work has been, as treating of School Government, more especially prepared for the teacher, it is one which cannot but be highly suggestive and helpful to the parent. The attention of the latter class is earnestly called, therefore, to its claims upon their interest and examination.

Such as the work is, it is now offered to the public, in the belief that it is calculated to render important service to those for whose benefit, and in sympathy with whose labors, perplexities, and trials, it has been written.

State Normal School, Albany, February 22, 1866.

# CONTENTS.

## CHAPTER I.



## CHAPTER II.



## CHAPTER III.



## CHAPTER IV.



## CHAPTER V.



## CHAPTER VI.

## CHAPTER VII.



## CHAPTER VIII.



## CHAPTER IX.



## CHAPTER X.



## CHAPTER XI.



## CHAPTER XII.



## CHAPTER XIII.

# SCHOOL GOVERNMENT.

## CHAPTER I.

### INTRODUCTION.

General definition of School Government—Importance generally granted—Results of its absence—Real necessity of government—General maxim—Improvement to have been expected—Expectation not realized—*Proofs of depression and neglect of government*—Rude forms of punishment—Teaching exclusively taught—Learning made the test of qualification in teachers—Should be examined in government—Employment of young teachers—High culture and experience needed for governing—Teachers absorbed in the work of instruction—*Causes of this neglect and depression of School Government*—Incidental obstacles in the way of governing—False theory of education—Theory diverts attention from government—The moral element suppressed—*Evidences of the fallacy of the theory*—Experience shows it—Shown from the laws of the intellect—Injurious results of overlooking these laws—Shown from the order of the human faculties—*Causes of this neglect of the moral nature*—Learning more easily appreciated than moral culture—Prejudices against moral instruction in schools—Disparting of the intellectual and moral nature in science—Ignoring of the religious element in the soul—Absurdity of this neglect of the moral nature—School Government more closely defined—Definition condensed.

School Government, as that branch of practical art to which the attention is to be given throughout this work, may be defined in general terms, as that just ordering of the affairs of the school, which is necessary to the successful attainment of its proper ends. Of its general importance in some reasonable and effective form, we apprehend few persons of intelligence or experience entertain any doubt. Even those, who are most disposed to take exceptions to its specific applications as pressing upon their children or wards, are quite ready to cry out against its marked absence from the school. Indeed, it needs no great sharpness of observation to reveal to any one, disposed to know the truth, the fact that the lack of it can only be productive of serious evils, such as the failure of the pupils to make satisfactory progress, the destruction of the teacher's influence, and the prevalence of disorder and ill feeling throughout the school. Accepting, then, even the current notion as to the nature of education and the functions of the school, ill calculated as that notion is to favor or secure right views of the importance of school government, it will be seen that that government is more than merely important to the succcessful completion of the daily round of instruction, and to the maintenance of general harmony throughout the little commonwealth; it is a thorough necessity. Indeed, in the school, as elsewhere, the general maxim is, "Order is heaven's first law;" to which may not inconsistently be added this other, "government is the soul of order."

From the general fact of its evident importance, it would naturally be supposed that government in the schools would be marked by a high order of excellence. Whatever might have formerly been its character, with our other advances in educational matters, improvement in school government was, as a matter of course, to be counted upon. As the old and somewhat nebulous luminaries, Murray and Morse, Pike and Daboll, descending through a right parabolic curve, sank at length "slowly and all reluctantly," below the horizon; as other and better lights began to brighten in the East, and men were seen casting about for better teachers and more enlightened methods of instruction, it was to be expected that the system of control and discipline existing in the schools, would come up for a corresponding interest and attention.

This expectation cannot, however, be said to have been realized. True, school government may not be found remaining in the exact chaos which prevailed in that earlier period, when the school entire was "without form and void, and darkness was upon the face of the deep." Yet it is quite certain that this important part of the scholastic creation has not kept pace with other things. It has not with equal interest and endeavor been evoked from the waste and darkness, and been reduced to true consistency and order. It has been rather neglected and left to its own chance of uncared-for growth and development. Hence, it still remains in a sadly depressed condition.

Of this neglected and depressed condition, there are various indications which deserve to be noticed on account of their practical bearing upon its correction. As the first, we notice the fact that the tide of progress has not yet swept away the older, ruder, and simply violent forms of government, which, while not altogether false in principle, were yet most rude and base in their application. The pitiless rod, the glancing ferule, the burdensome billet of wood, the stooping posture, and others of the banging and badgering devices of the former age, while passed somewhat into decrepitude and disesteem, are, neither in their more flagitious instances extinct, nor in their really legitimate instrumentalities, reformed and Christianized.

Again, even where these evil forms of government have gone into disuse, where better methods of instruction have sprung up, and where, consequently, especial means are employed for the training of teachers, it is quite commonly the case that the absorbing topic is *teaching*. We see no good reason why an educational school should not give the subject of *government* an important place in its curriculum; no reason why it should not as distinctly have a professor of the "Theory and Practice of Governing," as well as of the "Theory and Practice of Teaching;" at least, no good reason why the two should not be distinctly and equitably conjoined in one department, the "Department of School Government and Instruction." And yet, so far as we know, such an organization is not to be found in our normal schools, either in form or substance. In quite the larger portion, school government is taught inferentially, and even that as an incidental matter.

In the third place, were there nothing else to show that the proper government of the school elicits little if any attention on the part of the public, the fact that teachers are commonly examined and approved upon the basis of mere scholarship, might suffice. That which, in so important a preliminary as the testing of the teacher's qualifications, is hardly inquired after, must hold no very high place in the public estimation. Certainly, if school government were looked upon as of the first moment, we should find school officers suspending their wise explorations in the direction of geography, grammar, and arithmetic, in order to ascertain whether the prospective teachers are possessed of correct and adequate views of the nature and importance of school government. After they have been learnedly led through the mazy toils of describing the method of finding the least common denominator; of designating the barbarous boundaries of sundry ill-begotten chiefdoms in Asia; and of unfolding Brown's singularly philosophical and exhaustive mode of parsing "tweedledum and tweedledee," would it not be the next most natural thing to submit for their solution questions like the following: "What are the ends to be sought in school government? By what means are those ends to be secured? What are the respective relations of force, authority, and influence, in the government of the young? What facts should be taken into account in the administering of discipline? How is the correctness of a penalty to be determined? What course should be pursued with extreme or seemingly incorrigible offenders?" But no such questions are asked; and the conclusion already suggested is inevitable.

Another proof of the neglected and depressed condition of school government is, we think, afforded by the fact that young and inexperienced teachers find so ready and so general employment. The wise and effective government of the school is really a delicate and difficult work. For, consider how few are the accessible guides to the successful accomplishment of that work; how subtle and often profound are the principles embraced in its philosophy; how varied and perplexing must be its practical adjustment; how manifold the difficulties to be encountered; and how sad may be the results of failure to govern wisely and well.

Is this, then, a work proper to be undertaken by any other than a person of broad culture, of thorough self-discipline, of established character, and of mature experience? Can any other than such a teacher expect to succeed in it? What then must be the effect of entrusting it so commonly to young and inexperienced teachers; of entrusting it to those who, to the very possible, as very common want of native fitness, superadd the lack of any acquired fitness for the work of governing? This is the evil of which old Thomas Fuller complains, when he charges it as one of the causes of the defective performance of the duties of the schoolmaster, that "young scholars make this calling their refuge; yea, perchance, before they have taken any degree in the university, commence schoolmasters in the country, as if nothing else were required to set up in the profession but only a rod and a ferule." In such hands, what ex cellence can school government hope to attain; how can it, in fact, escape being well nigh destroyed? Why then place it in such hands? There can be but one answer to the question. It is because the importance of the government is not realized; the public concern themselves little about its fortunes; and, hence, the practical conclusion is, it may be entrusted to almost anybody.

As a final indication of this neglected condition, we notice the almost universal absorption of the teacher's ambition and the public interest, in the work of instruction. Few thoughtful educators can have failed to observe the fact that in our schools the matter of government has not merely dropped into a subordinate place; it has sunk almost out of sight. How very infrequent are the indications that the teacher ~~has~~ made the control of his school, and the wholesome discipline of the pupil, the subjects of careful study and systematic preparation? Where are the pupils found possessed with the idea that one of the first objects of their ambition should be to develop into noble subjects of the school government? Where do you find patrons or parents, upon the occurrence of school examinations, evincing a lively interest in the moral, as well as the intellectual progress of the child? On all hands, the interest taken is altogether in the results of the instruction; the pride evinced is altogether in the amount of knowledge that the child has gained, and his readiness and brilliance in exhibiting it. The government of the school, which should have made the child patient, persistent, high-principled, obedient, noble,—that is held as purely incidental and unimportant; it is "out of mind as soon as out of sight."

We pass now to notice some of the causes of this depressed and neglected condition of school government. And this must be done somewhat carefully, since, upon the conclusions reached, must depend the proper elucidation of points subsequently involved in the discussion. Of these causes, the first to which the attention may be directed are incidental in their character and influence.

Under this head, we summarily include all those accidents of our school systems and school operations, which throw obstacles, either mechanical or moral, in the way of the institution or maintaining of true and effective government.

Those defects, therefore, in the accommodations of the school; those errors in its organization; that ignorance or neglect of school officers; that antagonistic influence of parental government; and that inbred insubordination and lawlessness of human nature, which counteract or oppose the teacher in his efforts to institute, perfect and maintain good government in the school;—all these tend to defeat his efforts and, by making school government a failure, depress it, and cause it to be neglected. The principle applied here is a plain one. Man everywhere reverences success. Success is always an end; often an idolatry. Hence, the common tendency to treat whoever or whatever is attended with failure, as worthy of little attention or regard. Whatever then, by interposing obstacles in its way, goes to make the government of the youth in our schools either a partial success only, or, what is more often the case, a practical failure, tends to bring it into contempt.

Passing from these incidental and minor causes, we find back of them all, another altogether more profound and influential.

We refer here to what we shall endeavor to show to be a thoroughly false theory of education. The mistaken views which have long prevailed with regard to the nature and object of education, are not wholly unknown to our more sound and earnest educators. To such, no fallacy can be more apparent than that involved in the common notion that education is simply the development of the intellect, through the acquisition of knowledge. Its evil results are spread broad-cast over the whole field of public instruction, and the so-called development effected in the schools. Its direct influence, which, however, seems not so distinctly to have attracted notice, has been to create that diversion of the attention from the subject of school government, already mentioned.

This unfortunate result it has effected, not merely by elevating intellectual development too exclusively, but by altogether ignoring moral culture. Discharge education of the moral element or simply reduce it to a secondary position, and where have you any place for school government? What can it be other than a mere horse-boy to the work of instruction,—that is, a mere means of holding the will in obedient waiting upon the intellect in the prosecution of its exclusive demand upon the opportunities and appliances of the school? Not for one moment, we insist—not for one moment—can school government take its true place in that system of education in which the moral nature does not stand side by side in privilege, with the intellectual powers; in which the discipline of the susceptibilities and the will is not held equal, (we had almost said paramount) to the development of the sense, the understanding, and the reason.

That the theory which thus, to the discredit and damage of the school government, dissevers the moral discipline from the intellectual instruction, and indeed almost ignores it,—that this theory is a false one, will be quite evident without extended discussion. The practical workings of instruction in the schools show most clearly that the development of the intellect cannot proceed successfully except under the auspices of that thorough order which the proper discipline and control of the susceptibilities and the will can alone secure. In other words, the pupil will make progress in learning, only as the school is efficiently governed. This is the testimony of experience.

Besides this, the necessary laws of mental growth and progress are in proof. The development of the intellect must be the product of its self-activity. Such self-activity must owe both its inception and continuance to the susceptibilities and the will. What the pupil is led to desire, he purposes; and what he purposes underlies and determines the nature and extent of his intellectual application. Quite clearly then, that application and the consequent intellectual progress can attain the highest character and the most successful results, only as, under proper control and discipline, the combined desires and purposes are brought into a cheerful, steady, and growing accordance with the highest want of the intellect.

It is the very common overlooking of this important principle, which occasions so much waste of time and labor in our schools, so much unsuccessful study on the part of tho pupil, and so general a prevalence of a crude or one-sided culture and development among those who have ostensibly been educated.

Higher than this, is the proof found in the relative order and end of the faculties. The end of all rational activity is, internally, the attainment of the highest dignity or worthiness; externally, the highest benevolence. Hence, as the sense is for, and only for the intellect; so the intellect is for, and only for the susceptibilities and the will. Clearer perception is no end in itself; it is only a means to higher knowledge. Higher knowledge is no end in itself; it is only a means to the attainment of purer and more intelligent desires and loftier purposes. Develop, then, the intellect as completely as you will without making that development conduce to a corresponding discipline of the heart, and the product is either half abortive or fairly monstrous; it is either a crude Hercules or a dread Lucifer. Hence, whatever theory of education inverts this order, and subordinates the moral to the intellectual, is clearly and intrinsically false.

It is important here that we give some attention to the causes of this failure to do justice to the moral nature in our school training. We shall briefly notice three.

First, then, it is to be remarked that the economic value of the mere intellectual training makes itself more directly apparent to the vulgar mind. The advantages resulting from the boy's proficiency in "reading, writing, and ciphering," all can appreciate. How those acquisitions work into the business pursuits of life, and how they bear upon success in those pursuits, they know. But not so readily do men,—of whom the mass have no higher conceptions of the objects of life than the getting of a living or the making of money,—not so readily do they discover the value of true principles and a just self-control as parts of the boy's attainments and character. The bearing of these upon the price (so to speak) which he will bring in the market-place of men, or upon the success of his life-career, they cannot well estimate. We can hardly expect them to do it.

Again, a strange, an unwarrantable (we had almost said cowardly) prejudice against what has been called moral instruction in schools, has quite generally prevailed, and has, doubtless, in some part produced the evil to which we allude. How many, affected by that, for a free and brave people, pitiable fear of "sectarianism" and "priestcraft," have stood ready, not only to decry any attempt to introduce moral instruction into the schools, but to sacrifice outright the child's intellectual training, rather than to have proper pains taken to instill into his mind those moral and religious principles which are the crown of all learning, and to develop in his heart that manly and virtuous strength which is essential to a just education and a true well-being,—without which, indeed, not even that proper government, so necessary to the favorable prosecution of the intellectual training, can be secured! And yet, this is tantamount to entertaining so great a fear of some pharisaical or fanatical cleansing of the cup and platter, that it is preferred that they should remain intact in their original or accumulated vileness, so as to be neither endurable to the touch nor capable of containing anything pure or pleasant.

A third cause, perhaps less direct, but not less mischievous, may be found in the fact that almost all the current philosophies have studiously dissevered the consideration of the moral nature, from the study of mind, than which nothing can be more unphilosophical. It were bad enough to compound ethics with the philosophy of the moral powers; but to dissever the latter from the intellectual faculties, in the study of mental science, is an outrage upon the truth of the human soul. Were it possible to succeed in such an attempt to

> "Distinguish and divide
> A hair 'twixt south and southwest side,"

the only effect would be, as we have already seen, to

restrict or distort the views entertained of the intellectual nature, and to cast discredit upon the moral nature as neither essential to the former, nor of dominant importance in the soul.

Even in those treatises devoted ostensibly to the study of the moral powers, there has been a too common avoidance of all distinct reference to the spiritual or religious element in the soul, into which the moral element must ultimately be drawn up and absorbed, unless it is doomed, as if invested with the curse of the serpent, to go prone upon the dust in actual abandonment and degradation. The natural effect of this course must be, as may be clearly seen, to cast discredit upon that moral training which should form a recognized and revered constituent of all true education, and the essential basis, if not the complete substance, of all true school government.

But whatever may be the causes of this failure to do justice to the moral nature of the child, and to provide for his moral instruction, the failure is in the highest degree absurd and pernicious. What is your education, with all its intellectual completeness, if it does not secure that the child shall become the true man, the pure friend, the worthy parent, the noble citizen, to say nothing of the exemplary Christian? These are really what the self-conscious spirit, the dearer associates, the rising generation, the community, the organized state, seek. Without these, "the rest is leather and prunella." And yet, these higher qualities are to be secured only through the thorough disciplining of the moral nature under the wise control and the just sanctions of a proper government in the schools; not, however, as a substitute for, but as coöperative with, the government of the family. The latter is prior, and should be superior, instead of being, as is too commonly the case, both inferior and adverse.

From all this, it will be seen that school government is not only the proper controlling of the school, so as to make it practicable to secure the ends of true instruction, as looking toward the development of the intellect; but it is also, and in a higher sense, the effective disciplining of the school, so as to bring the appetites, desires, and passions of each individual under rational and virtuous control, so that they shall be as perfectly subject to the *right*, as, by instruction, the perceptions and judgments are made obedient to the *truth*.

School government is, then, the proper ordering of both the organic and individual action in the schools, so as to secure in the pupils the best possible development of the mind and discipline of the heart.

# CHAPTER II.

## OBSTACLES IN THE WAY OF GOOD SCHOOL GOVERNMENT, SPECIFICALLY CONSIDERED.

Importance of specific notice—*Obstacles accidental, organic, and social*—The accidental, external and internal—*External contingent*—Defective accommodations—The beautiful tends to order—*Internal contingent*—Insufficient apparatus—*Organic obstacles, external and internal*—*External organic*—Improper distribution of departments and labor—Excessive labor demanded—Paralyzes the teacher's energies—*Internal organic*—Imperfect classification and want of system—Want of competitive examinations—*Social obstacles*—Parental opposition to good school government—Neighborhood antagonism—Official unfaithfulness—Radical insubordination of human nature—*Practical inferences*—Difficulties demand improvement the more—Effort should be comprehensive—Duty belongs not to the teacher alone—Too much not to be expected.

In the preceding chapter, allusion was made to certain incidental obstacles which stand opposed to the improvement and perfection of school government, and which, as such, are a cause of its present depressed and neglected condition. Those obstacles deserve more than a passing allusion, for their importance is such that, without their removal in good part, even the general prevalence of just views of the nature of that government, will not avail to secure he desired reformation. Indeed, the efforts to remove the one and improve the other, must run parallel, to be either consistent or successful.

Furthermore, a proper examination of these obstacles bears directly upon some of the points to be subsequently discussed, affording, in case of some of them, a partial elucidation.

Proceeding with this examination, we find these obstacles to be threefold, those which are *accidental*, those *organic*, and those *social*, in their origin and character.

Under the head of contingent or accidental obstacles to good government in the school, we include all those that may be said to involve the material condition of the school. These are properly of two kinds, the *external* and the *internal;* the former including whatever pertains to the external accommodation of the school: the latter involving whatever may relate more directly to the convenience of its internal operations.

Among the obstacles of the former kind, the external contingent, must be included the unsightly location of school houses, bad or insufficient playgrounds, rude and ill-conditioned buildings, ("Gaunt, ghaistly, ghost-alluring edifices," as Burns would style them); buildings not only an outrage upon the possibility of architecture, but utterly insufficient in size to prevent the necessity of crowding the pupils; rough, unfinished floors and walls; uncurtained or unshaded windows, and a hard uncomfortable style of desk and seat. The direct tendency of all such insufficient and unworthy accommodations is to produce a rough, ill-tempered, insubordinate nature. And so directly do they tend to this savagery, and to the consequent destruction of all genial or humane control, that only the blindness which grows out of mere greed, can fail to perceive their baleful influence, and the pitiable folly of the "penny-wise" economy which allows them existence.

The true correction of some of these evils, that is, that correction which does not stop with attaining the nearer limit of mere comfort, doubtless comes within that nobler field which it is so much the fashion to decry, the culture of the beautiful. But decry it who will, the influence of the beautiful is humanizing, and, as such, it tends always to order.

Of those obstacles which grow out of internal contingencies, we may enumerate the lack of proper or sufficient appliances for carrying on the practical, or in other words, the demonstrative and illustrative portions of the work of instruction. The want of ample blackboards, of numerical frames, of explanatory cards or charts, of maps and drawings, of mathematical blocks, indeed, of apparatus generally, can not but so far narrow down the student's work to the simple book and the mere recitation, as to furnish no proper or pleasing outlet for his surplus activity and ingenuity. In some cases, that activity and ingenuity will doubtless sink back into sheer dullness and stagnation. But more often it will unfortunately work itself out in acts of disorder, mischief, and, perhaps, overt acts of insubordination, and thus burden or counteract the effort of the teacher to maintain good government in the school.

Passing to the obstacles which are organic in their origin and character, we define them as being those which belong to the constitution, or to the working of the school itself. These may also be subdivided as external and internal; the former including such as are determined to the school by the will of its patrons or local officers; and the latter, those that fall more immediately under the jurisdiction of the teacher.

Under the external organic, we include such evils as the want of a thorough system of grading, and of a consistent distribution of the departments, wherever such an organization is made practicable by the size of the school; the assignment of several teachers to one room; and what is, especially in our city schools, the most common, and everywhere a most intolerable evil, the want of a sufficient number of teachers for the aggregate of the pupils to be controlled and taught. These evils all tend directly to discourage every attempt at good government, by the unnecessary labor which they impose, and the inevitable confusion they create. A simple reference to the underlying principle as unfolded by Political Economy; namely, that of the necessity for a distribution of labor, will suffice to show the correctness of the position here taken.

With regard to the last of the evils specified, there is still a more serious cause of complaint. The difficulty is not that there is simply an unwise distribution of labor; it is rather that the amount of labor required, in order to any proper instruction or government, is utterly preposterous; for the teacher to accomplish any satisfactory portion of it, is among the practical impossibilities. Overwhelmed, as many teachers are, with such an excess of numbers as to preclude the possibility of individual observation, attention, and effort, and of any direct and adequate personal influence over the pupil, what can be the result other than that the attempt at government should be altogether in the direction of vague, irregular, and arbitrary generalities?

And, under the burden of an enterprise so perplexing and so hopeless as that of attempting to secure, in the face of such obstacles, a consistent order, general interest, close application, quiet obedience and habitual respect and subordination, what can be expected other than that the teacher's ambition will become utterly broken down, and his energies hopelessly paralyzed? If this is not the result, then you may safely set down his as no ordinary character; it is little less than heroic.

Under the head of evils which are internal as well as organic, and which, as such, stand in the way of good government, we include such as the lack of a proper classification of the pupils as to studies or relative advancement, the absence of a definite and fixed order of studies, the absence of a systematic order of study, recitation, and exercises, and the failure to provide for the school a system of special examinations determinative of excellence, and conditional to advancement. Some of these, it will be seen, directly counteract the interests of good government, by inducing general confusion, habits of irregularity or disorder, and, in one instance, positive self-will in the free choice of studies. The last, in failing to provide the highest possible stimulus toward superior application and attainments, indirectly leads to the same injurious result. It does this by not opening sufficient channels for the counter-diversion of the pupil's activity. In the case of every restless and enterprising nature, each new encouragement offered to a noble ambition is just so far an influence tending to withdraw the attention and the energies from what is petty or culpable. Every such influence favors successful government.

We pass now to the consideration of those obstacles in the way of school government, which are of social origin. We fear it is not generally realized that society is practically opposed to all really good and effective government of the young. And, among all the evils which such government is called to encounter, we apprehend this social counter-current is the most wide-spread and persistent. Considered with reference to its immediate sources, it may be designated as three-fold, *parental*, *social proper*, and *official*.

To begin with, good government in the family is the exception and not the rule. Parents indulge their children at home, nay, indirectly train them to utter lawlessness. Hence, the impressions of both parents and children, as to the nature and necessity of good government in the school, become perverted, and their feelings under its more personal and pressing operation become really demoralized. They neither think rightly of it, nor appreciate the good in it. The natural consequence of this is, they set themselves against such government just so soon as it touches them. When the lawless will of the child is put under restraint, or his insubordination subjects him to discipline, he rebels and appeals to the parent. When the indulgent or ungoverning parent finds his child under arraignment for his transgression, or suffering the just penalty of the law he has broken, he rebels and, at once, joins issue with the teacher.

This done, the evil spreads,

"Like fire in heather set."

Other children and other parents are in danger. Their feeling is, "Why stand we in jeopardy?" Their sympathies aroused, and their fears excited, they make a common cause in the conflict. And now Gog and Magog all in commotion, what chance has the teacher or his government? Either his cause must be so transparently just that even the dense dust-cloud of the general excitement cannot hide its merits; or he must possess both a consummate tact and firmness; or he must have seated himself too firmly in the confidence of the school officers, or a few considerate and influential patrons; or his cause is practically lost. But how many of our public school teachers can command all or any one of these contingencies? Comparatively few. With the rest, then, the case is clear; the government of the school must succumb to the home government, and must become as depressed and neglected as that.

Nor is this all. It is too often the case that the school officers, being of the community and quite in sympathy with it, fail to sustain the teacher; perhaps they even oppose him. Instead of standing up like men, and, true to their official responsibilities, checking and reversing the popular current, away they go with it, sometimes even drifting down on the foremost wave, perhaps adding to its destructive rush, by ostentatiously exercising their "little brief authority," in either censuring or removing the teacher. But what can the government of the school ever be under such treatment other than so despicable a thing that there can be found "none so poor to do it reverence?"

And this social counter-current is the more formidable because it is no mere surface-evil. It is the surface-manifestation of a deep underlying principle of insubordination in the human soul. Whatever theory may be chosen as accounting for its origin, there is little enough room for doubt as to the existence of the fact that the native position of the human will is one of incipient rebellion against moral restraint and authoritative control.

From the beginning, the outworking self prefers its own way, even to the countervailing of its own best welfare. And, as the general law, only the long-continued pressure of self-interest, the hard discipline of bitter experience, or the constant and constraining influence of acknowledged government, ever serve to correct, to any adequate extent, this "false nature." But not even these are sufficient to the work of completely restoring the moral nature to a true and loyal subjection to reason and right, and thus securing in it an abiding readiness to yield obedience to the demands of all just authority. Here is the "ineradicable taint."

There are certain practical lessons which it were well to learn from the foregoing. The natural effect of discovering such obstacles in the way of all attempts to institute and maintain good government in the school, will be to create discouragement. To the enlightened and resolute spirit, however, they will only serve as additional proofs of the need of a more determined effort toward the desired improvement. They, in fact, reveal the province of school government as, in a pre-eminent sense, the true field for the master spirit.

But it should be borne in mind, as has been already suggested, that all efforts in this direction should be comprehensive; they should not be confined to an internal manipulation of the government itself, but should also embrace a reformation of the outside influences which are so adverse. The scheme of order and the system of discipline must, of course, have their share of the attention, and must be made as nearly perfect as may be under the circumstances. But, parallel with this should constantly be kept the effort to remove whatever in the accommodations, appliances, and organization of the school, or in the condition and operation of society, interferes with the attainment of that perfection.

And this is broadly suggestive of the fact that not alone is the teacher responsible for the existence of good government in the school. Upon school officers and patrons of schools, upon every member of the community, rests a share of that responsibility. It is for them to see that whatever can be done to remove the external obstacles of which we have spoken, is done. It is for them to advance means, and to second measures for improvement in the condition and organization of the schools. It is for them to exercise a wise self-control and reticence as to meddling with the management of the school. It is for many of them to learn to be governed, and to acquire the power of governing well at home, before they presume to sit in judgment upon the teacher as governor.

And, still further, neither patrons nor teachers should expect too much. Great improvement may, by proper effort, be effected. To accomplish all that can be done in that direction, should be the persistent, life-long aim. But let it be borne in mind that many of the evils of human condition are remediless. Hence, perfection is not to be expected; and when perfection is not attainable, failures should not always be condemned as faults.

# CHAPTER III.

## DERIVATION OF SCHOOL GOVERNMENT FROM PARENTAL AUTHORITY.

Importance of this derivation—School government and the education of the young, united—That education an onerous work—Not to be undertaken by every one—Must be inspired by parental instinct and love—Necessary reaction on the child's nature—Child-education domestic—The idea often considered as Utopian—Not due to a fallacy in the theory—Due to a lack of knowledge and leisure among the poorer classes—To a lack of will rather than capacity among the rich —*The causes of these deficiencies twofold*—Too little rational love for the child—None live properly for society—The claims of society paramount—Society demands the proper training of the child—These causes proofs rather than objections—The government of the child goes with his instruction—Parental government the source of school government—It is in fact the key to school government——School government re-defined.

BEFORE proceeding to the discussion of the nature of school government, it is important that its origin, or derivation be ascertained. From that source, whatever it may prove to be, we may naturally look to obtain light sufficient for the distinct revelation of its more profound principles and of their practical application. In that direction, at least, we must look for the earlier indications of its radical characteristics. From what source, then, is the government of the school derived?

School government, from its very name, and from its definition as already given, must be seen to be inseparably connected with the education of the young. It starts with the first attempts to institute that work; it grows cotemporaneously and parallel with it; and only with its completion can it either be superseded or expire.

The proper education of the child, commencing as it must, with the earlier developments of its intellect, and extending over so large a portion of its existence; covering, as it must, a period of so much dependence and weakness, and inevitably encountering so many obstacles and adverse influences, is necessarily a lengthy and onerous work. Indeed, it is safe to say that, whenever it has been undertaken with any intelligent and realizing sense of its true nature, it has been felt and found to be one of the most trying that can fall to the lot of imperfect humanity.

But a work of this kind, especially one so removed from the chances of pecuniary gain or immediate reward of any kind, will not be ventured upon by those who are governed by no higher incentives than those of personal advantage. A work like this, which must be wrought out slowly year by year, amidst constant discouragements,

> "And all for love and nothing for reward,"

must find its potential inducements in the deeper instincts and the purer affections of human nature.

For such instinct and affection, it needs little argument to show, we must look alone to the parental nature and relation. Only in the parent's heart, may we expect to find the forces at all adequate to the inception and prosecution of this work. Out of the natural relations of the parent as parent and provider, must grow a sense of abiding obligation for the present support and development of the child; out of parental love and ambition, must spring parental concern and effort for the future welfare of the child; out of both this obligation and concern, must emerge the primitive attempt at the child's education; and just in proportion to the full sense of that obligation, and the intelligent maturity of that concern, will that attempt develop into an earnest and thorough system of domestic culture.

This parental derivation of his culture is also most necessary to the development of a proper filial temper in the child. Out of the child's habitual reference to the parent for the fulfillment of this responsibility; out of his daily dependence on the parent for his intellectual sustenance and development; out of his growing confidence in the amplitude of the parent's capacity as a "source and fount of light;"—out of all these, must grow that deep, abiding, and much needed regard and reverence which no other being can claim, and which should not be even shared with another. As the voice of the parent's heart must be; "Those whom I so love must be anxiously trained for their highest well-being, and by myself alone, since no work so solemn and so sacred may be intrusted to another;" so the answer of the child's heart must be; "To my parents I owe that developed knowledge, virtue, and power which are the very crown and blessedness of being; and to those to whom I owe so much, I am first and forever most in debt, and that beyond all possibility of too large a return of love and service." And so should the education of the child, as domestic, reduplicate the force of domestic care and sustentation, and the two bind together, as "with a two-fold cord not easily broken," both parent and child. Thus would the household be blessed with the only possible realization of a perfect and lasting unity.

Hence, we urge that the primary view of education, notwithstanding all that is contrary to it in the existing order of things, must be that of a purely domestic training.

But to many, doubtless, this idea of education will seem fairly Utopian. As they look over the whole field of society, and everywhere find the intellectual training of the child so completely transferred to other hands, and so many schemes on foot, and those often so vast, for its accomplishment elsewhere than in the home, they can hardly conceive any other system than that of parental abdication and scholastic vice-royalty to be the true one. The feeling cannot but be strengthened by the fact that, under existing circumstances, certain advantages, such as a higher mental stimulus, more extended acquirements, and general harmony in the popular intelligence, are the common results of the prevailing method.

These impressions are due, however, not to any fallacy in the theory, but to certain practical difficulties in the way of its realization, which grow out of the existing erroneous conformation of society. So grave are those difficulties, that we even admit that it would be quite impossible to make the education of the young conform to the true idea. What they are may readily be shown.

For example, among the humbler classes in society, where less ambitious aims and greater simplicity in the style of living might seem to allow opportunity for the performance of this work, insurmountable obstacles are to be found in the lack of the culture necessary to the parent's becoming the teacher, and in the lamentable absorption of the energies in making provision for mere physical comfort or material advantage. Hence, they have neither capacity nor time. So the greater interests are swallowed up of the less,—the seven fat kine are devoured by the seven kine lean and ill-favored.

Among the more independent and more highly cultivated classes, where the requisite learning and capacity might be found, either the energies are absorbed in the pursuit of the more ambitious ends of life, or the style of living adopted is such as to multiply to an excessive degree the fictitious wants of both the individual and the household. Hence, the heart is altogether pre-occupied, and the requisite leisure wholly forbidden. And so, ample tithes are paid in mint, and anise and cumin, in the merest fashion and frivolity, while the weightier matters of the law of parental obligation are neglected.

And the grand cause of this is two-fold. Near at hand is that of too little intelligent and real love of offspring. Love, merely instinctive or animal, there may be; but that which grows out of a careful and self-denying regard for the higher claims of the child's nature as spiritual and immortal, little enough is there of that. So far as these higher wants of the child are involved, and the parent's rational obligation to provide for them is concerned, the mass are like the ostrich, "which leaveth her eggs in the earth and warmeth them in the dust, and forgetteth that the foot may crush them, or that the wild beast may break them. She is hardened against her young ones as though they were not hers: her labor is in vain, without fear; because God hath deprived her of wisdom, neither hath he imparted to her understanding."

Somewhat less immediate, but not less serious, as a cause, is the fact that comparatively all live for themselves and not for society. Setting aside, as belonging to another and higher field, the religious aspect of the thing, we think it may be consistently urged that, in that associated form of being for which man was designed and adapted, and to which he is, in fact, so necessitated; namely, the community or the state, that sovereign selfishness which makes every man his own chief end of concern and activity, must be pronounced altogether abnormal and false. Doubtless, he owes somewhat to himself. The principle of self-love so pronounces. Self-preservation demands it.

But, to look only at that side of the question, every man has interests vested in society, and those of the most vital character. Indeed, so close and important are the relations of society to all his interests, that upon the condition and character of that very society, depends the welfare of most of those individual interests in which he is so apt to become selfishly absorbed. No man can be blind to the best interests of society, or wilfully neglectful of them, without offering a premium upon his own damage. But beyond this, society has a claim of its own as pre-eminent, and, by just so much as the whole is greater than a part, is the claim made urgent. The true dignity and tho true happiness of rational humanity requires that, in society, each individual should benevolently prefer the interests of the whole to his own. Men owe it to their own rational wisdom and moral excellence, that they live for society rather than for themselves.

But, we think it cannot but be seen, that, in a very important sense, to live for the proper training of children is to live for the perfected well-being of society. The children of to-day are to constitute the society of to-morrow; and he who may have little power to amend society among those who now compose its fullness and strength, may labor very effectively and hopefully among the young, for its future regeneration. The parent who, rising above mere sordid pursuits, and turning a deaf ear to all the seducements of ambition or frivolity, wisely and faithfully trains his child for the intelligent, able, and virtuous discharge of the duties, parental, social, and civil, which may ultimately devolve upon him, is doing society, as well as himself, his best service. Men, however, do not live for society, and hence, they do not thus give themselves to the education of the young in accordance with its primitive and perfect idea.

While, however, these causes are enough to make the realization of the true idea as thus advanced quite impracticable, a little reflection will suffice to show that they are practically proofs of the validity of that idea. They urge, and with no slight force, the native consistency and excellence of the domestic theory of education. In all the facts which they present, it cannot but be apparent that they lead directly back to the position that the education of the child should be domestic, and to the conviction that it is because men are either ignorant of their primal relations to the race, or are unequal to their proper care, or wilfully ignore them, that education is not the thing it should be.

Having thus traced the education of the young to the domestic circle as its original and proper territory, and to parental authority and duty as its primal source, we are prepared to assume the position that so soon as, for any cause, the work of education passes out of the house and into the school, just so soon does the moral discipline, or the government, which is one of its essential parts, go with it. The government must domicile with the instruction.

This, however, reveals the fact, of which we have been in search, that school government has its origin in parental government; it is, in fact, a contingence and growth of parental government, and, as such, must, in many points of character, be determined by the stock from which it springs. School government as thus determined, is the temporary and conditional transfer to the teacher, of all that part of the parent's authority which is dependent upon his exercise of the function of the domestic instructor, and which would be necessary to the successful education of the child in the home circle, according to the primitive idea.

In parental government, then, we are to look for the key to the real nature of school government. The latter must be, in the temporary and specific, much what the former is in the continuous and total. In the parent must the teacher find in good part his own prototype; and in the teacher must the parent cheerfully recognize his own natural vicegerent. And so closely will the authority of the two be found affiliated, that, to a most important extent, they must stand or fall together.

Hence, school government may be defined, as the exercising of that authority in the control and discipline of the child, by the teacher as the parent's substitute, which would be the right and duty of the parent were he to undertake the work of educating the child in his own part, supplemented, however, by such increase of power as will make it commensurate with the larger necessities of the school, as involving greater numbers and requiring a more stringent order.

## CHAPTER IV.

### THE CHARACTERISTICS OF SCHOOL GOVERNMENT, AS DERIVED FROM THAT OF THE PARENT.

The authority of the teacher as delegated—*The delegation or transfer complete*—Interference with it suicidal—The authority enhanced by the transfer—Parents bound to second and strengthen it—*The transfer a finality*—The authority not to be resumed—The child not to be withdrawn from under it—Such a remedy worse than the evil—Positively injurious to the child—Disregards even his natural rights—The one possible case of exception—School Government not necessarily invalidated by errors—*The authority of the teacher absolute*—The authority legislative *per se*—The school no democracy—Successful experiments in this direction not an objection—Self-government in the school involves a delusion—School Government looks forward to self-government, but should not formally institute it—False ideas as to self-government—*The authority of the teacher imperative*—Decisions to be authoritative, unargued—Logic not always invincible—Reasonings may be used as a supplementary means—*Decisions of the authority final*—Appeal or reversal reprehensible—Would destroy parental government—Interference of school authorities deprecated—The teacher must stand his ground against it—If overborne, must resign—The teacher may himself reverse—The teacher may himself refer to the authorities—This subject to objection—*The School Government to be benevolent*—Parental government too often selfish—School Government not exposed to this error—Too little wise forecast in school management—The ultimate good must be paramount—Temporizing expedients and present ends inadmissible—Passionate or vindictive measures reprehensible—Degrading or annoying measures objectionable—Ridicule restricted in its use—Satire condemned—*School Government catholic in scope and spirit*—The welfare of the whole the paramount consideration—Parental demands for specific privileges objectionable—The general economy of the school as a whole to be carefully studied.

Having thus traced the government of the school to that of the family as its natural source, we are now prepared to inquire what, in the light of this derivation, are the characteristics of the government which the teacher is to institute and administer in the school.

And, here, we observe, first, that the authority vested in the teacher, and exercised in governing the school, is substantially, though not formally, a delegated authority. It is in substance delegated, since it is identical with that exercised by the parent, and would in fact remain in his hands, but for his transfer to another, of his original functions as instructor. It is, however, not formally made over, since the transfer is no matter of stipulation, the whole being not an act, but a necessary consequence of the parent's demission of the power to teach. This resultant lack of formality in the transfer of the authority to govern the child, so far from abating any of the derived characteristics of the authority, only serves to add a new and necessary force to them. Were the authority formally made over to the teacher by the parent, the exercise of it might be assumed to be subject to either the expressed or implied stipulations of the transfer; but going over to him, with the educational functions as their necessary concomitant, it carries with it all its original attributes in their best and strongest character as not arbitrary, but inevitable.

Hence, out of this unrestricted delegation of the authority of the parent to the teacher, grow certain positive and practical conclusions. And, first, the transfer is complete, and the teacher's right to exercise the authority is entire. While there are authoritative rights vested in the parent, as parent and providential guardian of the child, which he may not abdicate, and which the teacher may not assume, yet all those which the parent might possess and exercise in the control of the child under the process of education at home, belong, under a system of education in the school, to the teacher alone. If, for example, the parent in training the child himself might insist upon punctuality or regularity; if he may demand implicit submission and without appeal; or if he may administer discipline or punishment in this or that form,—all this may the teacher do, and without subjection to question or interference. The parent has no right to refuse these prerogatives to the teacher, nor to disturb him in his necessary exercise of them.

Indeed, such interference with the teacher's prerogative is worse than improper; it is suicidal. Inasmuch as the school government is but a transferred part of the home government, by just so much as the parent restricts the teacher, he practically retrenches his own authority; and by so much as he disturbs the teacher's exercise of authority, he practically damages his own administration of government. Hence, it is commonly seen to be the fact that all such parental interference in the government of the school re-acts upon that of the home circle, and so, that which began by distressing the former, ends by hastening the demoralization of the latter. Thus, the parent plays the part of a principal who distresses an agent, but chiefly to his own detriment.

One very important principle evolved in this connection, is very generally overlooked. The prevailing impression is that the authority transferred by the parent to the teacher, is in some part diminished by the transfer. Few parents feel that the authority of the teacher is as important as their own. But the fact is, it is, within its sphere, even more important. The transfer of the authority is such as to intensify rather than to depress it. When it passes from the family to the school, it passes to a field in which its situation is more critical, and its success a matter of wider concern. The larger number grouped under one control, the wider diversity of dispositions and habits, the more stringent demands of the one common object, for perfect order and thorough discipline,—all these call for a stronger hand as well as a clearer head than are imperative in the simpler and more restricted field of the home.

The inference to be drawn from this fact is then necessarily, that, so far from any attempt on the part of parents or patrons, to disturb and thus weaken the authority of the teacher, their first and most imperative duty is to sustain and strengthen that authority to the full extent of its rightful demand as, for the time being, superior to their own. Hence, the only impression conveyed to the child's mind by either their opinions or actions, should be very distinctly this; no interference will be attempted except to second the efforts of the teacher, and sustain the law of the school. Complaint is, therefore, worse than useless, and rebellion only ensures a more complete subjection.

Out of the completeness of this transfer of the parental authority, grows another principle; namely, that, except in a single case, the transfer must be in an important sense a finality. The functions and prerogatives of instruction and government, as we have seen, go together. If now, because of his own incompetence, the parent transfers these to the teacher, he has no right under ordinary circumstances, to resume the one without resuming the other; nor may he resume both without providing for their better reinstitution elsewhere, and more, for their reinstitution in substance and form, enough better to counterbalance all the evils of change.

When then the child has been consigned to the teacher's charge, it is equally for instruction and discipline as one and inseparable. Nor is it competent for the parent or guardian to withdraw the child from under this instruction and discipline which go to make up his education, without providing so much better for his enjoyment of their advantages at home or elsewhere, that the evils resulting from the arbitrary change, such as the child's loss of time, the destruction of his confidence in teachers, the strengthening of his tendencies to insubordination, and the perfecting of his faith in his power to control the parent as well as the teacher, shall all be overbalanced by the greater good secured through the parent's transfer of him to some other field of training.

Unless the alternative here suggested is secured, it is evident that in most cases the remedy is worse than the evil which is the subject of complaint. Send the child to some other school, and, though he may have been practically in the right before, he is now, from the lesson of insubordination which has been taught him, quite sure to be thoroughly in the wrong at the first opportunity. In this case, either the original battle has to be fought over and fought out at last, or the doubtful experiment of change has to be attempted again, and under circumstances more dubious than before.

Retain the child at home, and without securing that the parent's exercise of the functions of instruction and discipline shall be comparatively faultless, and the gain is altogether ambiguous. The parent has practically discharged a quack from abroad, in order to turn empiric himself, at home. Even though the latter were in some respects better than the former, the disease may be aggravated by the loss of time, and so the patient is the worse for the change. So in the case of the child, it is a cardinal principle that the steady and sustained application and enforcement of even a less perfect tuition and rule, are better than a sudden and fractious change to those assumed to be better, or even really so.

If, however, as is more commonly the case, the child is simply withdrawn from the school without provision for his education at home, the whole is of the nature of a direct trespass upon his higher rights and necessities. Carlyle has somewhere said,

'For one to possess capacity for knowledge, and die ignorant,—this, I call tragedy." Yet for the enactment of this very tragedy, he makes direct preparation, who thus withdraws the child from such opportunities of training as he has, and leaves him where he has none.

It has been intimated that there is one case, and only one, in which the parent's resumption of the authority demitted to the teacher, is admissible. That occurs in the extremity of a *prevailing abuse* of the authority on the part of the teacher, or his *complete failure* to administer it effectually. But let it be observed that the conditions of the resumption are solely a prevailing abuse or a complete failure. The grounds for this limitation are plain. In almost every instance in which this resumption of the authority is attempted, it is based upon some partial ill-success of the teacher, or some isolated instance of faulty discipline. But here, as everywhere, action so radical and violent, upon premises so narrow and unsettled, is not only erroneous but reprehensible. He is not far from being the greater transgressor who, for a natural error or a single fault, makes a man an offender beyond both the enjoyment of rights or the chance of reclamation.

There are defects in the administration of the best governments. But until it is quite certain that a perfect government, and its faultless administration are immediately attainable, it is not wise to denounce the government we have, or to inaugurate actual revolution. Hence, occasional slips of the teacher in the exercise of discipline, while they of course mar his government, do not cancel or cut short in one iota the teacher's authority. Adopt the principle that they do, and you bring parental government also to the block, for, as a matter of fact, it is itself noto-riously wide of this very perfection. Indeed, bad as school government is, it is, in the aggregate, much better than the aggregate of domestic government; and it only fails to reach a still higher standard of excellence, because the latter, in its defectiveness, acts upon it as a perpetual check and counteraction. The parent or guardian, therefore, who pursues the course here reprehended, practically condemns himself, and only needs to carry out that course in order to be speedily "hoist with his own petard."

The second essential characteristic of the teacher's authority as derived from that of the parent, is that it is absolute. By this we do not mean that it is absolute in the highest sense as underived and irresponsible, but only that it is absolute with reference to the relative position of the teacher and the pupil. The authority of the teacher as sovereign in the school is in no way derived from, or dependent on the will of the pupil as subject; nor is the teacher in any way amenable to the pupil for his mode of exercising it. So far as the pupil-subject is concerned, the teacher is, in the better sense of the term, a true autocrat, and may both take his stand and carry himself as such.

Out of this essential principle grow certain practical inferences which not only go far towards determining the character of school government, but which decisively settle the false nature of some of the methods of government current. Of these inferences, this is to be observed, first, that the authority of the teacher in governing the school, is legislative *per se*. From that authority, as the sole originating source, springs the entire law for the school. Here, as elsewhere, true government originates of natural right, in the higher, more specific, and somewhat exclusive field of the superior intelligence and will, and goes down thence, according to its own clearer dictates and steadier purposes, to, and upon those who, as constituting the broader, less intelligent, less self-sustaining and self-controlled mass, are the proper subjects of government. To install the teacher in the school upon any other assumption, is both absurd in itself and false to the nature of school government as determined by the law of the domestic government; indeed, we may add, false to the nature of that domestic government as determined by the law of the divine government which is its natural antecedent. It is, then, for the teacher as the select one, and as the superior intelligence and the abler will, to originate the whole scheme of law for the school, and to wield its sanctions throughout the entire field of discipline. And these functions are imperative upon him. Except temporarily, for certain specific ends, he may neither suspend nor transfer them.

Hence, school government cannot, according to any true view, be taken as a democracy, either pure or representative. Its subjects are neither capacitated for the exercise of the functions of government, nor naturally entitled to them. To suppose otherwise is to assume that those, who are yet confessedly unequal to the work of self-sustentation and self-culture, are capable of self-government; that those, who could not originate the school, can wield its organization when it has been provided for them.

It is here freely granted that experiments have been made in this direction, and sometimes with no inconsiderable success. These, however, do not invalidate the principle. The democracy in these cases is practically a fiction, though a seemingly fair one; and its success, however promising, is equivocal if not deceptive, and otherwise fallacious in theory. It is due altogether to the tact and skill of the governor, and not to the self-active intelligence or power of the governed. Indeed, in such cases, the whole cast of the government is taken from the conception and leadings of the teacher. He is the power that wields the long arm of the lever, while, by his art, the pupil who sits astride of the short arm is induced to exert himself strenuously, as if he were really lifting the weight, instead of being himself the weight lifted. There is perhaps no harm in his making this deceptive effort, no harm in his indulging that flattering fancy; possible even, some incidental good may by the skill of the teacher, be induced from both. Still it may be doubted whether it is consistent for the philosopher to assume the appearance to be the fact.

Neither is the weight self-lifting, nor is the governing self-government, for such an assumption.

It is granted here, that school government, as perhaps every government should, looks forward to self-government, and, wisely managed, does prepare the way for it. But it does this rather by maintaining its own autocratic character, than by abdicating the throne and setting up a supposititious self-government, under the auspices of a delusive democracy. It prepares the way for ultimate self-government, by developing, through the observation and reflection stimulated by a true control, a just conception of the nature and applications of law and its sanctions. Still more significantly does it prepare the way for that self-government, by training its subjects to an habitual reverence for true superiority and to an implicit submission to the rightful authority which already is.

The idea of self-government irrespective of a constant and loyal reference to a government prior to, and higher than that of self, is one of the dangerous fallacies of the times which school government should vigorously endeavor to correct, rather than to weakly countenance. So also, the idea of the possibility of the fair institution and sustained exercise of self-government, previous to establishing the habit of simple obedience to the higher authority, is another fallacy as common and as fatal in its tendencies. He who has not learned to obey, has not learned to govern; and he who has not acquired the habit of reverencing the just requisitions of a higher intelligence and will than his own, cannot render a true obedience to the self-imposed regulations of his own moral impulses and energies. And how few are thus fitted for the work of self-government, is clearly indicated elsewhere in that significant and divinely authoritative maxim, "He that ruleth his own spirit is mightier than he that taketh a city."

Again, the teacher's authority as absolute, must be imperative, rather than deliberative or demonstrative. His requirements and decisions, in whatever form presented, whether that of request, demand or mandate, must be unargued. What he resolves upon and pronounces law, should be simply and steadily insisted upon as right *per se*, and should be promptly and fully accepted by the pupil as right, on the one ground that the teacher, as such, is governor. The faith of the pupil in the equity of the law must be begotten of the authority and the law themselves, and not of any reasonings thereupon. When the occasion rightly serves, some pains may be taken to demonstrate the rightness of the authority, but not the rectitude of the decisions. If that rectitude is neither accepted on the basis of simple faith in the authority, nor on the ground of its own self-evident claims, (which it will be, if the pupil is at all properly disposed,) your argumentation will be either thrown away, or it will only serve to suggest objections calculated to strengthen and embolden the rebellious spirit.

It is a great mistake to fancy that the sound con clusions of the logical understanding are necessarily invincible. That is or is not, altogether as the will may be positioned. Reason with the will accordant, and all goes "merry as a marriage bell:" reason against the inclination or fixed purpose of the will, and your logic "wastes its sweetness on the desert air." Especially is this true of the impulsive and unreasoning multitude; and the child's nature is precisely that of the multitude. With both, your reasoning has force only as it accords with the inclination. Hence, in the school, as in the family, faith in the authority is a far better basis for enforcing the decisions arrived at in governing, than any display of their logical consistency. Hence, further, the thorough subjugation of the will to the authority as absolute should always antedate any resort to discussion or demonstration: When effective discipline has reduced the subject of government to cheerful obedience, conclusive logic may sometimes happily follow up the work, and complete it by compelling the understanding to endorse the surrender of the will.

Once more, in the government of the school, as in that of the family, the decisions of the authority as absolute must be final, or in other words, must be substantially beyond appeal or reversal. To allow any such appeal or reversal as a recognized element in school government, is to conspire its speedy overthrow. Any such reference to the outside authority of parents or patrons is no more to be countenanced or endured than it would be in the case of the home government. Against its subversive influences, parental authority could not long make head; no more can the authority of the teacher. The principle is of equal application to both: here, they stand or fall together.

This is, in a certain shape, one of the very obstacles that parental government has to encounter. Many a conscientious parent understands its working. Some stringent but wise restriction is imposed upon his children. It soon gets to the ears of the neighborhood. It is at once caught up as indicative of pride or exclusiveness, or as involving a tacit rebuke of the ungoverned state of other families. Then it is openly condemned so that the censure passes from child to child until it reaches those under restraint. To them it comes with all the force of a sustained reference or appeal. Up springs from this an incipient rebellion. To meet this, the government of the parent is, perhaps, put upon its defense, and thus its authority is irreparably damaged. As with the domestic government, so with that of the school, only that, in the latter case, the mischief is the greater, since school government is more often, by both children and parents, held as a lawful subject of animadversion.

Nor is an appeal to the school authorities, whether it be informal or legally regular, less injurious. The teacher may err in his decisions, and, at times, his exercise of authority may be unhappy; yet, in the sight of the school, both should be fairly sustained. Reverse the one or denounce the other, and you attack his government in its most vital part; you impair its capacity to command respect and submission even where its demands are intrinsically perfect.

Everywhere among our youth, the spirit of insubordination is so predominant that it is not safe to relax the reins of government at all, not even when they have been improperly tightened. Doubtless, some incidental evils may result from this unyielding grasp of the authority; but let those who are governed charge them where they belong, that is, to their own insubordination. Hence, rather than touch the government of the school, let the school authorities, while, perhaps, privately counseling the teacher against future errors, promptly refuse to entertain any appeal against his authority. Let them bear in mind, that errors in government are nowhere unavoidable except in the fancies of fools, and that invariably a defective government is better than none.

Hence, also, the teacher who finds his authority thus, through the error or the weakness of school officers, made subject to appeal and counteraction, should, out of regard both to the preservation of his own dignity and the maintenance of government in the school, coolly stand his ground, and insist upon the enforcement of his decisions. If he finds this made impracticable by the stubborness or the magnitude of the opposition, let him promptly resign. To remain under such circumstances, is to acknowledge himself a subject; is to confess himself defeated, and, hence, he can expect but little more than to be treated as a conquered enemy. To maintain his authority and secure good government in spite of these adverse influences, will be found a difficult and a doubtful task. Both self-respect and just policy, then, dictate the one course. A change of base will tend to re-establish his character as a strategist, and secure a clearer field of operations.

While we object to any appeal from the authority of the teacher to any other extraneous source of power, we by no means cut off the teacher himself from the right to reverse his own decisions, or reform his own administration of government. As absolute, he may both make and unmake law, only let him bear in mind that the latter is the much more delicate work of the two. To take a position is easy, but to retrace the steps taken, that is the work. This retraction is, however, sometimes both a necessity and a necessary evil. In such a case, great must be his address who can effect it gracefully and with unimpaired influence. If he can do this, let him do it by all means; only let him carefully count the possible cost beforehand. Always, too, let it be undertaken at his own instance, and as his own exclusive prerogative.

Beyond this case of positive reversal or retraction, it may sometimes occur that the teacher himself chooses to refer the points in question to the constituted authorities. He may, for instance, be well assured of being sustained by those authorities, in which case, a reference only completes the discomfiture of the refractory pupil. He may also, in the case of matters which he does not consider vital, and as to which he has no choice, prefer a reference as a means of escaping a direct responsibility. Both of these are, however, open to the objection that the action of the teacher is politic and evasive, rather than frank and independent. In the first instance, the pupil is partially imposed upon, for there is no real intervention in his behalf; and in the second, the idea of a divided authority is directly countenanced. For these reasons, while the right of the teacher to allow the reference is clear, the propriety of resorting to it is doubtful.

On these general grounds, then, and with these exceptions, it is urged that the decisions of the teacher, as absolute in his authority, must be accepted and maintained as a finality.

Returning to the characteristics of the school government as derived from that of the parent, it is urged finally, that it must be benevolent. The end for which the authority is exercised in the case of the teacher, as in that of the parent, lies wholly out of, and beyond himself. The control and discipline of the child are not for the parent, nor for the teacher, but for the child only. An incidental good may accrue to both the former, but the good directly sought is that of the child alone. And that good must be sought even though no such incidental good, but rather a positive evil, seems to be the reward of those who govern. In this principle, is summed up the grand humanity of both domestic and school government. They are, neither of them, "finely touched, but to fine issues," and of those issues, this benevolence is the noblest.

But plain as this principle is, it is too often overlooked in both parental and school government, though most signally, as we believe in the former.

In the vast majority of cases, parental authority is exercised in pure selfishness. Not what is for the child's real injury is condemned and punished, but what is productive of inconvenience or loss to the parent. For example, the child, disregarding the parent's caution against carelessness, breaks a window. The fault, now, which is brought home to his conscience, and for which he is made to believe himself punished, is simply the loss he has occasioned by the breaking of so much glass. The real fault, however, was solely his disregard of the warning given him against carelessness. That warning was given altogether, (or, at least should have been so given,) to prevent his acquiring the always mischievous habit of being careless. And yet, little pains is taken to impress upon the child's heart a sense of his guilt in this direction. Not thus is he made to feel: "It was unfilial and unkind in me to give so little heed to that wise and loving caution against carelessness." More commonly the only feeling awakened amounts to this, "Confound that old window! I wish glass did'nt cost anything;" a finality that would be supremely ridiculous, were not the error it reveals so fatal.

In the government of the school, the tendency to this evil is not so great. The combination of systematic instruction with the exercise of authority, necessarily keeps the teacher's mind steadily under the influence of an object that can only be sought for the good of the pupil. Thus, the steady purposes of the instruction as a benevolence, serve to correct the possible tendency of the discipline towards selfishness; and so strong is their pressure in this direction, that it will be only a narrow and half-brutal nature, such as, we believe, is seldom to be found among our teachers, that can fail to be controlled by them. Hence, it is not, and cannot be at all common for teachers to govern according to the mere dictates of personal convenience, or to administer discipline under the irritated impulse of some sense of incurred discomfort or damage. If, however, the teacher's temptation to such departures from the spirit of true school government be less, it behooves him to see to it the more carefully that all his action is ordered the more perfectly in accordance with the truest good of the pupil as the only end to be sought.

But there is a point of great importance beyond this. There is in all our school operations, a lack of forecasting wisdom and beneficence, and a dominant content with such provisions and attainments as are altogether present and temporary. The child in the school is seen and held, only as the child he now is. What he is to be as the final growth of his present being is altogether overlooked. The school is nothing beyond its present necessities and effects. Its need, as looking forward to the largest ultimate result, is of no account. Hence, everywhere the insufferable school-house, the crude furniture, the naked walls, the absence of maps, blackboards, and apparatus, and the old books. Hence, also, the cheap teacher, the unstudied methods of instruction, and the temporary devices in government. But, were it borne in mind that the child is growing to be a man, and that under the training of these mean and miserable influences; were it realized how much these may have to do with making him in recollection, spirit and action, the very man he should not be, it would seem incredible that the provision made for the merely present in the school, should not be raised so as to conform to the necessary demands of the future.

All this should impress upon the teacher the importance of the grand principle, that in all his benevolent control of the pupil, he is to give the first and most anxious concern to his ultimate welfare. Present considerations may have a certain importance; but they must never come into competition with the graver elements of a future and more imperative good. What the child is to-day must not, either in the instruction or the government of the school, be overlooked; but what he is to be hereafter, as having been molded by that instruction and government, must be the paramount consideration. Not then what will suffice for the immediate pleasure or profit of the pupil, should be the teacher's guide, or his measure of content in determining the direction of the law or the sum of the discipline in the government of the school. The controlling question with the teacher must be, what, notwithstanding its cost to me, or its pressure upon the pupil now, is best for the prospective welfare of the latter as a member of society and a subject of civil government?

From the foregoing, the folly and the vice of all temporizing in discipline will be evident. The teacher is sometimes induced to rest content with temporary expedients and half-way measures. But the very sources of this inducement might suffice to reveal his error in yielding to it. Those sources are generally his own indolence or sensitiveness. The rationale of their influence is this; foreseeing a conflict as the result of adopting the latter, but more severe, course in discipline, the teacher is unwilling to make the strenuous and persistent effort necessary to a successful issue, or he shrinks from the pain which he must, for the present, both cause and endure, and so he falls back upon measures that promise the comparative attainment of the immediate end with less expense to the energies and the sensibilities. The natural result, however, of all such evasions of duty is "only evil and that continually." They commonly fail to secure even the present end which the teacher has in view; and the painful but important conflict which he seeks to avoid, is only deferred until the occurrence of some future and aggravated complication, in the adjustment of which, the labor and the pain incurred will often be more than doubled. And the failure to secure the truest welfare of the pupil in the direction of moral discipline and development is equally complete. Instead of learning the salutary lesson at once, and being thus enabled to grow from day to day, under its fashioning influence, into the perfect subject of just government, he goes on until the final struggle, unsubdued, stimulated by delay to a more stubborn resistance, and roused by the ultimate but unexpected overthrow, to the indulgence of far more bitter and revengeful feelings than would have been possible under a contrary treatment. Of the unhappy influence of all this upon the after ideas and temper of the man, every teacher can judge for himself.

As another inference from the benevolent character of the school government, all passionate, violent or vindictive measures must be condemned. Of these, little need be said. Act directly as an influence and an example, on the pupil's evil passions, to countenance, aggravate, and perpetuate their indulgence, they assuredly will. As certainly will they re-act unfavorably on the teacher's character, on his influence in the school, and on the authority of his government. The least that can be said of such measures, is that they are unwise and injurious. The truth more nearly is, they are unmanly and inhumane.

Not less severely must all means or appliances of discipline, which are of a merely degrading character, or which are simply calculated to badger and exasperate the pupil, without leading to real subjection, be reprehended. As it is inconsistent with the parent's self-respect that he should basely humiliate himself in the person of his child, and as his wisdom and benevolence must forbid all seeming effort at mere petty annoyance or retaliation, so must both these be inconsistent and reprehensible in the teacher's administration of government, resting, as that government must, upon the parental basis from which its derivation has just been traced.

Perhaps, also, no more fitting place will occur for

a proper reference to the use of satire or ridicule. It is true the topic is closely related to the consideration of child-sensibility, as developed in the following chapter. But commonly the use of these two elements is rather a matter of self-indulgence or self-gratification, and so bears directly against the principle of benevolence or unselfishness in government. A free use of ridicule or satire, regardless of their species and influence, is pure selfishness.

Here, then, there is occasion for discrimination and self-control on the part of the teacher. Within a certain restricted limit, a simple scholastic ridicule; namely, that employed purely for the purpose of correcting needless error in knowledge, or persistence in self-neglect, and where, from the pupil's known character, or from the nature of the error, no other means will subserve the desired end so well,—such a ridicule is legitimate. But whenever ridicule becomes purely personal, and touches defects which are not due to the failure of the voluntary nature, but are constitutional or excusable; whenever it is indulged in for the purpose of mere self-gratification, is mingled with any irritation of feeling, and is enjoyed with the keener relish because it is seen to sting and wound,—whenever any of this is true, ridicule is to be utterly condemned. As to satire, much the same is true, saving only this difference, that as satire is usually more extended and caustic in its character, it is even more dangerous than misguided or malicious ridicule. Assuming this as correct, it follows necessarily, that all harsh, discourteous, vituperative language is to be utterly reprobated, and for reasons the more evident, because it can not involve a particle of either benevolence or self-respect; it is more properly the very embodiment of coarse incapacity and incipient malevolence.

Lastly, like the parental government, that of the school should be catholic in its spirit and administration. Always considerate with regard to individual wants, the teacher must, nevertheless, order and govern the school for the whole rather than for a part. This is his only consistent and safe rule. Some things which are individually desirable may even be promotive of the general welfare. In addition to the specific comfort or advantage which they secure, they may reflect general credit on the government for discrimination and kindliness. Other personal provisions may not noticeably interfere with the broader interests of the whole. Others, again, may, as interfering with the general regulations, or as establishing subversive precedents, directly conflict with the welfare of the whole. In all these cases, the application of the principle of catholicity is clear. In the first, it fully sustains the propriety of the individual provisions; with reference to the second, it is silent; as to the third, its voice is a decided prohibition. The general law is, then, this; while, as will be shown elsewhere, all proper discrimination as to individual nature or need must be made, the general welfare must ever be the dominant consideration.

Ignorance or disregard of this principle often leads parents and guardians into the grave error of demanding individual privileges for the child which are inadmissible because inconsistent with the good of the whole. Thus, for example, an irregular choice of studies is demanded for one; for another, a privileged class or seat; for another, release from some prescribed duty; for another, exemption from some specific restriction or exercise of discipline. These, while, perhaps, in certain isolated cases possibly unobjectionable, may, and more commonly must, as disturbing the general order or establishing dangerous precedents, be positively injurious. It will, then, doubtless, be the wiser course to prefer no such claims. But in case, on mature reflection, they seem desirable, let them not be pressed upon the teacher against his convictions. Let him be left free to act according to the demands of catholic unity in the school, and catholic rectitude in its government.

From this, it will be seen, that the teacher, instead of acting from blind impulse or specific impressions, needs to study carefully the economy of his school and its system of government, as a whole, so that in their clear and full comprehension, he may be enabled to prevent any maladjustment or undue prominence of parts, to the disadvantage of the whole. Hence, also, his constant effort should be to impress upon the mind of the entire school, a sense of its prevailing unity, and of the rightful predominance of the general interest over every other.

# CHAPTER V.

## SCHOOL GOVERNMENT, AS RELATED TO THE SCHOOL AND ITS CONSEQUENT CHARACTERISTICS.

Importance of considering government with reference to its subjects—All government to be adapted to those controlled—True particularly of school government—School government to be applied to two classes, children and youth, more especially to children—More such in our schools—Children more governed than youth—Too much license allowed the latter—This practice reprehensible—*Child-character in the school*—Method of discussion—Careful classification necessary—Traits classified as individual and general—Individual traits classified as inherent and contingent, mental and physical—*Mental characteristics—Activity considered*—Mischief often a legitimate result of activity—Activity must be provided for—Neglect of this in public schools—*Objectivity*—Objective representations necessary—Indirect utility of apparatus—Direct application of objective means—Christ's use of this means—The objective a means, not an end—*Spontaneity*—Effect on observation, attention and memory—*Inferred laws*—Care as to involuntary impressions—Suggested particulars—Care in presenting things—Repetition necessary—Careless repetition injurious—*Lack of method*—Method indispensable—Government must be systematic—*Intellect ready but not strong*—Inferences prompt but invalid—Explicitness demanded—Principles especially applicable to the child's reason—"Do right" an insufficient rule—Practically deceptive—Its only advantages—*Sensibilities naturally acute*—Child often abused for feeling—Government must be sympathizing and gentle—Feelings to be diverted rather than suppressed—Double utility of their diversion—Child sensitive to praise and blame—Love of esteem radical and deep—Exceptional cases due to abuse—Government must be stimulating, not depressing—Stimulating kindness especially adapted to the worst cases—Method of its application—*The child's purposes fitful*—Fitfulness impairs development—Increases the teacher's labors—Government must counteract lack of persistence—Failure to do this a prevailing defect—Defect aggravated by so-called improved methods of instruction—Particularly by the exclusive object system—*Physical characteristics—Activity or restless-*

*ness*—Origin both mental and organic—The latter cause more especially considered—Exercise to be secured—No fixed rule for exercise possible—Common sense on gymnastics—Gymnastics restricted in their field—Absurd in case of young children—Nature's gymnastics superior—These principles applied to girls—Military drill compared with gymnastics—General inference as to kind, and management of exercise—*Child's frame immature*—Violent usage to be avoided—Evils possible—*General characteristics contingent on the constitution of the school*—*Mingling of the sexes*—Constitutional differences of the two to be regarded—Influence of these differences increases with age—May become the only means of control—Effect of contrasted sex between teacher and pupil—Error in instructional organization of boy's and girl's schools—*Heterogeneousness of pupils*—Variety extensive and complex—Organic adaptation consequently impracticable—Authoritative discrimination the only reliance — Discrimination not partiality.

THE study of school government as derived from that of the domestic circle reveals to us some of its original and more comprehensive characteristics. But the study of its nature in the opposite direction, as determined by the body politic to which it is to be applied, is equally important as calculated to unfold to view some of its more specific and practical traits.

No government, however perfect in theory, can be a true and proper government unless, in all its practical elements it is so framed as to be fitted as far as possible to the peculiar character and consequent wants of the commonwealth over which it is to be installed as supreme. That which is a true and good government for an intelligent and virtuous community, cannot be the same for a body ignorant and vicious; nor can one adapted to the wants of the mature, the considerate, and the self-controlled, be expected to answer as well for those who are young inexperienced, and dependent on others for both protection and guidance.

Hence, while school government must have its fixed original characteristics, it must also possess those which are in some sense acquired, that is, which must grow out of the character and condition of those who are to be subjected to its authority.

School government, then, as related to the school, we find applied to two classes; namely, to children and to youth, or those who have advanced so as to stand midway between childhood and early manhood.

Of these classes, the more prominent must be the former, since for several reasons, it is more generally applied to that class. First, it is quite evident that as our schools are constituted, our primary and public schools, or those chiefly made up of children, must constitute the largest class, so that even though their individual numbers may be less, their aggregate of pupils must exceed that of the youth, or the older class embraced in our higher institutions of learning.

Secondly, it is, we think, the fact, though an anomalous and unreasonable one, that the government is practically made to be more for the children than for the youth of the community; that is, it is made more continuous, systematic, and rigorous for the former than for the latter class. Indeed, it is one fault of the higher schools, that their government instead of increasing its demands with the increased capacity and responsibility of the pupil, tends contrarywise to greater irregularity and laxity, in many cases amounting to little more than an apology for government. Indeed, in the management of these youth, according to the usages of many of our higher schools, the only end directly sought seems to be that of acquired learning, the matter of discipline in training being treated altogether as secondary and incidental,—in fact, as a sort of necessary evil. The sum of the teacher's anxiety and inquisition is the mere result in recitation; the student's methods and habits of study, matters far more important to his after success, are left to his own ignorance and unconcern. If the student recites the prescribed amount correctly, his work is accepted as done, and the teacher's duty as discharged; and yet the student's study may have been exceedingly desultory and vicious, a thoroughly ragged compound of application and skylarking, to the correction of which the teacher has given no thought whatever.

Now, the least that can be said of this lax system of controlling the youth in our schools, is that it is exceedingly questionable. Instead of this general presumption in favor of the teacher's release from responsibility for the student's habits, and in favor of the student's capacity and disposition for self-control and discipline, it is a question whether it were not wiser to bring these half-grown candidates for future lawlessness and misrule, under the same exact discipline which is meted out to their younger, but no more needy, associates. It is a question whether, of the two evils which mark our management of our youth ; namely imperfect government, and too early emancipation from what government there is, the latter is not the least excusable, and the most pernicious. Against the former, human nature might offset its own weakness ; but over against the latter, it has nothing to place but its own culpable folly and indulgence.

Finding school government practically applied to children rather than youth, we pass to the consideration of child-character in the school as determinative, in some part, of the character of the government related to it. In a former portion of this work, we discussed the derivation of school government, and its consequent characteristics, in separate chapters. In considering, however, its application to children in the school, it is practically more convenient and effective, to present the facts and inferences together, so that the characteristics deduced shall be found in immediate dependence on the personal traits which give rise to them, and with which they are closely interwoven. Inasmuch, now, as the field upon which we are entering is somewhat intricate, a close and somewhat formal classification of the facts will be necessary. Aside from this, the importance of the conclusions to be reached, makes a certain degree of thoroughness imperative.

The facts or traits of child-character, to be considered in this connection, may be primarily classified, as *individual* and *general* ; or those which belong to the child as an individual, and those which mark the children of the school as a body. The class termed individual may be further divided into two species ;

the *inherent* and the *contingent,*—the former including such characteristics as belong to the child's nature in itself considered, and the latter embracing those traits which have been fastened upon that nature by peculiar external influences. Without running into the trite and, for our purpose unnecessary, threefold division of these characteristics, into the physical, intellectual, and moral, we shall content ourselves with distributing them, summarily without definition, under the two main heads, the *mental* and the *physical,* and with considering the inherent and the contingent together. We are now prepared to enter upon the consideration of the characteristics of the child's mental exercises.

Of these characteristics, the first in order, and perhaps the most noticeable of all, is *activity.* There may be cases in which the child's mind appears to be either sluggish or inactive. This, however, should be assumed to be altogether an abnormal condition. In most cases, it can be directly traced to physical malformation or debility. In proper health, mental activity is at once the symbol of the health, and the law of the child's mind. Idle, it cannot and will not be. Its whole nature revolts from it. What is currently stigmatised as mischief, is but the perpetual protest of the child's nature against lack of proper and sufficient employment. So far from being blameworthy for the ingenious and indefatigable inauguration of so much of this so-called mischief, the child is innocent, and, in the light of nature, even praiseworthy. He is but exercising as he best can, the powers he was designed to exercise, and through exercise, develop. It is the parent or the teacher who is at fault; and, in censuring the child, he stands really self-condemned, for he practically pleads guilty to the knowledge of active faculties, for which he has taken no care to furnish proper and sufficient employment.

The principle to be deduced from these facts, is unmistakable. The teacher must, in his management of the school, make ample provision for this superabundant activity. It is impossible, otherwise, for his government to be just. If he leaves the child to idleness during any portion of the school session, or throws him upon his own resources for proper employment or amusement, it will certainly not be competent for him to hold that child amenable to strict discipline, because, forsooth, his self-applied activity, in any part fails to accord with the aims or regulations of the school. But, inasmuch as it cannot consist with the teacher's duty or policy to license any such discordant activity, it is imperative on him to provide for it outlets that are both proper and profitable. In the case of the more active and somewhat restless minds, this must be a subject of careful study, and an object of ingenious and patient effort. In this direction, lies one of the gravest faults of our public schools, in their treatment of primary pupils. Not advanced enough to employ their time profitably or pleasantly in the study of assigned lessons, they are condemned, during the intervals between their exercises, to sit in irksome idleness, upon seats or benches which are only adapted to the purposes of torture, waiting painfully for the next exercise, or longing for the coming of the recess. With nothing provided for their pleasant employment,—no slates and pencils, no alphabet blocks, no picture cards, not even scissors and paper, or peas and sticks, they might well be pardoned, not only for occasioning disorder, but even for openly revolting against a system which seems expressly designed to oppress their natural activity.

A second characteristic of the child's mind, to be noted for its bearing on the government of the school, is its tendency to *objectivity*. Things taken in the abstract, or considered with sole reference to the subjective idea, are thoroughly foreign to his nature. Bring before him the objective form of which he may take cognizance through his ever active senses, and in which he may see symbolized the inward idea or the dry abstraction, and he is at once at home and on the alert. The world of sensible forms with all their variety, beauty and mystery, is eminently the child's world; in it, he dwells with living delight; upon it, his craving mental activity fastens for sustenance; through it, his perceptions feel their way to hidden truths; and out of its elements, his restless though simple and somewhat barbaric fancy is ever struggling to build new combinations of his own, often the prototypes of the ultimate creations of the manly imagination.

Out of this, arises the necessity of the teacher's availing himself, as far as is practicable, of objective reference or illustration, in his presentation of facts, principles and relations, in order that the child's observation may be attracted towards that which may be otherwise abstract or alien to his thought; and that his attention may be happily aided in its attempt to fasten upon, and fix in the apprehension, things that must be otherwise vague and unsatisfactory.

While the common idea is that blackboards, diagrams, maps, and apparatus generally, are only applicable to the purposes of instruction, a truer view discovers in them an important susceptibility of application to the uses of government. Certainly, just so far as the proper employment of these objective instrumentalities meets the wants of the child's mind, and absorbs all its activity in the new interest created, just so far does it divert his attention from unlawful objects, and forestall his temptation to indulge in idle mischief or actual disorder. To one conversant with school operations, no truism is clearer than this; the more interesting all the exercises of the school, the more easy its general control.

But still further, it is even possible to make a direct use of objective means in the administration of the government of the school. It is quite within the power of the skillful teacher to lead the child's mind, by some seemingly remote reference to objective facts, to an unconscious admission of principles that are ultimately discovered to have a close and conclu sive personal application. Take as illustrative of this, Christ's reference to the tribute-money and his demand; "Whose image and superscription is this?"

How readily he elicited the fatal admission that the currency in use as legal tender among the Jews was of Roman coinage! And this granted, how unanswerable the conclusion that the nation, being thus confessedly subject, might rightfully be laid under tribute! The consequent duty was thus put beyond all cavil.

Again, objective allusion or illustration, may often be employed to give additional vividness to the apprehension of truth, and consequently increased force to the resultant law. In exemplification of this, let us refer again to the same great teacher. Observe, how, when his disciples were contending for an idle supremacy, he adroitly "took a child and set him by him," and then, in the light of this objective lesson, proceeded to unfold to them, and to enforce upon them, the combined laws of personal humility, mutual condescension, and child-like obedience.

Without further exemplification here, which indeed our space does not allow, it is perhaps sufficient to refer the teacher to the scripture account of Christ's mission generally, as affording some of the finest instances on record, of both the intellectual and moral application of this method. Did his life possess no higher claim for diligent and reverential study, its value as affording models for the teacher, so sagacious and authoritative, might well commend it to the earnest investigation of every student in didactics.

Before leaving this topic, let one other thought be carefully impressed upon the teacher's mind, that is, that while he is to avail himself of the objective tendency in the child's mental exercises, he must guard against perpetuating it. This objectivity is a primal condition of the child's mind; but it is not designed to become a permanent or ultimate state. The facts of the outward world, and the exercise of the sense, are, of course, necessary to the development of the mind and to the uses of temporal existence. But there are higher faculties in the soul than the sense; and there is a world of fact within the thought, more refined and subtle, but not less real, than the sensible creation. The exploration of this field lays the highest claim upon the human energies, and the development of those faculties only, can lead the soul to its highest triumphs. Hence, in all objective training, there should be a constant endeavor to lead the mind from the sensible to the abstract, in order that its growth may be steadily towards a profound subjectivity, (if we may so speak,) in exercise and attainment. Objective instrumentalities must be kept rigorously subordinate as a temporary means to be steadily reduced from their maximum use in juvenile training, to their minimum employment in the maturer discipline of the adult mind.

We pass from this, to notice the third characteristic of the child's mental exercises; namely, *spontaneity*. Few observing minds can have failed to discover that rarely does the child think, feel or purpose under the guidance of antecedent reflection, or in obedience to deliberate self-controlled conviction. Some immediate object or incident serves as an occasion for those exercises, and determines their direction; and then comes the instantaneous and uncontrolled impulse, and arouses the faculties to action. And so generally is this true of all the child's activity, that it may be safely affirmed that in his nature, reflection is at the minimum, spontaneity at the maximum.

As a necessary consequence, observation, attention and memory, in the child, will be found subject to important modifications. So far as the exercise of those faculties is casual and spontaneous, it will be found marked by a not unfrequently singular sharpness and vigor. Whatever has come accidentally before the child's mind, or at least in the natural track of his unpremeditated activity, even though utterly unobserved by the mature looker-on, generally produces a somewhat permanent impression. But, on the other hand, whatever is brought before his mind for voluntary and controlled observation, attention, or retention, is subject to quite the opposite result. It will be seized upon by the observing spirit with less avidity; its construction in the attention will be more vague and incomplete, and its hold upon the memory will be altogether forced and transitory.

From these facts, there may be deduced several laws which must be recognized by the teacher in the government of the school.

And here, first, it will be seen that it is not enough for the teacher to be watchful as to whatever is directly set before the pupil's mind in the ordering of the school. It is necessary for him to exercise great watchfulness over everything that may appeal injuriously to this sharp thinking spontaneity. The peculiar vividness and permanence of the impressions produced unexpectedly under its auspices, make it imperative that objects and facts, principles and actions, that may create false impressions, should be zealously sought out and be carefully removed or corrected. It is, of course, not possible for the teacher to anticipate the existence or counteract the influence of all of these occasions of evil impressions, for it is their nature to exist and to operate unexpectedly. But he should not lack the will to be watchful, nor should he stint his endeavor to accomplish all that may be practicable.

All this is strongly suggestive of what has already been referred to; the importance of securing in all the external accommodations of the school a predominance of whatever is comfortable and attractive, and hence, naturally productive of refined, happy, and grateful impressions. Not less suggestive is it of the necessity of securing the earliest possible correction of such character and example in the leading spirits in the school, as must be malevolent in both their unseen and their outstanding influence. And if this, then what as to the teacher's own manners and bearing, and what as to the evident temper of his government;—what as to these, other than that the same jealous watch should be kept over them so as to secure in himself an example of whatsoever things are lovely and of good report? In the second place, it follows from the laws of the child's exercises as spontaneous, that great care must be taken in presenting to his mind, matters which call for the deliberate and somewhat arbitrary exercise of observation, attention and memory. Always, so far as may be, they should be brought forward in some way calculated to appeal to his feeling of interest. And if that be to any degree impracticable, they should be announced with a deliberateness, clearness, and positiveness that cannot fail to fix the attention and secure their thorough apprehension. To this should be sometimes added such a repetition of that presentation as will leave no doubt as to its immediate apprehension, and no excuse for any subsequent slips of the recollection. There is reason to fear that children, through the haste or carelessness of parents and teachers in this direction, or, perhaps, through their too ready assumption of the child's actual reception of the facts, are sometimes positively made transgressors, and are subjected to consequent punishment, when the alleged fault was simply an induced failure of the intellect, and not at all a willful trespass upon the reason and the conscience. Let it be observed, however, that the repetition which is suggested as tending to prevent this serious error just alluded to, is a thoroughly deliberate and pointed repetition,—a repetition with an earnest and well-defined purpose in it. Mere idle repetition, that which is ill-considered, hasty, and perhaps, confused, is injurious. So far from fixing the attention upon the matter presented, its only practical effect is to induce inattention. The law here, is the law of the school in everything else; whatever is not done deliberately and to a definite end, is done to little or no good purpose.

Another of the characteristics of the child's mind bearing upon the nature of the school government, is irregularity or *want of method.* Method is by no means a common trait among mankind at large. Of the two faults, ignorance of things to be done, and ignorance of a methodical way of doing them, the latter is certainly the more universal. In the child, we discover the germ of this prevailing evil. It is not strange that it should be so. It is the natural product of the objectivity and spontaneity already noticed. He whose thinking is determined by the mere contingency of objective occasion for thought, and whose mind ever follows the unsettled track of his own uncontrolled spontaneity, must be unmethodical. Method is a subjective accomplishment, and the result of discipline. It must be based upon penetrating and self-controlled thought. It must be antedated by analysis and classification. These, however, are operations both beyond the child's capacity, and contrary to his undisciplined nature.

But nothing can be clearer than that orderliness is indispensable to the harmonious and successful operation of the school. Just so far as the teacher can secure it, just so far he facilitates his management, and lightens the burden of discipline. Quite generally too, with the development of orderliness, or regularity of method in the pupils of the school, there will occur the simultaneous development of easy acquiescence in the system of control established by the teacher, and spontaneous conformity to its movements. Nor can there be any question as to the truth of this, so long as common experience testifies that it is the wild, impulsive, unorderly nature that is forever unexpectedly running athwart the legitimate track of the school order, and introducing some errant clash and jar into its otherwise harmonious movement.

Out of these facts grows the requisition that the whole ordering of the school should, both directly in its methods and requirements, and indirectly as an example and an influence, tend to the correction of this element of irregularity and disorder in the child's mind. Whatever the teacher himself does, and whatever he requires the child to do, should be carefully systematized, so that both the pupil's observation and action shall lead steadily in the direction of methodical habits. This, both the immediate claims of the school government, and the ultimate wants of the pupil clearly demand.

To pass from these more general characteristics of the child's mind, to those more restricted, we may remark that in the intellect proper, his conceptions and judgments, while rapidly formed, are apt to be vague and erroneous. From his very impulsiveness and disinclination to severe thought, the child is too ready to accept statements on faith, to the entire neglect of any search after their certainty, and of any examination of the details involved. For similar reasons, adopting premises hastily and with little question as to their soundness, it is quite common for him, notwithstanding he draws conclusions with curious directness, to reach results altogether deceptive. In short, the child's intellect is ready rather than strong; acute rather than comprehensive, and trustful rather than searching.

Hence, it behooves the teacher, in the government of the school, to see to it that every principle advanced, every regulation proposed, and every consideration urged, is made thoroughly explicit, and is unmistakably apprehended. Equal care must be taken to secure that the pupil is not misled by mistaken inferences the result of his own imperfect processess of reasoning. It is quite possible for the pupil to be led through these very errors and misapprehensions, into transgressions of rule for which discipline may be adjudged necessary, when, after all, the teacher may be the original occasion of the whole.

These principles are especially applicable to the reason in its apprehension of ultimate truths of either beauty or virtue. As the child's notions of the beautiful are essentially crude and barbaric, so also are his notions of rectitude. The gaudy and the glittering are to him, the beautiful, more often than the subdued, the natural, the harmonious. So also are the desirable or convenient more often to him, the right, than the just, the worthy, and the benevolent: This finds ample illustration in the well-known indefiniteness of the child's ideas as to the right of privilege or of property. Indeed, generally in his mind, the rational faculty is either in the germ or but feebly operative, and, hence, left to itself, it is by no means a safe guide for his action.

Hence, we are inclined to regard the generalized principle, "Do right," sometimes laid down by teachers as the sole law of the school, as, of itself insufficient, deceptive and dangerous. That it is insufficient, may be seen from the fact that it is not in any proper sense a law for the school, but only a fundamental principle, the basis for all law. Moreover, it leaves the specific applications, which are practically the law for the pupil, to his own judgment or reason, both of which, as has been seen, are unreliable.

That it is deceptive, may be seen in the fact that, instead of really leaving these applications to be determined by the pupil, the teacher practically reserves that right wholly to himself, inasmuch as he develops the general principle into specific rules, as fast as he finds occasion in the pupil's delinquencies for doing so. In this light, the so-called law verges closely upon an imposition, since, instead of being the sole law, it is more of the nature of a temporary device, and furthermore, ostensibly endows the pupil with a prerogative which is seeming and not real. Thus insufficient and deceptive, it needs not that we demonstrate the danger of depending upon it.

The only advantages that can result from the proposing of this principle at the outset are, *first*, that it enables the teacher to defer the promulgation of specific rules, until circumstances seem to present a natural demand for them. This enables the government of the school to conform itself to the principle of growth or development, and thus to adapt itself the better to the unfolding capacities of the pupils, and to the evident wants of the school. And, *secondly*, properly set forth, it makes itself as a general law, appear to be of the nature of a reason for each specific rule; indeed, wisely applied by the teacher, it becomes demonstrative of the rectitude of each individual provision. Hence, it should be proposed only with these ends in view.

Passing now to the sensibilities, it is important to notice the fact that in the child's nature, these, while fluctuating and transitory in their exercises, are yet peculiarly acute. How slight the word or tone, how seemingly trivial the act or circumstance, that saddens the young face and fills the eyes with tears! And thus it should be. It is the natural product of that delicacy of feeling which is yet a fresh and unwasted legacy to humanity, from the lost Eden to which the child is so much nearer than the man. In his normal state, the child must be a creature of much sensibility. If he is not found to be such, it may be depended upon that his sensibilities have been impaired by malconformation; or they have been deadened or brutalized by bad treatment.

The latter is the more sure to be the case, from the commonness of the practice of abusing children for giving vent to their feelings. Nothing is more common than for their outburst of sorrow to be made an occasion of false consolation, or of ridicule; or still more detestably, of angry crimination. Sometimes this abuse is visited upon them because their outcries are productive of inconvenient disturbance; or sometimes because they create apprehension of censure; sometimes even out of pure irritability, or, possibly, of intrinsic malevolence. In every case, it is unnatural and inhuman.

From this arises a natural demand that the government of the school, while just and firm, should always be marked by a sympathizing spirit and much gentleness of manner. Let the teacher sedulously avoid that current frigidity and folly which attempt to impose on the childish conviction, the belief that the ills lamented are unreal; and which would salve the wounds of the juvenile sufferer with consolatory falsehood or pitiless stoicism. It is the part of both true courtesy and sincerity, to accept fairly the child's trials according to the child's estimation of them, just indeed, as the teacher would desire his own afflictions to be entertained in the apprehension of his friends. Having done this, let him, without exaggerating those ills, or weakly humoring them, both unfavorable to the development of true patience and fortitude, proceed with mingled tenderness and tact to apply the proper remedy.

In all such cases, the legitimate mode of reaching the desired end, is through diversion of thought rather than suppression of feeling. As the sensibilities were reached before through the intellect, so the feelings, being the after-growth of the thought, must be reached again through the same avenue. Let the teacher, then, first enter into the feelings of the child, in a genuine sympathy, and then proceed adroitly to lead the attention to other and more pleasing subjects. Just so far as he can succeed in effecting this transfer of the thoughts, (and such is the child's volatility that it is not a difficult task to accomplish,) he will succeed in abating the feelings which were the object of his immediate concern.

In effecting this result, the teacher secures a twofold gain. It is something to have soothed the feelings of the distressed child; it is no less an advantage to have enshrined himself in the child's heart as a true and trusted friend. In this direction, the occurrence of these youthful trials are, if rightly improved, golden opportunities for the teacher. Out of them, he may develop the sweetest and kindliest regard of the pupil for himself, and a genuine and effective regard for his system of control. Thus employed, they will quite invariably prove that, in gaining the true mastery of the pupil and the school, an ounce of sincere sympathy, skillfully employed, is worth a pound of authoritative discipline.

In this connection, it is also worthy of remark, that while the child's sense of moral obligation, following in the wake of his yet unillumined reason, is by no means ready or acute, he is, nevertheless, more or less sensitive to praise or blame. Now, it is not assumed that the feelings he may evince in this direction are purely the product of his moral susceptibilities. They are more likely the combined product of his constitutional sensitiveness, and his insatiable craving for esteem and love. Whatever may be accepted as to their source, they are certainly a fact in the child's nature; and they possess a power over his conduct which cannot but make them an important element as related to the government of the school.

This latter feeling, the child's love of esteem, is peculiarly deserving of notice as one of the most deeply rooted in his nature. Seeming to be born of his instinctive sense of inferiority and dependence, his looking and longing for esteem and love, are like the reaching forth of the apprehensive spirit after the token and assurance of that concern in its behalf, among the higher and ruling natures around it, which may serve it as a sure ground of kindred feeling and peaceful trust. Imbedded thus in the very instincts of the feeble and dependent spirit, it will be found generally very tenacious in its hold upon the impulses, lingering about them long after the external aspect has been case-hardened by neglect or abuse.

That there are many children in our schools who appear to be comparatively insensible to praise or blame, and who appear destitute of the love of esteem, is doubtless true. This, however, by no means invalidates the main principle. Such cases are abnormal in their character. Some of them are very possibly due to an original moral obtuseness, just as there are cases of a constitutional stolidity of intellect. But much the larger proportion are solely the hard growth of unnatural training at home,—training in which the longing for love has been mocked with stony-hearted coldness and neglect, and the grateful emotions, ready to be warmed into life by the genial breath of approval, have been blighted and beaten down by the blasts of ridicule, censure or angry vituperation.

The influence of these facts should be to impress upon the teacher the importance of guarding the government of the school against degenerating, through the predominance of ridicule and satire, criticism and censure, into a mere engine for depression. Rather let him see to it that it everywhere evinces a delicate regard for the finer feelings, a watchful desire to discover the first traces of true merit, a hearty appreciation of the feeblest endeavor to do well, and a cheerful readiness to bestow upon the humblest and least promising claimant, every just meed of encouragement and praise. In this way, it is possible to make the government of the school a living and effective stimulus, by its steady appeal to the better aspirations of the child's heart, provoking it "to love and good works."

Especially let it be borne in mind, that this system of encouraging appeal to the love of approval and esteem is pre-eminently adapted to those who belonging to the hardened class above referred to, are seemingly the most incorrigible. This is so, first, because of the inherent power of that principle in the human heart, of which society every day furnishes the most striking examples. What alone has ever surely saved the drunkard? The clear, sun-bright evidence that he has yet a hold upon some one's esteem and confidence, and may regain that of others which he had fancied to be hopelessly lost. What alone prevents the glad redemption of the pitiful victim of seductive wiles? The crushing consciousness that a villainous proscription by a pharisaical virtue, has cut her off from all generous regard or hope of re-established esteem and confidence. Still further, the method referred to is the best for the more vicious pupils, because, secondly, it is so entirely opposite to their experience and expectation, that it, as it were, takes them unawares, and upon the side of their nature least fortified against approach, and therefore most susceptible to influence. The truth of this is amply illustrated in the history of every reformatory effort for the reclamation of abandoned youth. Ragged schools, schools of reform, industrial schools and the like, have everywhere been successful, just so far as they have skillfully availed themselves of the child's desire of approval and love of esteem. A proper appeal to those principles has in it the true magician's art; it will disenchant and restore to his better form the enthralled victim of demoniac wiles.

The method to be employed in applying this approbatory stimulus is exceedingly simple. In the first place, let the teacher avail himself of the first occasions, whether real or only seeming, for bestowing praise and evincing confidence, and carefully follow up each attained success, by judicious but increasing demonstrations of that character. In the second place, where, from the extremity of the case, no occasion seems to offer, let him adroitly create one. This he may do by politely appealing to the child's love of activity, or ambition to be helpful (a powerful feeling in most children), for some incidental but ostensibly important aid. Here is, at the outset, an unexpected exhibition of confidence which may at first puzzle the pupil, but which will ultimately and the more surely, because it puzzles him, beguile him like a fascination into the bestowment of the required assistance. This done, the way is open for a kind and deferential acknowledgment on the part of the teacher. The course is now clear. Carefully repeat the process until the pupil grows into the feeling that he is of some real value. This effected, you may openly and confidentially appeal to his ambition to become more useful and worthy. The utility and certain efficiency of this whole process might easily be illustrated by specific cases. Space, however, does not allow their introduction here; and, besides, to the minds of many teachers, they will occur spontaneously.

Passing from this discussion of points bearing on the susceptibilities, it remains for us to notice one characteristic of the child's voluntary nature, and that is, the prevailing fitfulness of his purposes; in other words, his lack of true persistence. Resulting, as this does, from the traits already noticed, it is not necessary to regard it as a fault, as is too commonly done. It is, however, a deficiency, to the correction of which the government of the school should be carefully adapted.

And this, first, because unsteadiness, or lack of persistence, must always stand in the way of the child's best development. Indeed, it might not inconsistently be urged that failure to develop a proper persistence is failure to develop the first manly element in the child's mind,—failure to develop in him the master-requisite to his future success in the active walks of life. This conclusion, all the current maxims of men relative to the power of perseverance amply sustain. These all show that while intelligence and perseverance are both necessary, the latter bears the palm as, single-handed, the better champion.

But, further, this lack of persistence tends directly to increase the demands made on the teacher's energies in the control of the school. It certainly stands in the way of his readiest attainment of the proper object of the school. When, for example, the pupil recoils from the determined pursuit of his study, he will either fall back on some schoolmate for aid, which at once tends to confusion, or he must resort to the teacher, in which case, the latter must undertake the pupil's work, as his substitute, or he must task himself to bring up the flagging energies of the little straggler, and command his faltering spirit again to the persistent attack. Or, if in another case, the pupil fails through lack of steadiness, as is the more common fact, to maintain a course of intended obedience, either the teacher must give himself promptly to the work of girding up the relaxing purposes, or he will have to address himself to the work of administering discipline in the correction of overt transgression.

Hence, it follows, that while the government of the school must recognize this lack of persistence in the child as a constitutional weakness for which in all judgments, due allowance is to be made, yet it must, in all its example, influence and requirement, work steadily for the counteraction and correction of the defect. In order to do this, it must, while always both properly helpful and hopeful, carefully avoid any relaxing of its own demands. It must be itself a model of considerate steadiness and inflexibility. So too, it must set itself persistently against all vicarious performance of duty. Duties should be judiciously assigned, but once thus assigned, by mingled encouragement and quiet demand, they should be pressed steadily home upon the pupil for his sole and unflinching performance.

The failure to do this, we believe to be a common vice in the government of our schools. The consequence is that no true foundation is laid in the will, for steady and thorough scholarship in the pupil's subsequent educational course, or for manly decision and persistence in his after business career. And so we find perpetuated throughout the community, a fitfulness of purpose, an unsteadiness in application, and an entire uncertainty as to the persevering attainment of proposed ends, which necessitate constant fluctuation in the currents of society, and ever recurring personal failure and disaster.

This lack of persistence is, we fear, constantly encouraged by the methods of instruction becoming every day more prevalent. No thoughtful educator can have failed to observe that the entire tendency of our assumed improvement in teaching is to simplify books, to elaborate all the processes of reasoning for the pupil, and to made the teacher more minutely helpful. In short, we are practically running into a system of study made easy. Now while it is clear that all the difficulty attending the work of learning, which grows out of preposterous or ill-adapted requisition, and needless obscurity or complexity in the presentation of truth, should be fully obviated, it is to be doubted whether that simplicity or helpfulness, which relieves the pupil from close application, earnest thinking, and resolute self-assistance, is anything less than a positive evil. There is every reason to believe that, while the youth who emerge from our schools may know more, and may be more sharp and confident than those of the former generation, they will lack that power of persistent application, of independent thought, and thorough self-reliance, which are only to be developed under the seemingly hard but yet salutary discipline of a system which compels the pupil to do for himself, instead of leading others to do for him. Not that which is the easiest and most agreeable, is always the wisest or the best.

In this connection, a grave question arises as to the influence of a too exclusive use of the "Object System," so prominently, of late, set forth before the public. Involving as it does an almost constant presence and prominence of the teacher as the author of the derived knowledge, how can it other than insensibly and surely lead the child into utter obliviousness of his own independent acquisitive power and purely individual duty? Always flinging around his attainment of the conveyed knowledge, the halo of the teacher's presence, interest, and attractive skill, how can it do other than envelop his solitary and unaided application, with a sadly contrasted cloud of dulness and uninterest? Our own observation leads us to the almost inevitable conviction that pupils who have been, to any great extent, trained upon this exclusive method, may really be quite acute and observing as to whatever appeals to the senses, or comes through some living source of presentation, but will, when thrown upon books and their own powers of reflection, be found painfully lacking in capacity for sober and persistent self-application.

Turning the attention now to those physical characteristics which the government of the school must recognize in the child, and to which it must adapt its management and discipline, we find two that require at least a brief notice.

It needs but little observation to show that in the child, while there is a lack of enduring strength, there is a high degree of physical activity; in fact, in proportion to his real power, his physical activity is at the maximum. So marked is this peculiarity, that it may not inaptly be styled the leading characteristic of his bodily nature, and the symbol of its proper conformation and perfect health.

This activity may be traced to two sources, the mental activity of which we have before spoken, and the superabundant vitality bestowed upon the youthful organism. Necessarily, the restless objectivity of the child's mind must call for a constant employment of his physical powers in ministering to the wants of his intellect. Then, too, the child, instead of holding the physical powers in abeyance in his thinking, from his very impulsiveness, commands them into the service of his thoughts, as vehicles of expression. Hence, we might almost say, he thinks with his whole body. It is thus that the child is naturally a pantomimist.

The more important aspect of its origin, however, is found in excess of vitality as subservient to bodily growth. Necessarily, as the child's frame must be a growing one, there must be in all its organic elements a vital energy more than adequate to the claims of mere sustentation. There must be in them a power capable of adding to what is, that which is to be, and so, adequate to the building up of the child into the man. And as this requires not only accumulation, but a growing assimilation, compactness and hardihood, there must also be the abundant exercise of all the maturity and power already attained. Nutrition adds, but exercise adjusts and establishes. Hence, exercise is one of the ruling instincts of the child. However much inconvenience, then, this activity may occasion to the teacher, it is idle for him to either disregard it or quarrel with it. It is a fixed fact in the child's nature, and must be provided for.

Hence, in his management of the school, the teacher must see that adequate provision is made for this physical want. He should, as far as he can, have a care that the confinement of the pupils during the daily sessions is not so lengthy or rigid as to produce a languor and exhaustion from which they do not readily recover. In the case of the younger class of

5

pupils who are not able to study, those of a feebler class whose tendency is to morbid inactivity, and those who are constitutionally over restless and active, he should strive to make especial provision. What these need, however, is not so much specific artificial exercise, as release from idle confinement, and opportunity for natural amusement. With regard, then, to all his pupils, the teacher's management must be governed by the general principle that, while the child's physical nature must experience some natural inconvenience from the necessary confinement and restraint of the school-room, his bodily health and development must not be made to suffer by allowing that confinement and restraint to be unduly extended or severe.

Beyond this, no fixed or invariable rule is possible. For example, in the rural districts, where the freedom of nature is enjoyed, and people are brought up to wholesome industry, school children rarely suffer for want of exercise. It is abundantly supplied by their home amusements and avocations, their journeys to and from school, and the recesses customarily allowed them during the daily sessions. But in the case of the children in the schools of our larger towns and cities, whose opportunities for natural, open air amusement and development are more restricted, greater attention must be given to the matter of artificial exercise. But whatever may be the locality, school, or class of children, the teacher must, to a greater or less extent, discriminate for himself as to the time, quantity, or quality of the exercise. No

specific rules can be given him. His guide under the general law indicated above must be simply sound common sense.

The reference, which has just been made to artificial exercise, suggests the importance of raising some question as to the utility of gymnastics. And this the more particularly, because, reacting from our former complete neglect of physical culture, there is among our educators, a growing tendency to swing to the extreme of making this species of artificial exercise everything. That gymnastics, like military drill, have their place and utility, it is useless to doubt. For example, given a class of pupils who have been trained in habits of physical indolence and inactivity; one precluded by the false feminine usages of society from active out-door pursuits or amusements; or one, by absorption in study, made oblivious of the physical wants,—given either of these classes, and an established order of gymnastic exercises is probably the only thing that can effectively supply the deficiency. Here, their use may be set down as a necessity; for, where natural means fail or are foolishly discarded, a resort to those which are artificial is inevitable.

But from this, it is quite apparent that the field within which gymnastics as an established mode of exercise and culture are applicable, is restricted. In the case of the pupils in our country schools, who enjoy the facilities for physical activity and development, afforded by rural life and industrious habits, and even in that of the children of the laboring

classes of our larger towns and cities, who, when not industriously employed, enjoy the wild freedom of the streets,—in the case of both these classes gymnastics are practically superfluous. What need of staves, or rings, or dumb-bells, or Indian clubs, to the young "sans culotte" of the streets and alleys, or to the farmer-boy, who, in addition to the games of the recess and noon-spell, has his mile walk in going to and from school, and his "chores to do" morning and night at home?

This, however, is not the limit of their restriction. In the case of young children, their application is little other than absurd. And this because, with a

"Vaulting ambition which o'erleaps itself,"

it claims to be a wisdom above nature. Nature has indicated with unmistakable clearness, the means by which the young child is to secure the physical activity requisite to a proper development of its bodily powers. Its own spontaneous vivacity, its own restless curiosity, its own ever-ready imitation of the movements of men, its own insatiable love of associated sports,—these are nature's occasions for exercise. Through the activity thus secured, she has provided for them a means of physical development more accessible, more varied, more extensive, more practical, more completely pervaded by an intelligent interest, and to the child, every way more delightsome. To all this class, formal gymnastics are a forced and unnatural work. Their simple appearance under its processes is a continual protest against

these factitious devices. Their difficulty in effecting accurate movements, their strained and anxious look of attention, and their lack of hilarious interest, show that nature's law for the child's exercise is spontaneous and unconscious activity. Now, if the indi cations of nature are worth anything, (and the attempt of some modern educators is to make them paramount,) this is the very field where they are most clear and decisive.

Beyond this, we question whether these principles should not be applied to another class to whom the modern gymnast holds out his exercises as a desideratum; we mean to our incipient and precociously developed young ladies. Give them open grounds, a common-sense attire—one adapted to both activity and cleanliness—full liberty of action, and the choice games of their brothers, and we verily believe nature would soon evince the superiority of her modes over all systems of artificial training. Put into the girl's hand the hoop and stick instead of the staff, the ball and bat instead of the dumb-bells; let her run and jump instead of striding extravagantly by rule, in prescribed dirctions; get her enlisted in "hide and seek," "prisoner's base," or "I spy," instead of twisting and twirling herself in unimaginable curves and spirals, and depend upon it, the physical development will not be found lingering like "a laggard in a lady's chamber," but will speedily show itself foremost in the field. The only difficulty in the way is this; gymnastics are fashionable; games for girls, vulgar!

It is, perhaps, not improper that some reference

should here be made to military drill as a means of physical culture, since, in the minds of many educators, it has come to hold an important place. Of this we think it may be said, that, whenever it is applicable, it has its advantages, and is, in some respects, superior to mere gymnastics. In the first place, it has that moral superiority which is a cardinal virtue in any exercise; namely, a recognized end beyond itself, and beyond that of mere bodily development. The influence of this to create a sustained and sustaining interest, and to dignify its whole routine, is unmistakable. Beyond this, it is impossible for it to run into mere conceits or absurd and repulsive exaggerations in movement. Hence, also, its influence on the mien or carriage generally, is more manly and ennobling, than it is possible for that of gymnastics, with its larger license and purely material ends, to be. Lastly, its power to establish habits of implicit obedience is necessarily greater, inasmuch as that obedience is not merely enforced by the present command, but is also fixed by all the associated ideas of the sublime art to which it is subordinate, and in which that obedience is seen to be a beauty and a power. But, as was suggested, the application of military drill is limited, for it requires numbers, a certain degree of maturity, and is altogether a masculine exercise.

The general inference to be drawn from these facts is, that while gymnastics may be employed where they are adapted, more attention should be given by teachers to the natural means of exercise enjoyed by their pupils. Hence, the teacher should recognize it as one of his duties, not only to provide proper and sufficient occasions for relaxation and amusement, but also to personally oversee the out-door or play-house sports (for every school should have its play-house) of his pupils. He should do this, in order that he may influence them in the choice of their games, advise with them as to the conduct of those games, secure to all a proper participation, guard any against excess, or exposure, or serious accident, and provide against the occurrence of injustice or angry contention. We believe that the common neglect to perform this supervisory service is a great mistake both as to duty and policy. Not only do physical evils result from it, but not unfrequently moral complications arise, which affect the harmony of the school, and, in the end, severely tax its government.

Returning from this somewhat divergent discussion, to the child's physical characteristics, it is important to notice that, even when healthy or stoutly built, the child's frame is not mature or well knit, and that, in the majority of cases, it is even slender or positively feeble. It is consequently not at all adapted to excessive physical effort, or to rough and violent usage. Hence, where either of these evils is allowed, serious mischances may not only result, but must rather be expected.

This, it will at once be seen, enforces the duty just suggested,—that of carefully supervising the sports of the pupils. It renders it equally imperative upon the teacher to be watchful against roughness or sudden violence in the administration of discipline.

Nothing is, however, here determined as to the question of corporal punishment. It is only affirmed that, if it be accepted as legitimate, it should be administered in such ways as will not endanger the child's frame as yet immature or slender. No sudden and violent jerking of the pupil or whirling him about the room should be tolerated. Either may easily result in the dislocation of some joint, the fracture of some of the small bones of the limbs, or in the infliction of some injury to the spine, ultimately producing weakness in the back. Nor should any heavy implements ever be employed in inflicting blows upon the child; and, above all, no blows should ever be inflicted upon any part which, from its direct connection with the nervous centres, must be dangerously sensitive to any severe shock or contusion. All such treatment of the pupil is undignified and brutal. It is simply the outbreak of passionate unreason. It is not discipline.

Having thus somewhat fully discussed the individual characteristics of the child's nature, as subject to the government of the school, we have to turn the attention to those which are general, and contingent on the constitution of the school. These traits, unlike the preceding, must mark the many rather than the few, and, hence, require the children in the school to be taken into view as a body.

Here, then, it must be observed that, necessarily in the great majority of our public schools, the children must be of both sexes. Even were it the better course to separate the sexes, which admits of question, in the larger number of cases it would be impracticable.

Hence, in these schools, boys and girls must be taught and trained together; and the teacher who would govern justly or most successfully, must recognize this necessity, and adapt his government accordingly.

But to do this, he must keep in mind the fact that there are distinctions in the character of the two, which render a common adaptation insufficient. There are specific traits in each, which require specific modifications. In the earliest or comparatively infantile period, the divergence in these traits is less marked, and a common method will avail equally for both boys and girls. But as they advance to childhood, the divergence is marked, and demands discrimination. For example, the boy's nature responds more readily to appeals made to his manly ambition; the girl is more sensitively alive to personal appreciation and love. The boy will better bear a frank and somewhat bluff manner; the girl instinctively craves an approach marked by the sympathizing look, the gentle word, and the kind caress.

And these influences grow severally stronger as the two advance to the keener self-appreciation of youth; for both then comprehend more clearly the import of the teacher's bearing toward them. The boy discovers in it the distinct and generous recognition of his manhood; and the girl feels in its fine courtesy and considerate regard, the first dawn of the homage her womanhood may always claim from the true man.

It is quite possible also for these means of influence to become of the first importance, since, with growth in years, the force of mere authority over the mind diminishes. Hence, the feelings just indicated in the boy or girl, may come to be the only available sources of control. Happy, then, will be the teacher who has fixed himself in the hearts of both, as a generous and appreciative friend,—in that of the boy, by a hearty confidence in his trustfulness, and pride in his manly energy; and in that of the girl, by a refined and chivalric attention and esteem.

A fact, by no means to be overlooked here, is this; that in the exercise of this influence, a contrast of sexes between the teacher and pupil, reduplicates its power. Hence, often, a boy, who would be quite insensible to the confidence or praise of a man, will be completely taken captive by the same means skillfully employed by a genial and attractive woman; and, contrariwise, a girl, whose supreme delight would be to contemn and caricature a teacher of her own sex, will evince a most considerate and obedient regard for a preceptor who gives her, by his tact and courtesy, the always pleasing assurance that he both understands and appreciates her character. Hence, it is seriously to be questioned, whether a grave mistake is not made in our boys' schools, by employing tutors exclusively, and in our female seminaries, the corresponding one of placing the pupils almost wholly under the instruction and control of lady teachers. The natural tendency of this course, we believe to be, the perpetuating in the former, of rough manners and unamiable passions; and in the latter, the thorough consummation of boarding-school diablerie.

But we pass, in conclusion, to notice the heterogeneousness of the school, as giving rise to contingent traits of character, that bear a vital relation to the government. As our schools are constituted, it is well known the pupils must be marked by the greatest possible diversity of age, constitution, temperament, character, social condition, and antecedent training. Some are hardly past sheer infancy; while others are verging upon manhood and womanhood. Some are slender, even to helplessness; and others are hardy and domineering. Some are sensitive; while others are rough and unfeeling. Some are ready and versatile; and others slow and even pitiably obtuse. Some are burdened with conscious poverty; others are full of pride of position. Some have been humored, and perhaps enfeebled, by over indulgence; while others have been hardened and almost imbruted by passionate and unnatural abuse. And between these various extremes, the individual character may run through a whole gamut of the most perplexing gradation.

Now, it is quite clear that no government that does not in some way, and to a good degree, reach these differences, can be either just, merciful, or effective. And, yet, it must be quite impracticable to frame a government that shall in its organic structure be able to effect this object. A surface of collective character so tortuous in its corrugations can not easily find any organic whole that will readily touch it at all points. To endeavor then to secure adaptation by specific provisions would result in such multiplication of details as would destroy all simplicity, intelligibility and effectiveness.

The great want can then be met only by the application, under the teacher's absolute prerogative, of the one principle of authoritative discrimination in the application of either requisition or discipline. In dealing with the individual pupil, as comprehended in his condition and character by the teacher, the various provisions of his government must be fearlessly suspended or modified according to the case, so as to make the pressure, as far as may be, practically equal. Hence, from the beginning, the teacher should explicitly avow his right and his determination to do this; and the school should be made to see and feel, not perhaps the justness of each specific application, that must rest on the teacher's simple authority, but that of the general principle.

Nor should such discrimination be charged as partiality. While it is not to be doubted that the government of the school should be comprehensive, that is, that it should be a government for the whole, and not for a part to the detriment of the whole, nothing can be clearer than that to neglect or refuse to discriminate in behalf of any part according to its natural claims, whenever that can be done without injury to the whole, is to dispense with both adaptation and justice, and make the government the iron engine of blind theory and arbitrary will. Hence, the teacher who exhibits a deference or regard for a thoroughly good pupil, which he would not evince toward a vicious and disobedient member of the school; who extends a lenity to a feeble and uncared-for child, which he withholds from one robust, or possessed of ample advantages; who bestows a painstaking kindness and labor upon the dull, the timid, or the easily depressed, which he denies to the ready, the resolute or the forward; who allows privileges to the infantile members of his flock, which he refuses to grant to the older ones; who, in a hundred such ways, while planning for the whole, discriminates for the benefit of the parts;—such a teacher is not partial; he is simply sensible and just. Partiality is discriminating or showing favor without, or against, just reasons. But discriminating or showing favor for wise and sufficient reasons, although often thus stigmatized, is no partiality; it is rectitude. Let the teacher, then, see to it that his government is neither from ignorance nor fear, undiscriminating; nor from blind prepossessions or prejudices, simply partial.

# CHAPTER VI.

## GENERAL ELEMENTS OF SCHOOL GOVERNMENT IN ITSELF CONSIDERED.

Main theme resumed—General elements classified, as Order and Discipline—Necessity for the two, common—Order defined and classified, as Arrangement and Management—*Arrangement defined*—Characteristics of arrangement—*Simplicity necessary*—*Definiteness considered*—Rules a necessity—School, mechanical as well as moral—*System important*—Secures harmony—Secures thoroughness—System liable to abuse—Must be practical—*Specific applications of arrangement*—To juvenile class exercises—To outside study—To recesses—*Management defined*—Its characteristics—*Promptness*—Evils of tardiness—Causes loss of time and confusion—Promptness induces general punctuality—*Steadiness*—Fluctuation a prevailing evil—Steadiness produces respect—Creates faith—Cultivates popular stability—*Earnestness*—Promotes proper confidence of manner—Creates enthusiasm—*Geniality*—Pleasure as well as profit of the pupil to be studied—Importance of sympathy—Induces a loving regard—*Quietness*—Not mere sluggish unconcern—Quietness favors intelligent apprehension—Tends to quiet order in the school—Favors proper reticence in the teacher—Induces higher respect for the teacher—*Good management promotive of general order*—Reduces the need for discipline.

THE preceding topics, which were in some sense general and preparatory, have been already seen to be of vital importance. As possessing such importance, and yet, as too generally securing only a passing notice, it was judged proper to discuss them with a good degree of thoroughness. In doing that, some points belonging to the main subject were, of necessity, anticipated, and that at the risk of subsequent repetition. Notwithstanding that fact, they will be noticed in what follows, in their proper place, and according to the just demands of the occasion. This will be considered as fully justified by the too common neglect of them; by the new light thrown upon them by their immediate relations; by their intrinsic importance; and by the necessary claims of our whole scheme to systematic completeness.

We pass then, after so much delay, to the consideration of the main theme, or school government in itself considered. Bearing in mind the fact, as before stated, that school government is the proper ordering of the organic and individual action in the school, so as to secure in the pupils the best possible development of mind and discipline of heart, with reference both to present and future welfare, we proceed to the consideration of its general elements viewed as those distinct parts of the teacher's exercise of his intelligence, skill, authority and virtue, which make up his entire system of control. These we classify under two general heads; namely, *Order* and *Discipline.*

A very common error of the public, and probably of a majority of teachers also, is that of regarding the government of the school as summed up in the discipline alone. This is possibly due to the fact that the discipline is the higher and more striking element, and as such, appeals more forcibly to the apprehension of the common mind. Were the estimate rested upon this comparative superiority, and the discipline accepted as simply representative of the whole, there would be no particular ground of complaint. But when it is allowed to overshadow and conceal the other element, the thing is altogether inconsistent and injurious.

For a variety of reasons, both of these elements, though in some features distinct, are inseparable and alike necessary. That they must be so taken, will appear from the following facts stated in brief; their general institution and conduct must run quite parallel; their perfection must depend on the same executive qualities; and their facts are, all the time, mutually emerging from, or re-acting upon, each other. Indeed, nothing can be clearer than that the right ordering of the operations of the school must bear strongly, both upon the amount of the discipline required, and upon the ease with which it may be administered. Certainly, no ill-ordered school can be, without a corresponding multiplication of offenses; nor can those offenses be corrected without a corresponding draft upon the power to be exercised. Contrariwise, also, the just discipline of offenders must re-act powerfully upon the regular operations of the school, making the mere conduct of its daily system the more easy and successful. The thorough defeat of misrule in any school, is the certain triumph of its general order.

By the order of the school, we mean that which includes its general system, or which covers all its ordinary operations as determined by the teacher. This will, of course, include the two subdivisions, *Arrangement* and *Management.*

Arrangement is inclusive of all that pertains to the systematic disposition of the sessions and recesses of the school, of its studies, recitations and exercises. Of the absolute importance of arrangement, little need be said. As being simply the nice adjustment of the regular machinery of the school, it bears too directly upon its daily running, to be at all obscure or doubtful in its influence. Nothing can do more to secure the movement of the whole machine against irregularity, friction or jar, and retardation. Indeed, a proper arrangement may justly be styled the better half of good management.

A proper arrangement must be marked by four leading characteristics; simplicity, definiteness, system and practicality.

First, it must be *simple*. Such is the defective organization of our public school systems generally, that, in most schools, any disposition of the daily operations will be complicated enough. But that the arrangement may not burden the teacher's mind to the detriment of other parts of his work, and that it may not, through any needless cumbrousness, be prevented from being successfully carried out, it is quite clear that it should involve as few parts, and be subject to as few rules as possible. Whether the teacher is able to reach any ideal, or prescribed model of simplicity or not, let *simplicity* be carefully studied and persistently sought.

While, however, simplicity is to be a constant aim, let it not be secured at the expense of *definiteness*, There should be no vagueness or uncertainty in the operations of the school. Purely incidental matters may, of course, be left to an incidental or impromptu adjustment. This will serve to cultivate in the teacher, both that quick perception and ready skill which are necessary to his perfect mastery of his position, and to secure in the adjustment effected, a truer adaptation to the immediate wants of the occasion. But for everything else, there should be a well-determined time and place, otherwise the scheme of the school will operate somewhat and somewhere to the discredit and, perhaps, the embarrassment of the teacher, and to the disadvantage or the injury of those under his charge.

From this, it will be quite apparent that rules will be necessary. Certainly, the teacher can have no fixed or definite arrangement, without laying down specific rules for himself; nor can he expect to secure conformity to his own laws of arrangement, among his pupils, without laying down rules as specific for their guidance. Some educators are accustomed to set forth with an ostentatious flourish of supposed philosophy, the doctrine that the teacher is to make no rules for the school, and that he who does it is, *per se*, unfit for his business. As is usually the case with superficial thinkers who would be wise overmuch, they fail to discover one very important fact; namely, that as an organized body, the school is mechanical as well as moral; it has parts and operations that must be fixed by positive regulations, as well as those which must be determined by moral principle. The general law, "Do right," upon which these theorists lay so much stress, and which has been somewhat carefully noticed elsewhere, even if it answered the ends of the moral element in the school, would be utterly absurd if applied to its mechanical operations. For example, such questions as, where, or in what order pupils shall attend to such and such exercises, are questions of scholastic economy, and not personal rectitude. They are to be determined by the judgment, and not by the reason. They find their claim to obedience in the positive authority of the teacher, and not in the enlightened impulse of the pupil's conscience. The same is true of many other requisitions which will be noticed hereafter under this general head.

Again, both for the sake of its own perfection, and in order to secure various important ends, the arrangement of the operations of the school must be *systematic*. Some of these have already been noticed in the discussion of government as applied to the child-nature. Another will be found in the simple power of system to reflect the teacher's capacity as a practical analyst and comprehensive manager. Furthermore, system in arrangement favors the simplicity and definiteness to which reference has just been made. Indeed, it is only through the clear analysis which must antedate and determine the system chosen, that the teacher becomes able to simplify his arrangement by rejecting non-essentials, and to render it definite by applying rules according the relative demand of its various parts.

Beyond these, system is necessary to harmony both in the arrangement and the conduct of the school operations. Not until every part is adjusted in its place under the inspiring spirit of true system, can the whole become a self-consistent unit; and not until this pervading unity is attained, can the whole movement be secure against possible friction or conflict. System is thus in the school, as elsewhere,

"The hidden soul of harmony."

But to this very harmony, *thoroughness*, or comprehensiveness is necessary. It is only under the light of a systematic classification of the facts of the arrangement, that the whole field stands clearly revealed in all its parts, their proportions and relations, so that the judgment may determine whether aught is wanting to the just completeness of the whole. And the importance of this completeness is seen in the simple fact that it is the only safeguard against specific or incidental legislation, which is always wasteful of power and injurious to harmony. As in building, the thrusting of modifications into the original plan, always enhances the cost disproportionally, and endangers the ultimate symmetry of the edifice; so is it with the thrusting in of impromptu regulations to meet overlooked contingencies in the order of the school; they endanger its consistency, and unduly burden its movements. While, however, the teacher must hold system as essential, he must not forget that it is susceptible of abuse. He must not forget that just in proportion as it aspires to perfection, it is in danger of withdrawing itself from the conservative influence of circumstances, and of becoming consequently altogether speculative and impracticable. Such a system is necessarily unfitted to the wants of our schools, in which, so generally, stubborn facts both confront and confound fine-spun theories. It is also the more to be guarded against, because under the existing and growing passion of education for absolute schemes based upon exhaustive analyses, the, perhaps, dominant and most dangerous tendency of popular education is to swing to impracticable or vicious extremes, and not unfrequently, through arcs of oscillation either tremendous or absurd.

Hence, the arrangement of the school operations while systematic, must be *practical.* While in constituting it, the teacher may be guided by well-considered theory, he must still see to it, that the insufficiencies or aberrations of his theory are constantly corrected by a careful induction of facts,—the very facts which his method must meet and master, or prove a failure. Better, if need be, sacrifice somewhat of theoretical perfection than come short of practical adaptation.

As illustrative of what we mean in this connection, take the following specific applications of the principle. In every public school, there are commonly, some general exercises in which the larger portion of the pupils may engage simultaneously. Rightly managed, these are quite desirable, as they serve to develop skill and energy in the teacher, and unity of feeling and harmony of action among the pupils. The studies adapted to such exercises are gymnastics, singing, spelling, and reading. Now the principle of arrangement, under consideration, requires that these should be set apart for the opening or the close of school, for the reason that they will then least interfere with individual application to study, the pupils having either, not begun their work upon their lessons, or having already finished it. So too, of these exercises, those should be set down for the opening, which require the least antecedent preparation, because there has yet occurred no time for such preparation. Still further, those that are most exhausting should come in the same connection as the preceding, because at that time, the physical powers are most fresh and vigorous.

Again, the training of the juvenile classes in the alphabet and reading, the object exercises if there be any, and the reading lessons of the larger classes, should occur in the early part of each session, so as to afford time for the preparation of the various lessons to be recited by those who are mature enough to study. Among the first of these, may also be included the recitation of lessons prepared the evening beforehand, at home, for the obvious reason that they are in readiness, and should be put out of the way of the daily study.

The assignment of those lessons to be learned at home should not be made without regard to principle. They should embrace studies which the pupil can pursue independently to the best advantage, and which will require the least transportation of apparatus or materials, or those which require results in writing rather than those in abstract retention.

In the distribution of exercises or studies between the two sessions, those should be assigned to the morning session, which are the least interesting or the most severe, since during that portion of the day, the powers of both the teacher and the pupils are most fresh and vigorous.

The assignment of the recesses should also be carefully regulated by this principle of practical adaptation. Nothing can be more absurd than the common custom of having one and the same recess for the older and the younger pupils; for those who can, and those who cannot study. The latter should have two or three recesses rather than one, for it is little other than cruelty to compel them to sit idly and wearily waiting the coming of the, to them, long-delayed recess. Of the former class, there are frequently some to be found who should almost be ashamed to take one recess, as if it were practically an impeachment of their power of fixed application.

The principle of practical adaptation will also raise the inquiry, whether the recess should occur precisely in the middle of a session, at which time, while the pupil has not become fatigued, his mind has only just got most closely and vigorously at its work; or nearer the close when his study is done, or is nearly so; when he is actually fatigued; and when a recess will refresh his powers preparatory to the work of recitation.

But we pass from these illustrations of the bearing of practicality upon the arrangement, to the subject of management. Management is that part of order which includes all that belongs to the proper conduct and complete carrying out of the system of arrangement adopted. It hence, covers the whole of the teacher's bearing and action during the progress of the various parts of his system, and in carrying his school through them, whether they are sessions or recesses, exercises or recitations.

A proper management must be marked by five general characteristics; namely, *Promptness, Steadiness, Earnestness, Geniality* and *Quietness.*

First, it must be prompt. Generally in the public schools, there is an excess of work, and hence, a deficiency in time. It is rarely, if ever, the case that the teacher is able to carry the whole daily order through with sufficient or invariable thoroughness. Either all of the parts must be somewhat abbreviated or hurried, or some of them must be practically neglected. Promptness, then, as a means of saving time, is indispensable, for this saving of time is necessary to the perfection of the teacher's work. Hence, the teacher must be instant to the time, as the peal is to the flash.

Then, again, tardiness is necessarily confusion. An exercise delayed is either an exercise cut unduly short, or inconsistently crowded upon its fellow. Whichever it may be, the order of the school is out of joint, and so far the result is confusion. Not unfrequently, too, the first pressure caused by the loss of time, throws the teacher into a nervous hurry for the whole session, and thus the disorder is perpetuated. The only preservative against such hurry and confusion is promptness.

Still further, promptness in the teacher operates

both indirectly and directly to secure punctuality and readiness throughout the whole school. Of the bearing of these upon the general harmony and success, little need be urged. Prevailing dilatoriness is little better than prevailing insubordination. It is the necessary concomitant of lack of interest; and lack of interest is lack of order. Hence, it is always safe to conclude that unless the teacher's management is prompt, his discipline must be defective, if not a failure.

Again, the teacher's management must be steady. One of the most common evils in both parental and school government is that of constant fluctuation. There is no steady and continuous pressure of the authority, in the direction chosen, and to the very end of a complete attainment. To-day decisive measures are adopted and pressed with vigor. To-morrow the effort is relaxed, and the preceding policy practically contradicted. It may be even worse than this; through fickleness of purpose or love of novelty, the old measures or methods may be summarily abandoned, and new ones fitfully introduced in their place.

One of the necessary results of this unsteadiness is loss of respect for him who has the management of affairs. Unsteadiness argues either ignorance, lack of forecast, or weakness of purpose, any one of which is enough to secure the just condemnation of the teacher. But, very clearly, the finest attainment of order must depend very largely upon the respect which the teacher commands. Without that respect, he can carry neither methods nor measures to a happy completion. His sole dependence must be mere arbitrary authority, perhaps what is still worse, mere brute force. But however proper these may be in their place, without the concurrence of respect, the success they may win is half failure.

Beyond this, unsteady management destroys faith in the certainty of things. Few principles are more productive of uniform and orderly action among men than that of the invariable uniformity of nature. Since the mountain will not come to Mahomet, Mahomet must go to the mountain. Nature will not change, hence, man conforms to nature. So the regularity of nature begets regularity in man. Thus, in the school the inflexible steadiness of the management creates among the pupils, unwavering faith in the certainty of results, and a fixed conviction of the necessity of conformity to the consequent condition of things. This is itself *order*. Order thus begotten is habit. And habit is self-controlling. Hence, steadiness itself is power.

But aside from its direct bearing on the management of the school, this steadiness has a most important prospective influence. As tending to the creation of habitual steadiness of action among the pupils of our schools, it operates ultimately as a corrective of one of our worst national characteristics, popular instability. With us, everything, from the action of individuals to the gravest matters of national legislation, is in a state of constant fluctuation. Violently receding from one extreme, only to rush as violently to another; up for a measure like a flood-tide or an inundation, and then, under the influence of some counter excitement, subsiding or ebbing until, in the old direction, nothing is visible but dreary mud-flats or barren sand-spits; it becomes a question whether we are really susceptible of becoming stable. This much, however, is certain, that if that stability is ever to be established as a national trait, its foundation must be laid in the individual character as developed in the home and in the school. And yet there is reason to fear that unsteadiness in management is one of the most common and most incorrigible faults of both.

Again, the management of the school must evince earnestness. Promptness and steadiness carry with them the appearance of mere power, and are, hence, liable to give to the teacher's bearing and action an air of stiffness and coldness, which can never prove favorable to the best development of the young mind. This evil can only be countervailed by the presence and pervading influence of some heart-principle in the management. Hence, it is every way important that all that the teacher does should be characterized by thorough earnestness. For more particularly, a thorough earnestness always produces in the teacher an air of firm assurance that carries to the mind of the pupil a full conviction of the teacher's ability. Proper self-reliance, or confidence, is itself a source, as well as an evidence, of power. This is eminently true of the confidence or assurance begotten of true earnestness. But, for the possession of that earnestness, the teacher's entire business is a continual plea.

Hence, for the lack of it in his management, he has no excuse.

Still further, this earnestness on the part of the teacher, in all the various exercises of the school, is contagious. It passes beyond himself. It flies from heart to heart throughout the little commonwealth. It finds and arouses in each a kindred spirit. Up springs through all ranks and classes a kindred zeal. This general earnestness, or zeal, at once commits the whole school to the order which the teacher has instituted, and in which he is so deeply and evidently interested. In this way, the teacher's earnestness, by commanding spontaneous co-operation, reduplicates his power and ensures success.

Partly out of this demand for earnestness, grows the demand that the management should be genial. That earnestness is supposed to be generous, not wrapped up in the attainment of ends concerning the teacher alone, but ever looking forward to the welfare of the pupil as the highest good. A genuine interest in this latter object will naturally shed over the teacher's whole bearing and action in the conduct of the school, the light of a constant and considerate good will. Hence, so far as it can be done without destroying dignity or infringing upon order, the teacher should come down pleasantly to the pupil's level, evince a sympathetic feeling for him, and skillfully adapt things to the production of his pleasure, as well as his profit. This, by no means argues that he should humor the pupil in what is weak or injurious, nor that he should stoop so far as to mingle in his rough sports,—himself a mere boy among boys. But it does imply that he should comfort the child when he is in trouble, encourage him in his efforts to do well, evince an interest in his amusements, and lend him a helpful aid in planning or perfecting such as are really wholesome and gleeful.

The natural influence of all this, it is easy to see, will be to enlarge the pupil's confidence in the kindliness, as well as the ability, of the teacher, and to draw both together in the bonds of a common and a growing love. The effect of such a love is to secure on the part of the pupil, a hearty co-operation in all the plans of the teacher, and to ensure to his management a perfect success. It is in reaching the sources of this love, as will be elsewhere shown, that the teacher attains the seat of his highest influence and power.

There is, however, one tendency of high earnestness which must be guarded against, and the more carefully, because the influence of all this pressure upon the teacher in the direction of perfect management, goes to increase that tendency. We speak here of the liability of the teacher to a sort of over energy in his management, degenerating, perhaps, into mere boisterousness. As opposed to this, it is demanded that the management be quiet.

And by this is intended, not the quietness of sluggish unconcern, not the quietness that grows out of a fear of trouble, a dislike of labor, or a love for the comfortable but debasing recesses of an easy chair. The quietness proposed is not so much constitutional or involuntary, as deliberate. It is the quietness of one who has carefully taken his own measure, and that of the objects he seeks to effect; and who, confident of the end, calmly moves on, without haste, without perturbation, without tumult, without violence, towards its attainment. Nor is there anything in this which conflicts with the penetrating glance, the firm tone, the animated movement; it conflicts only with whatever is fussy, vociferous or violent.

As a result of this quietness, it will be seen clearly that it favors the most intelligent understanding on the part of the school, of what is desired, or what is being done. All needless noise or parade of energy, by distracting the attention, and, perhaps, stunning the senses, tends to impair the distinctness of the pupil's perceptions, and so stands in the way of his receiving the clearest and most enduring impressions.

Aside from this, as in the preceding instances, the tendency of the teacher's manner is to reproduce itself in that of his pupils. A quiet teacher may have noisy pupils, but it will be because the quietness is negative, and is, hence, coupled with positive inefficiency. It is, nevertheless, the natural effect of the true quality, to repress the noisiness so common among children. Rightly employed, it is one of the most powerful means of securing an orderly silence in the school.

Again, this rational quietness is favorable to the exercise of proper reticence, and may even produce it. By this reticence, we mean a wise reserve in the teacher as to the antecedent betrayal or proclamation of his intentions or plans, to the school. There are, as has been stated, cases in which this previous announcement of measures, as a means of intelligent understanding among the pupils, and as guarding them against unwitting errors, is necessary. But the object here, is to guard the teacher against a thoughtless habit of gossiping about his proposed measures, or of conceitedly flourishing them before the school. It cannot but be seen that it adds little to his credit, to be unable to keep his own governmental secrets. Besides, any such heedless or ostentatious parade of his plans much beforehand, leaves no room for unobserved modifications in case of difficulty or disappointment; it operates directly, by taking off the edge of novelty or newly expectant interest, to impair their effectiveness; and it sometimes actually leads to graver complications in the matters involved. A reticent quietness is, therefore, one of the finest attributes of the teacher's management.

As a last excellence, this quiet management tends directly to create a higher respect for the teacher. To the observing pupil, nothing in the teacher can be more suggestive of manly self-control, and of power in reserve. It is easy for him to see occasions enough for very natural outbreaks of vehemence in voice, or haste and disorder in action. It is easy for him to see how the teacher, by means sudden and startling, although tending to disquietness and violence, might summarily secure the ends he seeks. But when he sees all this calmly forborne, and unmoved quietness, and quiet immobility still the teacher's sole reliance, he can not but feel a profound reverence for a character so self-poised, and an authority so significantly reticent. The influence of such a reverence, on the teacher's success in the order of the school, is too apparent to need further discussion.

It only remains then, for us, under this general head, to urge upon teachers a closer attention to the arrangement and management of the operations of the school, as a part of their government, eminently adapted to reduce the occasions for any uprising need of discipline. It is, indeed, the proper field for the finest exercise of judgment and tact in the application of the old maxim; "An ounce of prevention is worth a pound of cure." Discipline is chiefly curative: arrangement and management are eminently preventive. They are the shrewdest allies of that master-art in the control of the young,—the art of counter-diversion, to which, as applied to individual cases, reference has already been made. What is true of its power over the child as an individual, is as true of its influence on the school as a whole. Hence, it is quite possible for the school when ready, either from prevailing weariness or general irritation, to break out into overt acts of insubordination, to be, unsuspectingly to itself, swept by some skilful counter-diversion, into a new channel or new current of aroused interest or restored good feeling. For the attainment of such results, the teacher's management is responsible.

## CHAPTER VII.

### GENERAL ELEMENTS CONTINUED—DISCIPLINE—REQUIREMENT.

Order and discipline related—*Discipline distinguished from order*—Discipline defined—Elements classified, as Requirement, Judgment and Enforcement, or Correction—Discipline as specifically related to school government—*Requirement distinguished*—Specific duties of the pupil classified; as, Personal, Associated, and Filial and Scholastic—Claims of these self-evident—*Requirement restricted*—Illustration—Duties required out of school—Offences *in transitu*—School jurisdiction limited—Influence but not authority to be employed—Exceptional cases considered—Characteristics of requirement, moderateness, naturalness, fairness and firmness—Moderateness distiuguished and enforced—Naturalness distinguished and enforced—Fairness distinguished and enforced—Firmness considered.

In passing to the consideration of discipline, it must be premised that it is so closely related to order, that it is difficult to treat them so far separately as to have no points in discussion common to both. And yet, general convenience and the real differences that exist in their nature, require them to be thus separated.

But in order that their points of approximation and divergence may be clearly distinguished, we shall place the two in careful contrast, as follows. Order in the government of the school, embraces whatever is merely mechanical, or organic; discipline is inclusive of whatever is moral in its nature or ends: order has jurisdiction over the field of practical economy or convenience ; discipline extends its sway over that of personal responsibility or duty : order stands upon the claims of positive authority ; discipline is founded upon the ultimate principles of rectitude : order regulates the exercise of the faculties as all subsidiary to the development of the intellect ; discipline exerts control over the moral faculties, the conscience and the will, as determinative of their own conditions, or of character. Hence, finally, the grand law of order is expediency ; that of discipline is rectitude. Discipline, in its highest sense, may then be defined as the proper control of individual power and responsibility in the school, with reference to the higher laws and aims of pure morality.

The elements of discipline, as thus defined, may be arranged under three general heads ; the legislative, judicial, and executive, and, as thus classified, may be specifically designated as ; *Requirement*, *Judgment*, and *Enforcement*, or *Correction*.

In the light of this classification, it will be seen that discipline, as here treated, while bordering closely upon government as commonly understood in the state, is only a specific part of government as required for the school. The reason why government in the school is thus made more comprehensive than government in the state is clear. In the state, the maturity and independent capacity of the citizen, the necessary variety of his pursuits, and the freedom of application demanded, render a fixed and comprehensive method of action inconsistent, if not impracticable. In the school as a commonwealth, from the immaturity and dependence of its members, and the necessity for the united and harmonious pursuit of a specific end, order becomes an essential part of the general control, and, hence, must be included as the first grand element of the government, as discipline is the second.

Under the head of requirement as the first general element of discipline, must be included all demands made upon the pupil as susceptible of moral relations, and subject to moral obligation in the school. In other words, whatever the teacher may either positively or negatively require as based upon principles of morality; as apprehended by the reason and felt in the conscience to be obligatory,—all this may be made a matter of disciplinary demand. Requirement, then, covers the whole ground of the pupil's moral obligation as a member of the school.

The specific duties embraced under the head of requirement may be classified thus:

1. Personal, or those the child owes to himself as pupil, as, for example, self-improvement:

2. Associated, or those the pupil owes to his companions as members of the school; namely, Equity and Kindness:

3. Filial and Scholastic, or those the pupil owes to the parent so far as his commands reach the school, and those he owes to the teacher as its ruler,—or Obedience and Reverence.

Upon these duties severally considered, little need be said. The obligation of the pupil to fulfill them to the best of his ability is self-evident. That he should be a member of the school, necessarily involves his hearty co-operation in the effort of the school authority to secure his best development and discipline: he could not be anywhere associated with his companions, much less in the intimate and important relations of the school, without being bound to respect the rights and feelings of all: from the duties of filial obedience and regard, no place or position can release him, much less his membership in the school which the parent has provided for the better advancement of his highest interests: and his obligation to obey and reverence the teacher as the specific representative of the parent, for the time being, and as the rightful and necessary head of the school and soul of its operations, is founded on the very nature of things.

It will be observed, however, that the moral obligation involved in all these duties, is restricted, as if bounded by the pupil's relation to the school. This must be of necessity. School government is specific in its aim, and limited in its field of application. While, then, ethics entire may be properly embraced in the instruction given in the school, only such of its principles as are distinctly applicable to the control of the child as a member of the school, can be properly embraced in its system of government. These principles as constituting the body of school ethics, are all those which may be consistently noticed here.

As illustrative of this restriction of school ethics, the following specific cases may be taken. The principles of ethics bearing upon "Duties to the State," can have no place whatever among the requisitions of school government; for, neither is the child yet a citizen, nor would the school be held responsible for his treatment of those duties, even if the pupil had attained his majority. All *that* belongs to the relations the pupil (if he be of age) holds to the state, and hence it is altogether within the province of civil government. The state, it is true, recognizes the school, but surrenders to the school none of its prerogatives.

Again, the "Duties to the Parent" belong in general to the domestic relation, and properly come under the cognizance of the home government alone. It is quite clear, however, that out of the relation which the parent holds to the child in the school, and out of the relation which the teacher, as his agent or substitute, holds to the parent, there may arise specific duties to the latter, which the former must recognize in his government. The parent may, for instance, with the consent of the teacher, lay certain specific requisitions upon his child as a member of the school; and the government of the school may claim and enforce obedience to these requisitions. The duty of obedience in this case, while a *quasi* duty to the teacher, is primarily a duty to the parent. Such, and such only of the child's duties to the parent come within the jurisdiction of the teacher.

Similar illustrations might be drawn from the duties of the pupil to the teacher, to his associates, and to himself. It is not necessary, however, to cite them, since the general principle is sufficiently clear; namely, that whatever the duties may be, to fall properly under the cognizance and authority of the school government, they must both practically come within its reach, and must evidently pertain to the facts and relations of the school as the commonwealth concerned.

This general principle may be profitably applied to the solution of the question often raised as to the teacher's jurisdiction over the pupil's duties out of school, and especially over offences occurring *in transitu.* With regard to any school duties required to be performed at home, it must be clear that the teacher has no original prerogative whatever. His right to assign such duties or to enforce their fulfilment, must rest wholly on an understanding with the parent, either tacit or explicit. Even in this case, his application of authority must be indirectly to the deficiency evinced by the pupil in the school, rather than directly to the delinquency that occurred at home. For instance, in the case of lessons to be learned at home, it is competent for the teacher only to take cognizance of the fault of failure in recitation; it belongs to the parent alone to correct the indolence or misappropriation of time at home, which was the real offence.

The question as to offences occurring during the the period of the pupil's transition from his home to the school, and *vice versa,* is more intricate. And this, for the simple reason that the limits of the school jurisdiction are somewhat obscure. But the very cause of the difficulty is suggestive of the direction in which we are to look for the chief responsibility in such cases. We may accept this, then, as a first principle; that where the limits of jurisdiction are the broadest and most definite, there is to be found the direct responsibility for the correction of the offences in question. Any other responsibility in this direction, must be wholly conditioned and incidental. It needs now no argument to show that only the authority of the parent is thus comprehensive and complete in its application. The parents' jurisdiction over the child, and responsibility for his conduct, are subject to no restrictions of either place or time. Not merely within the precincts of the home, nor during certain set periods of employment, is the child held to the duty of obedience to parental law. It is a duty for all time and place.

But it will certainly not be urged that the jurisdiction of the school government is thus far-reaching and comprehensive. Limited alike in its object, time, and place of action, nothing can be more evident than that the application of its authority must find a necessary circumscription within corresponding limits. Not for the child's general conduct in society, at the home nor any more in the highways; not for his behavior upon holidays, at morning or at night, nor any more during any time not within the immediate neighborhood of the school sessions, can the teacher, as teacher, be justly held responsible. The parent's authority may rightfully maintain its hold upon the child until he comes under the eye of the teacher, and within reach of his voice and hand; but the teacher has no right to extend his rule contrariwise over the child until the moment when he passes into the sacred precincts of the home, and into the parent's presence and power. It is demanding for the less, what can only be due to the greater.

This, however, is not to take ground that the teacher may evince a stolid unconcern as to the conduct of his pupils elsewhere than within the precincts or the periods of the school; nor is it taking from him the power to do anything outside of those limits, to effectively subserve the pupil's welfare and the ends of good order. As a citizen and as a friend, he may, so far as he can, keep a kindly and careful eye upon the pupil's conduct during the periods of transition from the home to the school, and *vice versa*, and may exert all his influence to prevent the occurrence of offences, or to secure atonement for them; but it is influence which he is to exert, and not authority. And not only may he do much in this way; but it is believed that the very regard which he thus evinces for the rights of relative jurisdiction will add weight to his influence, and secure in the end better results than would be possible under what must necessarily be an arbitrary exercise of power.

This, however, must not be construed in any sense, as ignoring the possibility of exceptional cases. For example, flagrant outbreaks of injurious violence for which there is no parental preventive or correction, may come to the immediate notice of the teacher. Here it may be necessary for him to interfere, and the interference may be justified on the ground that arbitrary rule is better than licentiousness. So, too, cases may occur in which evil-disposed pupils may avowedly take advantage of the supposed absence of jurisdiction, to do after school, what the teacher has forbidden in school. In this case, the teacher may take cognizance of the act as an insolent evasion equivalent to *quasi* insubordination. The case sometimes cited, of a pupil's playing by the way, and so becoming late to the detriment of the school order, is not properly an exception; for while the teacher may not claim jurisdiction over the act of loitering which was the major fault, the tardiness itself is an immediate and legitimate occasion for discipline. The distinction and the method involved in this case, will be found applicable in many others, and their proper application will enable the teacher to avoid the two injurious extremes of arbitrary jurisdiction and allowed disorder.

Having thus defined the proper limits of requirement as a department of the school government, we pass to the consideration of its general characteristics. These may be enumerated as chiefly four; *Moderateness*, *Naturalness*, *Fairness*, and *Firmness*.

The propriety of these characteristics, especially as determined by the traits of the child's nature as subject to the government of the school, has been partially considered under a previous head. It is, therefore, only necessary that they should be briefly noticed here and more especially with reference to their bearing on the government in itself considered

By moderateness in requirement, we mean that the

teacher should, in all his demands upon the pupil as subject to moral obligation, study to avoid severity or excess. It is better policy for him to fall somewhat under the full measure of exact requirement, than to incur any risk of overgoing it. Aside from lenient adaptation to the child's feebleness or imperfection, it is far easier to secure the perfect enforcement of moderate demands, or if need be, to bring them up to the full standard of just requisition, than it is to maintain those which have been strained at the outset, to their farthest limit, or to abate successfully those which have been found to be excessive. In school government, as in every other, practical excellence is to be determined, not so much by the absolute perfection of the laws, as by their capacity to be perfectly administered.

By naturalness in requirement, we mean, not so much naturalness in the demands themselves, as in the method of their successive development. It is here considered as tantamount to that progressiveness in school legislation, which has been elsewhere noticed. The ground consequently taken, is that of the inexpediency of pre-enacted codes of requisitions, or laws for the moral government of the school. And this, for the general reason that no such code can be made for any commonwealth, as it were to order, and be either wise or just. Law for the government of any community, has its grand principles which are co-existent with the possibility of a community. But beyond those principles, law is the creature of the common need; and what that need is can only be determined by the developing power of circumstances. Hence, all specific laws should be, as it were, the natural growth of circumstances. So in the government of the school, specific rules, to have a natural origin, fitness, and power, should be made, only as facts develop a need for them. Let the teacher pursue the opposite course, and he will burden his system of discipline with minute and ill-digested provisions, many of which he will either have to repeal or violate as unreasonable or oppressive. This, however, is not to be interpreted as contravening the careful promulgation of general principles, elsewhere urged as necessary.

Beyond this, it is demanded that the teacher's requisitions in governing be thoroughly fair or honest. By this we mean, first, that all the means and ends of the requirement should be transparently what they purport to be. No subject of the school government should ever have occasion to suspect that he has been misled or overreached by policy or artifice. Any such impression will prove destructive to his confidence in the teacher, and respect for him; and when those are wanting, authority may compel submission, but it cannot command true obedience. Again, the requirement should be explicit so as to be beyond the possibility of misconception. Pains should be taken, not only to unfold the demand fully and fairly, but also to ascertain whether it has been as fully and fairly understood. The government which, failing in this direction, exposes the pupil to unwitting transgression, stands itself impeached as first in the fault. Still further, there should be no sudden revival and application of rules which, having lain dormant or lacked recent use, have passed out of the pupil's mind, or have been practically accepted by him, as inoperative. All such action will assume the aspect of *ex post facto* legislation, and will appear, if it is not even what it appears, narrow and unjust. The government of the school must then in all its requirements, be thoroughly frank and fair.

The presence of the foregoing qualities in the school government, it will be seen, prepares the way for the existence of that firmness without which it hardly deserves the name of government. Given, requirements which are moderate, the product of a natural want, and thoroughly sincere and fair, and the teacher may press the demand for obedience, with the most inflexible firmness. Nay, in such a case, the greater, the more stubborn, the firmness, if we may so speak, the higher the rectitude of the school government, and the more absolute its claim to obedient regard. It is in the power of this unalterable firmness to dignify even the dying struggles of a bad cause. Much more is it able to gather about the upright front of righteous rule, the radiant symbol of divine excellence. Not only, then, for the pupil's sake, as has elsewhere been urged, but for its own, let the government of the school, in the firmness of its requirements, be

> "Constant as the northern star,
> Of whose true-fixed and resting quality
> There is no fellow in the firmament."

# CHAPTER VIII.

## GENERAL ELEMENTS CONTINUED. DISCIPLINE—JUDGMENT.

Judgment defined—Importance considered—Elements classified, as Detection, Investigation, Judgment Proper or Decision—*Detection distinguished and classified*, as Spontaneous, or Immediate and Mediate, or Circumstantial—Kinds distinguished—Spontaneous detection justified—*Its rules stated*—Every offense not to be known—Knowledge of offenses, not always to be betrayed—Offenses to receive the most favorable construction—*Mediate detection classified, as Incidental and Concerted*—Importance of the latter—Especial difficulty arising from the school code of honor—Folly of condemning the code summarily—*Course to be pursued*—Pupils must be taught right views—Severer punishment in case of conspiracy to conceal—*Rules for concerted detection*—Must be the sole means of discovery—Offenses must be of a flagrant character—Detection must be prosecuted for no inferior or private ends—*Grounds of consistency*—Detection demanded for the general safety—The offense is necessarily covert—It is one of practical outlawry—*Method to be pursued*—Detection should be devolved on a subordinate agent—Propriety of setting a trap for offenders—Caution against seeking personal ends—Against the use of positive deception—Against undue exposure of the innocent—Objection to the use of temptation answered—*Investigation described*—Importance of investigation—Need of attention to practical logic—Logical process in investigation considered—Evidence classified, as Personal and Circumstantial—Kinds distinguished and illustrated—Testimony the chief reliance—*Confession by stratagem unwarrantable*—Practically dishonest—Impairs the teacher's self-respect—Demoralizing to the pupil—Particular caution as to the evidence of personal appearance—*Requisites in witnesses*—Opportunity, direct knowledge, capacity, veracity, freedom from prejudice—Caution as to the testimony of children—*Kinds of testimony*—Simple, Accumulated and Concurrent—Defined—*General characteristics of testimony*—Must be definite, accumulative, concurrent—*Grounds of strength in concurrent testimony*—Logical and practical illustration—*Decision* — Defined — Characteristics—Must be positive, overt, explicit—*General characteristics of judgment*—Must be deliberate, comprehensive, righteous and decisive—Popular decisions in the school condemned.

PASSING now to the second general element in the discipline of the school, we observe, that under the head of judgment, must be included whatever belongs to the decision of cases involving discipline.

The importance of this element will be readily inferred from the fact that, not only does the influence and success of the discipline depend on its proper performance, but, without its antecedence, no discipline in any just sense, is practicable. In fact, this judgment bears much the same relation to the correction of wrong, that the diagnosis of a disease, in medicine, bears to the subsequent treatment. Depending upon shrewd intuition and well-defined experience, rather than upon rules and authorities, that diagnosis is *the work* of the physician,—the work which most tries and evinces his skill. Indeed, the measure of diagnostic accuracy is the measure of success in the treatment. So, we may say, the proper judgment of the case in discipline determines quite as fully the course of the subsequent correction; and as such, it is one of the highest and most important elements of the teacher's art of governing.

The elements of judgment may be classified as threefold; *Detection, Investigation,* and *Judgment Proper*, or *Decision.*

Of these, first, detection is simply the discovery, by the teacher, of offenses and offenders. It may be of two general kinds; namely, Spontaneous or Immediate; and Mediate, or Circumstantial. In the former, the teacher comes to a knowledge of the offense and the offender, personally and directly, through the exercise of mere ordinary vigilance in observing the operations of the school: he spontaneously witnesses the original act himself. In the latter species of detection, the teacher either alone or through his agents, in the exercise of some extraordinary scrutiny, reaches a satisfactory knowledge of such related circumstances as, to a practical certainty, fix the offense upon the offender. This involves the employment of circumstantial evidence. It differs from investigation, to which it is nearly related, in the fact that it stops short of any open inquiry and public measures, and, hence, in its operations and results, may be wholly unknown to the school.

Of the propriety and importance of spontaneous detection, there can be no question. It is clearly the duty of the teacher to be always in a position of discovery. It is necessary that he should have some correct knowledge of so much of whatever transpires in his little commonwealth, in the shape of responsible action, as will enable him to understand fully the general drift of conduct in the school, and will thus fully empower him to make proper preparation for possible emergencies, and to wisely select for discipline, such offenses as may have a noticeable bearing on the general welfare.

This, however, is not to take ground that the teacher is to be suspiciously on the alert, or always watching for the occurrence of offenses. This is to be vigilant at the expense of some of the finest qualities of his true character, almost at the expense of his manhood. Such a suspiciousness the teacher is, by all means, to avoid. It is a vice of weak minds and weaker governments.

Hence, let the teacher carefully observe the following rules as bearing on spontaneous detection. First. It is neither necessary nor wise for him to know all the minor misdemeanors, or peccadilloes of his reckless, unthinking, and ill-trained subjects, especially those of the younger class. A knowledge thus minute, will only tend to impair his confidence in his pupils, and may thus induce in him a consciousness of evil character and conduct, calculated to affect his manner unfavorably, perhaps even to the extent of impairing their confidence in him.

Secondly. Even if he knows so much, it is all important that he should not evince his knowledge of it. To do this is practically to compel himself to take judicial cognizance of the offenses involved, since hardly anything can be more demoralizing in its influence upon the moral sense of a school than a teacher's evident neglect of known infractions of law. And yet, as many of these offenses may be altogether venial and quite destitute of any important bearing on the general order of the school, for the teacher to subject them to discipline, would only be to harrass himself and his pupils with an over government hardly less injurious than insufficient government. For a teacher to do this, "is wasteful and ridiculous excess." Of either extreme, it is better to govern too little than too much. Except in the family, nowhere more than in the government of the school, is there need of that noble charity which covers a multitude of sins,—nowhere so much advantage in its wise and patient exercise.

And, lastly, with reference to all facts which, as ostensible misdemeanors, really come to his knowledge, let the teacher, while retaining them in thought, as possibly susceptible of grave but yet undiscovered relations, carefully guard against assuming their worst interpretation as a foregone conclusion. Let him rather, habitually assume the probability of a fairer explanation, and generously hold to that opinion until it is, by subsequent developments, rendered either dangerous or impossible to do so.

Passing to mediate, or circumstantial detection, which has already been defined, it may be classified as of two species; namely, incidental and concerted detection. These rest alike on the same basis of observed facts, but differ in the manner of reaching the facts. As is indicated by their names, the circumstances involving detection under the former species, come to light of their own accord, in the teacher's exercise of ordinary watchfulness, and are only voluntarily woven, in his judgment, into a web of satisfactory evidence: under the latter species, they are, upon pre-determination and by concerted action, dragged from their concealment and set in such array as effects full detection.

Of the former species, nothing further need be

urged in this place, since its specific laws are the same with those already considered under the head of spontaneous detection. Of the latter, distinct and thorough notice must be taken both for the reason that it is more complicated in its nature, and far more difficult in its proper exercise. Indeed, in the pre-determined exercise of the function of detection, the teacher will find occasion for the employment of his largest knowledge of human nature, and his highest skill in dealing with character and circumstance. Instances will not unfrequently occur, which will, for a time, perhaps even finally, baffle his most strenuous efforts.

A special cause for this difficulty is often met with in the prevalence of a false sense of honor among pupils, which leads them to conceal the misdeeds of their associates. Sometimes, even where there is a better conception of duty, native lack of resolution, or fear of retaliatory abuse, strengthens the tendency to connivance or concealment. In this forced absence of the only direct testimony possible, the teacher is left altogether to circumstantial indications or the developments of time, and will not unlikely find even these insufficient.

In cases of this kind, it is altogether idle for the teacher to take ground before the school, that this concealment is a wrong, and to insist that those cognizant of the offender's criminality shall expose him; and it is the height of impolicy for him to betray any uneasiness or irritation (if he be indeed so weak as to allow such feeling) at the persistent adhesion of the pupils to the school code of honor. Nor does the fact that there can be no more question as to the pupil's duty in the premises, than there is in the case of the citizen cognizant of crime committed against the laws of the state, mend the matter. The evil is the result of a misguided conscience; and, until the teacher can correct the misguiding cause, he must be content with the exercise of patience rather than justice.

In endeavoring to correct this evil tendency to shield offenders from justice, the teacher may adopt two methods. First. He may labor to impress upon his pupils correct views of their relation to the government of the school, and a sense of their duty to sustain its authority as superior to any possible consideration due to their delinquent companions. Generously excusing concealment in the case of a first transgression, in which the witnesses have given the culprits no warning of the course that must conscientiously be pursued, he may urge it as due to their own manly courage, moral honesty, and just convictions of the general necessity, that, on any proposed repetition of the offense, they shall hold themselves absolved from all duty to become *particeps criminis* by shielding wilful offenders, and shall give the same, unmistakable assurance that they will be denounced as such without fear or favor.

In the second place, in all such cases of concealment of flagrant offenses which ultimately come to light so as to admit of correction, the teacher may, upon previous announcement, punish the offenders with the greater severity, on the ground of having not only transgressed, but also of having instituted a conspiracy against the order of the school. He should also, by a distinct withdrawal of confidence from the accessories, until their future amendment becomes probable, indicate his sense of their practical disloyalty and partial guilt. This course, if frankly explained and firmly pursued, will tend to produce better views and feelings in the school, with regard to the whole question, and it gives the only promise of any ultimate removal of the evil under consideration.

It has already been observed that no question can be raised as to the consistency of spontaneous, or incidental detection. With regard to pre-determined, or concerted detection, the case is different. Involving the exercise of extraordinary scrutiny, extending perhaps beyonds the periods and precincts of the school, and even involving a species of espionage, it is of a more serious character, and not unfrequently gives rise to grave and anxious questionings in the minds of earnest and conscientious teachers. The position is, nevertheless, here squarely taken, that within certain limits, this species of detection is thoroughly legitimate and necessary.

The restrictions to which its use must be subjected are these. First. It must be resorted to, only in those cases in which detection is in no other way possible. Detection itself may be a necessity; and, while we may not accept the maxim; "Necessity knows no law," we must urge that, as a general principle, necessity must be a law unto itself. Hence, that detection cannot be a necessity to the welfare of the school, without involving the means necessary to its accomplishment.

Secondly. The misdemeanor must be one of a positive and flagrant character. It must be of the nature of actual vice or crime, and must be clearly demoralizing in its influence upon the school. No mere peccadillo involving the simple occasioning of disorder, or only productive of individual annoyance, can be a sufficient warrant. Grave measures are to be instituted that can only be countenanced by grave offenses. Of this class of misdemeanors, perhaps the best illustration is to be found in that, sometimes petty, sometimes serious theft so painfully common in certain kinds of schools. Not only is it illustrative of the criminalty referred to, but also of the difficulty of detection specified under the previous head. Often the vice of pupils from the better families, and the direct product of the prevailing social extravagance and home indulgence; infecting not only boys, but, sad to say, an older class of girls, who are even worse than boys, it is by the very force of family pride, the more studiously concealed in its perpetration, and the more dangerous to the teacher in his efforts at detection,—so dangerous that its occurrence and exposure are alike his terror.

Thirdly. The detection of such offenses must be solely and sincerely prosecuted for no inferior or private ends, but only for the sake of the general welfare. It must also be carefully guarded so as to touch for the sake of discipline, only the actual culprit. For reasons which will appear as we advance, others who may possibly become involved in its disclosures should be proceeded with, only in the way of salutary instruction and warning.

Applied within these limits, the considerations which establish the propriety of this concerted detection, are brief and positive. First. The moral or organic welfare of the school is of paramount importance. Crimes so demoralizing can not be tolerated, and the teacher is set forth "for the punishment of evil doers" no less than "for the praise of them that do well." Hence, cost what it may; strike whom it will, the detection of the offender is no matter of mere option; it is imperative.

Secondly. The offense is necessarily covert, and as such, admits of no other species of detection. But it is a recognized principle in criminal law that the capacity of a crime to be concealed so that detection becomes difficult or next to impossible, aggravates its character, and justly operates to enhance the penalty. This is founded on the fact that, while not intrinsically worse than others, it is vastly more dangerous to society. But it is clear that this very accession to its dangerous character, renders the demand for detection the more pressing, and justifies all means really necessary to that end.

Lastly. The act of the offender is one of practical outlawry. In its commission, he puts himself beyond any claim upon the school government, other than that of strict justice, of which the first element must

teacher has the right, as in the case supposed, to put any such articles where he chooses. The school-room is his proper domain, and property is presumed to be justly safe anywhere within the school precincts. Again, the real temptation lies in the depraved propensity of the offender; "He is drawn away of his own lust and enticed." Still further, the induced act, as leading to his detection, is the only means of rousing him, before some final and fatal crime, to a sense of the peril and certain ruin of the course he is pursuing; it is the only hope of his salvation. Once more, even in the case of the innocent, much the same is true. If he can yield so easily to the commission of crime, his only safety lies in the prompt discovery of this liability, and the consequent counsel and warning made possible through it. And, lastly, it is quite clear that temptation is not necessarily an evil. "Temptations," says Bishop Butler, "render our state a more improving state of discipline than it would be otherwise; as they give occasion for a more attentive exercise of the virtuous principle, which confirms and strengthens it more than an easier or less attentive exercise of it could." Were this otherwise, and temptation intrinsically a wrong, then the trial of our First Parents in the garden of Eden, which was practically just as much a temptation as any of the acts heretofore supposed, would stand utterly reprehended as evil and malicious.

Passing now to the second general element in judgment; namely, investigation, we observe that it is inclusive of all that formal examination of the truth of facts bearing upon any supposed case of discipline, either as determinative of its actuality or its relative demerit. It will be seen from this, that it differs from detection, in being always premeditated, but without involving any concerted scheme of forced discovery; it applies to cases in which a partial detection is already attained, which however needs to be tested and made complete; it is formal and open in all its processes; and it attains its ends only through logical conclusions resting altogether on the basis of evidence.

These characteristics of investigation, and the evident difficulty to be experienced in determining, through a logical process, both the actuality of the offense and its relative demerit, are at once suggestive of the extreme importance to be attached to this part of discipline. Were not this enough, a simple reference to the laws and usages of civil courts would argue the same. All this array of witnesses and jurymen; all this careful educing and sifting of testimony; all these elaborate reasonings upon the evidence, and all this patient deliberation upon the whole case preparatory to the rendering of a verdict, are so many grave indications of the importance to be everywhere attached to the proper investigation of offenses. While the extrinsic interest may be the more pressing in the applications of civil government, the intrinsic importance to the school, of well-guarded and certain decisions under its government, cannot be overestimated. In the state, an erroneous decision is injurious; in the school, from the comparative helplessness of its subjects, a false judgment is tyranny.

From this, it follows that inasmuch as, in the administration of school government, the teacher must be sole jury and judge; and inasmuch as he be comes himself an offender if he trusts to the blind guidance of mere impressions, or the doubtful reasonings of a crude understanding, it becomes imperative on him to possess some consistent knowledge of practical logic, at least so far as it involves a knowledge of the laws of evidence and the deduction of sound conclusions. Hence, not only should a specific training in this direction be afforded to the teacher, by our normal schools, but a concise treatise on evidence should be regarded by him as an indispensable part of his library. And this is the more imperative, from the fact that throughout the community, so many evils result from the prevailing ignorance of the very knowledge to be derived from such works. What those evils are, is patent to every one conversant with the proceedings of our civil, and especially our ecclesiastical courts.

As has been already intimated, investigation, or judgment proper, involves a logical process. In fact, in every such case of discipline, the teacher has before him the proper consideration of the disjunctive proposition; "*Either A is innocent or he is guilty,*" which proposition we have taken express pains to state, so that it shall conform to that necessary and noble maxim; "Every man should be presumed to be innocent until he is proven to be guilty," since, above all other adjudicators, the teacher should be most mindful of its observance.

The evidence upon which the teacher is to rely in the solution of this proposition, is two-fold: *Personal Evidence*, or *Testimony*, and *Circumstantial Evidence.*

Personal evidence, or testimony proper, as employed by the teacher, must be understood in a restricted sense, and as embracing only the statements made with reference to the offense itself, by his pupils or others, claiming to have a direct personal knowledge of its occurrence or non-occurrence. This is evidence direct and positive.

Circumstantial evidence, as employed by the teacher, embraces the statements made by his pupils or others, with reference to such remoter facts as do not involve a direct knowledge of the offense itself, but which are, in the nature of things, related to it, and which so concur in their relation to it, as to find their best, or their only explanation in either its reality or non-reality. This evidence is indirect, and may be either corroborative, or, in itself, sufficient. It is, however, not to be accepted as positive evidence.

To illustrate this, let X be charged with cutting his name on his desk. If it is in testimony that A saw him do it; or that B saw the desk just before X took his seat, and it had not been cut then; B or C saw him doing something unlike anything belonging to his proper business, or only like the work of cutting the desk; and B, C or D noticed the name as freshly cut immediately upon X's leaving his seat;—this would be of the nature of direct or personal evidence.

If however it is in testimony, rather this, that A saw the freshly cut name soon after X left his seat; B or C saw fresh whittlings adhering to his clothes after he left the seat; D found the point of the knife blade broken off in the wood, which point corresponds with a broken blade in X's knife; E found blood about the cutting, and X's finger proves to have been freshly cut about that time; these, with the fact that it was X's name, or that the carving resembles other carving of his name indisputably done by himself, and no evidence appears that any one else did, or could have any motive for doing the mischief, would be of the nature of circumstantial evidence.

From what has been thus far suggested, it must be evident that in the government of the school, circumstantial evidence, elsewhere in the administration of justice admitted as affording sufficient proof, ought not, except in rare cases, to be received as in itself conclusive. In a commonwealth whose subjects are so often weak and helpless, and over whom the authority is so absolute, probability however strong can not afford safe ground for the infliction of punishment. Hence, the teacher's main reliance for proof should rather be placed upon personal evidence, or direct testimony. It is true, in cases of even grave offense, it may be difficult, perhaps even impossible, to obtain such evidence. Shall then the offender "shove by justice?" Doubtless: so long as certainty in judgment cannot be attained, discipline must be suspended. But the influence of impunity in the commission of offenses is evil. Certainly, were such cases the common rule. They are, however, more likely to be incidental, and will, to some extent, be counterbalanced by the moral effect of an evident determination on the part of the teacher, to forego even justice until it is competent to stand forth, in its severity beyond doubt or challenge.

In this connection, it is important to caution the teacher against an error into which some unhappily fall; namely, that of compassing a confession by stratagem. It is sometimes the case that, in the conscious absence of sufficient testimony, the teacher, in laboring with the accused, puts on the show of having established the fact of his guilt, in order to produce in his mind, a conviction of the uselessness of further concealment, and thus to induce an actual confession of the fault. This course is objectionable on several grounds.

In the first place, it is practically dishonest. It involves falsehood by implication. The teacher says by his action; "I know all the facts. I am fully assured of your guilt. I do not need your confession. I only seek it for its influence on yourself, and its bearing on the amount of the punishment." But not one particle of this is true. Now the teacher should take good heed that he does not attempt to establish virtue through the intervention of an immorality.

In the second place, the use of such means cannot but impair the teacher's own upright self-consciousness, and so must naturally tend to destroy that clear open sincerity and confidence of manner upon which so much of his influence over the school depends.

He who can resort to such means, without himself wearing the look of a conscious culprit, is either to be pitied or detested; certain it is, that if he deals much in such base artifices, he will not long retain in aspect, the fine upright glory of conscious purity and honor. Hence, the teacher may better forego the administration of presumptive justice rather than demoralize himself.

Lastly, the pupil is not always so obtuse or simple as not to penetrate the deceitfulness of the artifice. If he does pry into its hidden secret, an irreparable blow has been inflicted upon the teacher's character and influence. Even if the pupil does not clearly discover the imposition, he will, in confessing his fault and being punished, rebel in heart against both however just, as having been reached in some way, to which he has unwisely and half-inexplicably allowed himself to be made an accomplice. The influence of any such conviction cannot but be injurious. The civil law wisely relieves the accused from the necessity of testifying against himself, and not merely that he may be saved from the temptation to perjure himself, but that, when he is condemned, he may the more deeply realize the certainty of justice and the righteousness of the authority. This lesson from civil affairs should not be lost upon the teacher. Let his discipline wait patiently until it is able to stand on its own proper basis—sufficient evidence.

It remains only to give expression to a caution or two in the use of circumstancial evidence, and we pass from it. Regarding it chiefly as a species of mere corroborative proof, it is incumbent on the teacher always to accept it with great caution, and to sift it with the utmost care. Especially let him be upon his guard against that species of evidence supposed to be found in personal indications of conscious guilt. A look of surprise, of apprehension, or even of seeming shame, so often taken as proofs of a child's guilt, is, by no means necessarily such. Nay, in the case of children of a nervous, timid, or aspiring character, it may be rather the natural and conclusive indication of innocence. Let, then, such appearances be searchingly scanned, and be clearly discovered to be the foreboding shadow of a clouded conscience, before they are allowed to fling their darkness over the frowning judgment.

Reverting now to testimony proper, it will be observed that its validity must rest upon the existence of proper qualifications in the witness. A brief statement of those qualifications will suffice for the present purpose. Their propriety will be more or less self-evident. They are these:

First. The pupil testifying, must have been clearly in a position enabling him to be personally cognizant of the facts whereof he affirms.

Secondly. He must claim to have been, and to all appearances, must have been, thus directly cognizant of those facts.

Thirdly. He must be of sufficient capacity to really know, and to correctly make known, the facts he claims to have witnessed.

Fourthly. He must be generally accepted by those who know him, as properly veracious.

Fifthly. He must be free from any especial inducement, from either impulsiveness, interest, fear, or personal animosity, which might naturally cloud his perceptions, or bias his representations.

Under this last head, it is necessary to caution the teacher particularly against the peculiar tendency of the child's haste in judgment and vividness of imagination, to control his convictions and shape his testimony. Nothing is more common or natural, than for the child, on finding facts leading to a conclusion, to overleap, at once, the remaining steps, and assume what is really to be proved, and then to create, as it were, in his own conceptions, the very appearance which he assumes to have witnessed. Any one who has observed how perfectly the child's imagination effects the most radical transformations in his conceptions, and the absolute faith in which he will deal with the transformation thus effected, as reality, will realize the force of the caution here uttered. While, however, the teacher keeps this caution in mind, let him not fall into the error and injustice of charging such perversion of fact to a want of truthfulness in the child. Their source is, as suggested above, in the intellect, and not in the heart.

The testimony obtained from proper witnesses may be of three species; namely, *Simple*, *Accumulated*, and *Concurrent Testimony*.

Simple testimony is that which stands by itself,

and which is unsustained by anything beyond the character of the single witness.

Accumulated testimony is that which, going beyond the single witness, stands with other testimony of a like kind obtained from multiplied witnesses. It is sustained not only by the character of each witness but by the very fact of its accumulation.

Concurrent testimony, like accumulated testimony, involves a multiplication of witnesses, and is, like that, the stronger for this multiplication. The evidence involved, does not, however, like that of accumulated testimony, rest for its verity or force upon the character of the witnesses, but only upon their *concurrence.* This is because the concurrence, in this way, involves the fact; namely, if the fact really occurred, then such a concurrence becomes clearly possible; if it did not occur, then a concurrence is, as the case may be, either not probable or not possible.

The characteristics of the testimony as a whole, upon which the teacher may rest a decision, may now be briefly stated. They are as follows:

First. It must be definite; not vague or general.

Secondly. It must to a reasonable extent be accumulated. Simple testimony should not be deemed sufficient to conviction. No more in the school than in the state, should the fate of the culprit lie in the hands of a single witness.

Thirdly. It should be generally concurrent. A proper concurrence is in fact the crowning element in its strength. This may be seen as follows.

The grounds of the strength of concurrent testimony are twofold: namely, first, the impossibility or improbability of collusion on the part of the witnesses: secondly, the absence of any motives in the individual witnesses, which are adequate to lead to the given testimony, without supposing the reality of the fact to which they testify. If both these points can be established, or if it is impossible to detect anything to the contrary, the evidence is valid and conclusive. And this will be so, unimportant differences in the individual testimony, to the contrary notwithstanding. Nay, so long as there is a clear concurrence as to the main facts, the evidence is really the stronger for these divergencies.

This may be illustrated by a simple formula. For example, let the several testimonies be represented by A, B, and C; the main fact by D; and the unimportant divergencies by e, f, and g. We have then the following:

$$A=D+e,$$
$$B=D+f, \text{ and}$$
$$C=D+g.$$

Combining these by addition, we have:

$$A+B+C=3\,D+e+f+g.$$

Here it is clear that D, in which there was a concurrence, has acquired a threefold strength in itself, and so much further importance as is embraced in the sum of e, f, and g.

Even if the divergencies in minor points, are contradictory, the result is still decisive. Let

$$A=D+e,$$
$$B=D-e, \text{ and}$$
$$C=D+f.$$

Combining as before, we have:

$$A+B+C=3\ D+f.$$

In this case D's force in itself is reduplicated as before, and is still further supplemented by f, so that it is stronger for the divergencies, although some of them were contradictory.

To apply this to a practical case. Suppose that, as in a previous illustration, X has been charged with cutting his desk. Now, A testifies that he saw him do it, and with the little blade of his knife; B testifies that he saw him do it, but with the big blade instead of the little one; and D that he saw him do it, did not see which blade he used, but heard the blade break, and knows that the point found in the desk belongs to a large rather than a small blade. Here the main fact is raised to a threefold certainty; and the certainty is the greater because the divergence in the individual testimony evinces intelligence and independence in the witnesses. Nor does the contradictory divergence of A's and B's testimony impair the force of the evidence, since it is every way probable that both are correct. For it is easy to see that C might have first used the smaller blade, and afterwards, because of breaking it, changed it for the larger one, before B's attention was called to the act he was perpetrating.

Other illustrations might be given, but we think the teacher will now be able to apply the foregoing principles for himself. We have taken the pains to develop these logical points so that, in the absence of other sources of information, he may have at hand enough to answer any such individual and immediate want.

The element in judgment as a part of school government which remains to be considered, is Decision. Decision is the final determination in the teacher's mind, of the innocence or the guilt of the accused; and, if the latter, of its relative demerit and proper measure of punishment.

This decision to be valid and complete, must be marked by two characteristics; namely, it must be *positive, overt* and *explicit.*

As positive, it must embrace either the one or the other result, either that of actual innocence or actual guilt. No halfway conclusion should be accepted. If the guilt be not established, whatever may be the possibilities, assume, as has been before demanded, that the accused is innocent. We hold this principle to be even more imperative in school government than in civil government.

It is necessary, too, that the decision, when distinctly attained, should be publicly declared. It is neither just to the culprit nor good for the school, that it should be allowed to remain delayed or concealed and consequently inoperative. The steps of the investigation are known: so should be the end reached. And the announcement of the decision should be prompt and explicit. Any halfway, dilatory, or equivocal statement of the teacher's real conviction and determination is discreditable to him and injurious to the school. Let the teacher, at once, kindly but fearlessly render a clear verdict and pass the just sentence. Nothing can well be more unreasonable and even hateful than the timid or malicious procrastination or prevarication involved in the too common announcement; "I cannot attend to the matter now:" or "I will let you know my decision by and by." It not only impeaches the teacher's judgment or his courage, but it aggravates the pupil's spirit and perhaps determines him upon a fiercer resistance to the subsequent discipline.

From what has thus far been urged, it will be quite evident what must be the general characteristics of judgment in the government of the school. It must be, beyond a doubt, *deliberate, comprehensive, righteous,* and *decisive.* Without proper deliberateness there can be in the teacher, neither that air of quiet strength nor that evident care to secure even-handed justice, which are necessary to his highest influence as a ruler. Without such comprehensiveness in judgment as embraces both sides of disputed questions and all the facts bearing upon their full elucidation, no teacher can be secure against undue bias, and against the ultimate impairing of the general confidence in the candor and rectitude of his decisions. And without that prompt and explicit decisiveness which, after due investigation, brings a case to a clear and unmistakable conclusion, his government will fail to command that conviction of its strength and determination, which must underlie just reverence and implicit submission. On these points, no further enlargement is necessary.

It only remains to add, that it will be seen that no

provision whatever is made for what may be termed popular decisions in the school,—that is decision by the voice of the pupils. This has been for the reason that, while it is not denied that, in certain limited cases, and for the attainment of minor ends, they may be admissible, they are held to be incompatible with the true view of the school government as autocratic; with the just duty of the teacher as sole ruler; and with his proper dignity as truly capacitated for his place. Any common or important resort to them must therefore be either deceptive, or if not deceptive, practically absurd, and dangerous. The specific development of this in application must, however, be reserved for another place.

## CHAPTER IX.

### GENERAL ELEMENTS CONTINUED—DISCIPLINE—CORRECTION OR ENFORCEMENT, PREVENTIVE.

Correction defined and classified as Preventive and Penal — Preventive correction defined—Related to arrangement and management—Specific measures—*Rewards defined and classified as Consequential and Authoritative*—Kinds distinguished—General grounds of lawfulness—Authoritative rewards of the nature of positive institutions—Desire of approval inherent—Abstract virtue beyond the child's comprehension—Authoritative rewards classified as Public Approval, Conferred Privileges and Formal Gifts—*Public approval considered*—Its use of symbols—Requisites to effectiveness—Must be formally expressed—Must be protected against discredit—*Conferred privileges distinguished*—Superiority of this class—Classified as privileges of Regard; of Comfort; of Recreation; and of Improvement—Kinds exemplified—*Requisites to effectiveness*—Must obtain the teacher's interest—Must be held as resumable—*Gifts classified*, as Gifts of Pleasure and Profit—Kinds distinguished and compared—Gifts of pleasure appeal to the fancy or the imagination—Superiority of the latter—Gifts of profit classified as, affording recreation, real advantage, and æsthetic improvement—Kinds distinguished, and worth compared—Grounds of bestowing gifts twofold; as the basis of mere achievements, and of worthy effort—The latter superior—*Manner of bestowment*—Must be bestowed publicly—Must evince interest—Must be bestowed with discretion—With careful adaptation—Common failure as to adaptation—Bestowed as a grace, and not as a compensation—*The error of offering prizes*—Induce mercenary effort—Are not resumable—System of "Demerit Marks" deferred to a subsequent chapter.

WE come now to the last of the general elements of discipline in school government; namely, Correction or Enforcement.

Correction we understand to be inclusive of whatever means the teacher may employ to secure the freedom of the school from offenses against its order and welfare. Correction will, hence, naturally resolve itself into two kinds; namely, *Preventive* and *Penal Correction.*

Preventive correction naturally includes all the measures adopted by the teacher, to preclude the occurrence of occasions for transgression, or to counteract any positive temptations to wrong-doing, which may exist or arise in the school.

Of these measures, many of the more general cast will be found included under the head of order, as previously discussed. Hence, nothing more will be needed here, than simply to call the attention of the teacher to the fact that whatever he may do to secure sufficient employment or proper relaxation for his pupils; whatever he may do to awaken their interest or secure their respect; whatever he may do to make his regulations simple, explicit, and reasonable, and to render his management animated, reliable, and genial, will, while bearing more directly upon the order of the school, operate effectively also upon the discipline, to prevent the occurrence of either opportunity or inducement to the perpetration of otherwise unthought of misdemeanors. And thus will the wise and masterly ordering of the school serve as admirable and, to an important extent, effective means for the prevention, or precautionary correction, of probable offenses.

But, besides these general means, opportunity may

occur for the wise adoption of specific measures not definitely provided for in the foregoing suggestions. For example, the teacher may find certain contingencies of location, association, amusement or personal feeling, practically offering a premium upon mischief or violence. Thus, a pupil of a mischievous habit may be occupying a seat which so screens him from observation as to favor his roguish projects, and thus multiplies them. Again, two of a like restless and disorderly nature may, by being seated together, become the very flint and steel of mischief in active contact, from which, "like fire in heather set," nothing can be expected but speedy and, perhaps destructive, conflagration. Or, a child of feeble and yielding nature may be so situated as to fall under the constant influence or control of a vicious boy who will lead him into evil he would not otherwise have contemplated. It is also quite possible for certain sports, in themselves innocent enough, to favor the rise of disturbances which could not occur in the case of others that might be substituted for them; or pupils, from antecedent collision, may be so affected towards each other that, for them to be left to go their way at the same time, or to get together away from under the teacher's eye, will lead to new difficulties.

In all such cases, the teacher must promptly anticipate the movements of the enemy, and, if possible, flank his position. This he may do, by, for fair reasons, or without indicating any reasons, changing the seat of the secluded rogue, bringing him "to the front;" by separating those pupils whose influence on each other will be detrimental; by directing the school amusements into better channels, and by shrewdly preventing communication or simultaneous and unobserved movements on the part of belligerents. No detailed directions can be given him for effecting these objects successfully. The method must be his own, to be either legitimate or effective.

A still more important preventive means of correcting the possible occurrence of offenses, must be found in the right use of *rewards* as a stimulus to application and obedience.

Under the term *rewards*, we include whatever of either pleasure or profit, a person may, from either the constitution of things, or the positive provisions of authority, attain or win for his obedience or well-doing. Rewards may hence be classified under two general heads; *Consequential Rewards* and *Authoritative Rewards.*

Consequential rewards are such personal benefits in either condition of body, state of mind, or associated relations, as naturally follow a course of action accordant with the laws of things. Thus, he who is frugal in his fare and temperate in his habits, is rewarded with sound health and physical comfort; he who obeys the laws of rectitude, is blessed with an approving conscience and a mind at rest; and he who conducts himself with uniform fidelity and good will, wins the confidence and co-operation of others in his own behalf. All such rewards are commonly regarded as the consequences of right action, and, hence, are considered as rewards only in a restricted sense. This is due to the fact that they are the original and invariable results attached to primal and universal laws, the institution of which is so far removed from our knowledge, that the whole appears in our consciousness, not so much the product of authority, (which it none the less is,) as the mere spontaneous ongoing of cause and effect.

Authoritative rewards are such favors or benefits bodily, mental or social, as are bestowed in the rightful exercise of authority by the higher power, upon those who are judged as especially meritorious, generally, as meritorious beyond anything attaching to the naked performance of express duty. This species embraces those rewards commonly understood as such, and it is concerning the use of these in the school that there arises so much dispute among teachers, resulting simply in the unfortunate confusion of many minds, and the practical waste of much logic.

Of the proper use of rewards in school government, as elsewhere, it is thoroughly certain that it is legitimate, and that, whether that be admitted or not, no efforts to the contrary will avail under the present constitution of things, to discharge it from its practical place and power among the elements of human influence and control. And this, for the following reasons.

First. Authoritative rewards are of the nature of positive institutions, or those institutions which, while they do not arise in the line, and under the laws of natural cause and effect, and are not, therefore, necessary to the existence or operation of things as originally constituted, are still neither contradictory to that original constitution of things, nor in anywise dispensable under its present modifications and necessities, but are the clear practical product of a potent and provident authority which, through them, rightfully meets and satisfies existing and otherwise unmanageable emergencies in the operation of the moral system. Of this nature, are all such institutions as the church, civil government, even the school organization itself; and also all such regulations, as laws of marriage, laws of contracts, rules for political action, rules for judicial trial, and penal statutes; and until all these, evidently not necessary under the original constitution of things, nor necessarily related to the natural operations of cause and effect, can be abrogated, the institution and use of rewards stands with them, immovable.

Secondly. The desire of approval for well-doing finds an ultimate and steadfast foothold in the very nature of the moral susceptibility. Until the spirit be constituted so as to abjure all claim for approval, and the conscience shall no longer assume the power of "accusing or else excusing" the moral agent, the desire for rewards, and the impulse to bestow them, must remain imbedded in the first instincts of our nature. For what is a gift or a reward, other than an outward and substantial symbolizing of the inward approval of the course pursued or the act performed? Hence, always, the natural prompting of the highest satisfaction, gratitude or love, is to get out of mere fleeting looks or words, and into a something more tangible and enduring, that, in its possessed and treasured substance, shall seem to set forth more fully the power of the inward affection, and shall, when the personal exhibition of that affection has passed away, stand out clear and impressive before the sense, as its hallowed monument.

Thirdly. Whatever may be possible in the mature man, in the line of that sublime abstraction, "virtue is its own reward," the child is neither equal to such abstractions, nor are they demanded of him. They may, it is true, be gradually wrought by instruction into the body of his thought, for the sake of their ultimate effect on his principles as a man. But, embraced as he is, in a world of perceived realities, and only capable of attaining the subtler ideals by passing to them through the fine gradations of a progressively reduced and sublimated reality, it is absurd and tyrannous to rob him of the stimulus, guidance and aid of proper rewards as outward realities foreshadowing the ideal of absolute virtue, and rendering possible both its conception and attainment.

On these grounds, then, we hold the use of rewards to be legitimate and necessary, and regard the objections commonly urged, as only valid when applied to their misapplication or abuse. That such abuse is quite possible and, indeed, too common, we readily admit. Some notice of this abuse may be taken hereafter. But it is sufficient, here, to urge that the abuse of a thing, so far from demanding its condemnation, is often indicative of a higher excellence in its proper use, since, as Luther has remarked: "The best of God's blessings are often the worst abused."

Authoritative or positive rewards, as thus recognized, may be distributed into three kinds: *Public Approval, Conferred Privileges*, and *Formal Gifts.*

By public approval, we mean such a marked recognition of merit, before the whole school, as distinguishes the pupil from his fellows, and declares him to be worthy of general esteem and imitation. In the state, it finds its parallel in the deliberate vote of thanks, or the decree that the 'citizen has deserved well of the commonwealth.'

As in the state, such public commendation may be accompanied by some tangible symbol, such as medals, badges, or decorations; so in the school, the teacher may make effective use of corresponding means for giving to his public approval of the pupil's course, a sensible and permanent manifestation. In the case of the larger number of pupils, some such badge or symbol is almost necessary to a full appreciation of the reality of the praise bestowed. The grounds of this necessity will be readily apprehended by those who have carefully considered the child's nature as presented in a previous chapter.

There are, however, certain requisites to the effectiveness of this species of reward, which, we think, are too generally disregarded, and the absence of which is, we believe, the real cause of the doubt which teachers entertain of its utility. All such declarations of merit, to command the real respect of the school, must command the marked attention and regard of the teacher. Given carelessly or informally, and without his subsequent steady and respectful recognition, they will be regarded by the school as mere idle words, and, as such, will degenerate into mere occasions for mischievous innuendos, than which, nothing can exert a worse influence upon the meritorious pupil and others sincerely emulous of his example. Let the teacher then see to it, that due solemnity attaches to the act of public approval, and that the use of its appropriate symbols is always protected against ridicule. Indeed, all such ridicule should be treated as itself an offense, not only against the rights of the pupil, but also against the respect due to the teacher.

Private commendation is not here considered, not because it is excluded, but because it belongs under the head of natural or constitutional rewards, before mentioned. It comes more within the natural line of moral cause and effect; for the worthy pupil has just as much right, and indeed the same right, to expect the private approval of his course by the teacher, as its approval by his own conscience. That such approval, under only the restrictions of prudence, is to be bestowed when deserved, needs not be argued. It is a law of the moral instincts.

Under the head of conferred privileges, we include all such liberties, favors or personal advantages, as may, in the teacher's wise exercise of his supreme authority, be, by positive provisions, conferred upon the meritorious pupil. These privileges must, of course, involve no subtraction from, or infringement of, the rights of others. They are simply of the nature of higher or supplementary individual rights, open to the ambition of all, but due only to those distinguished by specific and really attained merit.

The bestowment of such privileges, it will be seen, involves a public approval, and is subject to the same requisites with that. It, however, transcends public approval in rank and effectiveness, inasmuch as it involves more substantial tokens of recognized merit. Approval involving the use of some distinguishing symbol or badge, approaches these privileges somewhat, but still differs from them in the fact that it is a mere honor conferred, and not a real advantage attained. This real or substantial advantage, or one regarded as such by the pupil, is a cardinal element in this species of reward. It must be the teacher's study to secure its actual presence in the conferred privilege.

These privileges may be conveniently classified under several heads; as, *Privileges* of *Regard;* of *Comfort;* of *Recreation;* and of *Improvement.*

Without resorting to any formal definition, these kinds of reward may be briefly and practically presented with sufficient clearness by simple illustrations. It will now readily occur to the thoughtful teacher how, according to the different susceptibilities of deserving pupils, he may extend to one the privilege of sitting by, or walking with the teacher, or of being allowed to do him some special service; to another, the right to occupy some favorite or peculiarly attractive seat; to another, some additional means of amusement or time for play, or a part in some especial scheme of pleasure or recreation projected by the teacher; and to another, the right to engage in some exercise or study beyond his ordinary course;—in these ways distinguishing each as worthy, and practically rewarding him according to his merits.

These rewards possess some peculiar advantages. Rising, for example, above the possible emptiness of a mere honor, they involve a substantial benefit which appeals to the better feelings rather than to the mercenary impulses. Beyond this, there is the advantage resulting from the fact that they may be temporarily conferred, or may be resumed in case of delinquency. Thus they may not only be endowed with double value by the simple possibility of their being forfeited; but they may, by being conferred on others, be made susceptible of a wider use and application.

But in order that these rewards, too little esteemed or employed in the government of our schools, may be made thoroughly effective, proper provision must be made for their application, and a real interest in their bestowment must be evinced. This interest must also be not only evident but permanent, for necessarily the pupil's esteem for them can not be expected to rise above the manifest value attached to them by the teacher. At least, the expert in reading human nature will not expect the child to prize for any length of time, the things which he finds others, and especially those above him, holding as practically more or less worthless. What is held as dear by one, is very naturally held to be desirable by another.

In this direction also, important use may be made of the principle of resumption upon forfeiture, as already indicated. A steady conviction of the possibility and the propriety of such a resumption of the conferred privileges, will, not only serve to demonstrate the teacher's regard for their unimpaired worth and justice, but it will serve also to perpetuate in the pupil's mind a just idea of their true nature and end, and will also operate as a steady stimulus toward persistence in the meritorious course so auspiciously begun,—all of them objects too important to be, for one moment, overlooked or disregarded.

We now come to the last class of rewards enumerated; namely, *Gifts*, a species sufficiently defined by their title. These may be conveniently classed as of two kinds; *Gifts of Pleasure* or *Profit.*

Under the head of gifts of pleasure, may be included all articles bestowed as rewards, which are of a kind appealing to the child's love of amusement, or to his sense of the curious or the beautiful. These naturally arrange themselves under three divisions, including severally such as address themselves to the active powers, to the fancy or to the imagination. Of these, the two former are the more available in the case of the younger class of pupils; but the latter are of the higher order both as it regards their relation to a purer taste and a more enduring influence. It is worthy of observation, however, that the child's imagination is not so much cognitive as dramatic: he readily creates character and scenes in his daily amusements; but he does not at all penetrate through the outer shell of the beautiful, to the hidden soul enshrined within, by the exercise of the creative imagination. Hence, whatever is addressed to his fancy, and to that fancy as somewhat barbaric in its character, will most commonly give him, for the time being, the greater pleasure. The value of such gifts, however, is fancied rather than real; and their capacity to produce pleasure is, consequently, limited and short-lived.

Under the head of gifts of profit, we include whatever rewards may be applied either chiefly or purely to some economic or useful end. These may be briefly enumerated as of three kinds. First, those which, while affording the child a means of proper amusement, carefully shape that amusement to some useful end of either development or improvement. As examples of these, we may mention the various historical, biographical and geographical games so abundant at the present time, and the numerous illustrated books upon useful subjects.

Secondly, those susceptible of conducing to the supply of the child's substantial wants either bodily or mentally. Examples of this kind of gifts may be found in articles of apparel, (applicable in the case of the more destitute class of pupils); appliances for toilet use; articles important in the lighter domestic employments of girls; such as are useful in writing, drawing, or the care of books, and, lastly, books of solid merit and practical utility.

Thirdly, those gifts which are of a mixed character, possessing, not merely a substantial utility, but giving large prominence to the demands of the æsthetic nature as requiring culture and gratification. As examples of these, some of those mentioned under the preceding head, when they are of a peculiarly ornate or artistic character, may be cited. Others may be found in illustrated works on natural history, science or art, or works of a standard character in the field of polite literature,—the whole ranging from the simple engraving or oil painting, to the choicest specimens of the English classics. Of this last species of gifts, it is to be observed, that, within their proper field of application, they possess a marked superiority over all others, and for the two reasons, that they extend their influence over more of the pupil's susceptibilities; and, touching the æsthetic faculty, they bring themselves into closer adjacency to the moral nature, towards which, as will be seen hereafter, all such appliances of discipline must faithfully and firmly look and labor.

And this brings us naturally to the consideration of that most important topic, the ground upon which alone, rewards may be properly conferred. Its importance will appear in the simple fact that the reward often takes its substantial character from the cause for which it was conferred, or the principle which determined its bestowment. It is here, much as it is in the case of moral action, the character of which is often purely dependent on the inspiring motive.

These grounds of bestowment may, we think, be twofold; the ground of *achievement* and that of *effort;* that is, you may bestow rewards for something that has been done, or for something that has simply been worthily attempted. In the former case, the measure of the reward must, of course, be the measure of the amount accomplished; in the latter, it must be guaged altogether by the sum of the effort made.

It is too commonly the case in our schools, that rewards are bestowed exclusively upon the ground of achievement. Now, we grant that there may be occasions for the choice of this basis of bestowment as necessary to the attainment of desirable ends. But it will be quite clear to the observing manager and moralist, that these should be sternly classed and considered as the exceptions, and not as the rule. And for this reason, that the measure of actual accomplishment is by no means always the measure of true merit, since, either because of higher natural endowments, or because of manifold more helps and advantages, one pupil may, with even less regard for the law of the school, and with really no noble intention or endeavor, accomplish more than another who finely exhibits these higher characteristics, but who has been less favored in both endowments and circumstances.

Hence, the bestowment of rewards upon the ground of the worthy effort made, must commend itself to every one as, in all respects, the better course,—nay, as the only one which can be either wisely or justly adopted as the law of the school. For, upon no other basis, can the discipline of the school as administered in the bestowment of these incentives to right action, either place itself on a proper moral foundation, or reach those characters which, before all others, need and claim its correcting or elevating influences. Bestow rewards upon this basis, however, and you recognize, not mere abstract results, but motive, spirit, character, which is, after all, the real thing you are endeavoring to reach and develop under your discipline. Bestow rewards on this basis, and you will reach and inspire with better hopes and aims, many a pupil susceptible of actual redemption from his worst failings and faults, who, under any other course, would sink into the complete stupor of hopelessness and self-abandonment.

Before leaving this topic, some attention needs to be given to the characteristics which should mark the manner in which rewards are bestowed; since, it is quite possible here, as elsewhere, for manner to outweigh matter in the production of results. Indeed, we are fully of the opinion that many of the objections urged, as it is often supposed with valid force, against the use of rewards, hold good, not at all against their use, but only against the manner in which they are bestowed.

We urge then, that rewards, to have their best effect, must be bestowed *publicly* and with due ceremony. From the objective tendencies of children, as before noticed, it must be seen that they are creatures of pomp and show, and borrow largely from the outward symbols of an act or an instrument, their ideas of its intrinsic worth and dignity. Hence, rewards of whatever species they may be, if bestowed in private or informally, will come to be seriously cheapened in the child's estimation, and will not long be regarded as objects deserving of high ambition or strenuous effort.

Besides this, the teacher, if at all possessed of his true place in the minds of his pupils, is their standard: they conform their measures of value or importance, to what they apprehend to be the teacher's estimate. Hence, let the teacher turn off the bestowment of rewards in a careless uninterested manner, and the pupil will, sooner or later, turn off his reception of them in similar style. It is a fixed law of all dealing with human nature, that, if you would make others count much upon anything, you must first make much of it yourself. Make as much, then, as you consistently can, of the bestowment of favors and rewards.

Something in the direction of this deep interest can be done by after notice and inquiry as to their nature, the use that has been made of them, and the pleasure which they have produced. In the case of gifts possessing a literary or artistic excellence, some pains should be taken to direct the pupil's attention to the peculiar points of admiration. A gift, wisely chosen with reference to some such subsequent use, may be made a means of especial interest and influence in the school. Called up as a subject of public remark, and skilfully presented in the light of its excellence or utility, it becomes a double prize to its owner and a double incentive to the school.

Bestow your rewards also with great *discretion.*

They are an extraordinary means of attaining an important, though not properly an extraordinary end. Hence, nothing can be more injudicious or absurd, than a lavish or undiscriminating bestowment of them. Confer them where there is not a clear and outstanding merit, and they become practically a lie: deal them out broadcast, as is too commonly done, and they become even worse than a lie: they are a mere farce. The former method, unjust as it is, is quite compatible with strength and character in the government of the school: the latter is only consistent with goodish weakness and want of sense in the teacher.

Still further, let proper *adaptation* in the rewards conferred, be carefully studied. The only sensible law on this point, is this: that just as age, condition, and character vary, so must the rewards. As well fail to discriminate in requirement and correction, as neglect to discriminate in the specific adaptation of conferred privileges or gifts. Such a mark of approval as would thrill the very heart of one pupil, would, to another, possess little or no interest, and to still another, would prove only a subject of ridicule. It is, hence, both idle and wasteful to mete out gifts to all in the same style and measure. It would compare well with the wisdom and economy of the farmer, who should gather into one inclosure his entire stock of animals, from his trotting horse, down to his pet bantam, and should scatter broadcast before them the same general kind of provender.

It is for the lack of a just observance of this principle, that the rewards of merit, commonly conferred in our schools, so often fail to excite the interest or produce the salutary results expected. It is, hence, in this direction, that the teacher may, not only evince his nice discrimination of character, and his fine tact in touching individual peculiarities, but may exert a most salutary power to give proper effectiveness to his means of precautionary correction, and to secure a truer appreciation of his measures, and a higher style of sentiment, throughout the school.

Lastly. Let rewards be conferred purely as a *grace*, and not as a matter of mere compensation. This involves two points; namely, first, their bestowment as a free exercise of simple authority, and not as a necessary duty; and, secondly, their bestowment purely as a provisional consequent upon proper well-doing, and not at all as its stipulated price. It is neither inconsistent nor injurious for the pupil to receive the reward, feeling that it is an authoritative result of his well-doing, and a positive symbol of his approved merit. But, for him to become impressed or influenced by the notion that he is to do well that he may obtain the reward, is utterly false in principle and vicious in effect. It is practically, to make the fulfillment of duty a mere matter of barter.

It is in this direction, that we are to look for the real objection to the offering of prizes. Offer a prize for the performance of any duty, or the accomplishment of any proper work, and, whether it be a mere honor won or a gain acquired, the pupil is subjected to a direct and powerful temptation to sink all true and noble motive in mere mercenary ambition and endeavor. He will be hardly human, if he does not sooner or later, under their deceptive stimulus, degenerate into a mere hireling. And the natural consequence of such a submergence of principle, and such a practical degradation of character, will be the uprising of that selfishness which so commonly, in connection with the offering of prizes, develops itself in evil arts, in narrow rivalry, and in subsequent heart-burning and recrimination.

Hence, while we are not prepared to condemn the offering of prizes altogether—for, we can conceive of cases in which, with all their concomitant evils, they may appear as a necessary means to an indispensable though imperfect good—yet, we must urge that they are to be held as a purely occasional and extraordinary means, and not at all as a fixed or desirable element in discipline. Rather than suffer them to usurp this latter place in the least degree, let them be proscribed altogether.

It is proper to add further, that prizes bestowed as rewards, are subject, like gifts, to this grave defect; that they are, in their very nature, irresumable; they are beyond reach of forfeiture. However immediately or grossly a rewarded pupil may abandon or reverse his praiseworthy course, you have no power to inflict censure by the retraction of the reward. You are, moreover, by the necessary finality of its bestowment, cut off from the power to hold out the possibility of a forfeiture, as an incentive to continued and persistent well-doing, the securing of which is the real end sought in your approval. Hence, the superiority of the former species of rewards becomes evident. Hence, also, it becomes clear that prizes are more consistently ultimate; that is, they more properly find their place at the end of a pupil's course under the school authority.

It may occur to some, that under this general head, some notice should be taken of the so-called system of "demerit marks." The discussion of that system, like that of several others of a specific character, will, however, be deferred for the present. And for the reasons, that it is somewhat mixed in its character, partaking both of the nature of rewards and of punishments,—a fact which properly assigns it a place elsewhere; and because the variety of considerations connected with its examination in detail, together with their somewhat diversified relations, and their grave importance, renders a distinct examination both more consistent and convenient.

## CHAPTER X.

### GENERAL ELEMENTS CONTINUED. DISCIPLINE—PENAL CORRECTION—THEORIES OF PUNISHMENT.

Penal correction defined—Punishment defined—Restricted use of the term—*Theory of "natural reactions"* (SPENCER'S) *stated—Objections to the theory*—Based exclusively upon assumptions with regard to reactionary discipline in physical nature—These assumptions unwarranted—*The theory framed with reference to physical rather than moral being*—Hence, inadequate to reach the higher offenses—Illustration—It ignores fixed distinctions between mind and matter—*Ignores cardinal facts in the condition of the moral nature*—Depraved will may nullify internal moral reactions—The external reactions may be wanting—Moral reactions altogether contingent and uncertain—*Theory fails to distinguish the authoritative from the consequential*—Does not distinguish the authoritative from the non-authoritative—Government can symbolize its displeasure only through positive inflictions—Cardinal distinctions between government of nature and of authority—Assumed superiority of the "natural reaction" scheme a fallacy—*Humanitarian scheme*—Relation to the reaction scheme—Animus of both—Infliction of pain as punishment, a necessity in nature—Pain in physical nature a means to a moral end—Human power to inflict pain under authority, not usurped or tyrannous—Non-infliction of pain not necessarily humane—Source of the objection to pain, excessive sympathy with the individual—*Reformatory scheme*—Discipline, not primarily, nor chiefly reformatory—The grand end, the protection of the innocent and the conservation of the body politic—No practical escape from the use of punishment in the school—*How reduce its amount*—By removing occasions for transgression—By the institution of exact and effective discipline—By the use of moral instruction—The introduction of moral instruction into schools argued—As necessary to the attainment of the end of true education—This sustained by history, philosophy and common sense—*Moral suasion scheme.*

WE pass now to the second general division of correction or enforcement; namely, Penal Correction.

Under the head of penal correction, or the corrective enforcement of law, we include the use of all means calculated to suppress offenses; to sustain the government of the school against the encroachments of offenders; and to prevent the lapsing of the innocent into transgression. These means, as such, are customarily termed *punishments.*

For the sake of guarding against error, we define punishments in precise accordance with the common apprehension of mankind, as being the authoritative infliction, by some properly constituted sovereignty, of some species of evil or suffering upon wilful offenders against the requirements of law.

By a mere license in speech, growing partly out of convenience in expression, and partly out of a somewhat oblique analogy in the mere condition of the transgressor of natural law, and that of the violator of the positive regulations of government proper, the term punishment is sometimes applied to the ordinary occurrence of consequential evils. Thus we say of the child who persists in playing with fire and gets burned, or of the person who disregards the laws of health, and incurs some severe illness, that he is richly punished for his misconduct.

But it is simply a contradiction of the common sense, of mankind, and a perversion of proper language, to insist that this is, in any true or honest sense, punishment, or to covertly accept and treat it as such. No government has ever accepted the subjection of the transgressor to these consequential evils, as, in any part, sustaining the majesty of its laws, or fulfilling the ends of justice; nor has law ever regarded the occurrence of these consequences as at all forestalling the application of penalty, or in one iota justly abating its measure of infliction. Hence, a somewhat noted modern theorist, while practically treating them as the only proper species or standards of penalty, cautiously admits that "they are not punishments in the literal sense."

Notwithstanding this admission, these consequential results are, by that writer, practically pressed as the only legitimate species of penalty, and with so much plausibility and earnestness, that it becomes important to notice the theory critically. According to this *natural reaction scheme,* proper punishments "are not artificial and unnecessary inflictions of pain." It is their peculiarity "that they are nothing more than *the unavoidable consequences* of the deeds which they follow." It is to "be further borne in mind that they are proportionate to the degree in which the organic laws have been transgressed." These natural reactions "are constant, direct, unhesitating, and not to be escaped," and "they hold throughout adult life as well as throughout infantine life." In behalf of "this system of letting the penalty be inflicted by the laws of things," it is assumed, "not only that the system by which the young child is so successfully taught to regulate its movements, is also the discipline by which the great mass of adults are kept in order, and more or less improved; but that the discipline humanly devised for the worst adults, fails when it diverges from this divinely-ordained discipline, and begins to succeed when it approximates to it."

Before entering upon the examination of those defects in the theory which bear most directly upon our main subject, we desire to call the attention to certain general positions taken by its author, which we believe involve mere unwarranted assumption, and form the basis of much sophistical reasoning. The radical facts upon which these positions are sought to be established, are drawn from physical nature and its laws of cause and effect.

Now it is assumed, first, that these natural reactions or punishments "are nothing more than the unavoidable consequences of the deeds which they follow;" that is, they are not artificial or positive provisions of authority. But is this the ultimate truth? So far as man, the subject, is concerned, they are doubtless immediately apprehended as simply consequences fixed in the ordinary round of nature. But, considered with reference to the originating sovereignty, (and it is that with which we have to do,) were they not primally, in the act of creation, really positive provisions authoritatively introduced into the physical scheme of things? Man's shortsighted disposition to rest content with their immediate phase as merely consequential, by no means changes the fact that they are ultimately the pure mandates of the Divine will, and just as truly so as any specific provisions subsequently thrust into the system.

Again, secondly, it is assumed of these consequences,

that "these painful reactions are proportionate to the degree in which the organic laws have been transgressed." But how wide this is of the truth, every day's experience fully and often painfully demonstrates. For example, one child carelessly tumbles over the door step and suffers consequences severe enough to remind him of the necessity of future caution. But who does not know that another may experience the same fall without receiving the least injury, while still another is well-nigh killed out-right? So too, one child wilfully, and in flagrant disregard of express warnings, plays with fire, and escapes with impunity, while another, engaging in precisely the same act through pure ignorance, is actually burned to death. So far from these natural reactions being proportionate to the inducing acts, their singular disproportionateness is one of the most perplexing mysteries of the present state of being.

It is further assumed "that these natural reactions which follow the child's wrong actions are constant, direct, unhesitating, and not to be escaped." But we have just seen that cases may easily occur in which the wrong act may be, and without the painful consequence at all. Beyond this, who does not know the power of mere repetition, to practically nullify or destroy the proper reaction? For example, the boy takes tobacco, chews it, and he is made sick; but he continues the practice, and finally ceases to experience the reactionary penalty; nay, he will be made sick by the attempt to abandon the hateful practice.

Once more, it is assumed that the transgressor

"soon recognizing this stern though beneficent discipline becomes extremely careful not to transgress." Now while this effectiveness of the natural reactions as a corrective, may be measurably true of the mere minor and aimless violations of physical laws, it is utterly untrue of all that higher and more dangerous class of transgressions, in which the incentives of pleasure or immediate gratification come into play, Society is full of examples of the most painful nature, in which the constant experience of the saddest consequences altogether fails to deter men and women from known violations of the laws of the physical nature.

Without pausing to notice here the various and singular failures of the writer in question to discover the thorough inconclusiveness of many of his inferences; his entire disregard of the most evident distinctions between the facts of the purely physical system and one as purely moral; and his sometimes winding and painful evasions of the real question at issue, we pass to those more vital errors which vitiate the whole system as one of moral discipline and governmental correction.

In the first place, then chiefly, the theory is one developed from the physical constitution of things rather than from the facts and laws of the moral nature. It finds its predominant types and leading principles in the operation of physical causes, and the laws of their effects, or consequences, and not in the exercise of the moral powers and the necessary principles of their just control. Hence, unless there can be established an exact parallelism between the two, or unless the latter can be shown to be merely the ulterior development of the former, the analogy instituted between the two must sooner or later fail, or, if still pressed, must prove utterly deceptive. But no such parallelism or principle of continuous development can be proven.

This may, perhaps, be more clearly seen in specific illustration. Thus, if one runs a pin into his finger, pain follows: the consequence is immediate and certain. But, if he tells a lie, the moral sequence,—conscious guilt and remorse,—is not, as all experience shows, immediate and certain; nay, it is more commonly uncertain, and is reached only through intervening pressure and struggle. Again, if one tumbles over a door-step through heedlessness, the slight accident produces a slight pain, whereas a more serious accident would occasion a greater pain. But it by no means follows, that this gradation of effects holds good where action purely moral is concerned: it by no means follows, that he who steals fifty dollars will feel five times the self-condemnatory pain, or will incur five times the opprobium which falls to the lot of him who has taken but ten. Still further, he who spills boiling water on his hands may learn from the resulting scald, a lesson so effective that no persuasion will induce him again to disregard the laws of his constitution in that way. But no man of common sense needs to be told, that it by no means follows from this, that he who has basely defrauded his neighbor, experiences so keen a pang in consequence, or is visited by such naturally resultant evils, that no inducement of avaricious desire will persuade him to do the same again. Nay, experience teaches that he who has done it once, is, if anything, the more likely to venture upon a second experiment of the same kind, and that one still more flagitious.

Without multiplying illustrations, it will, we think, be clearly enough seen from the foregoing, that this method of moral discipline must prove wholly inadequate to the proper correction of the higher offenses. While, as a subsidiary means, it may render important service in the treatment of all offenses which, involving distinctly the violation of some law of material being, are subject to the rigorous imposition of natural consequences; when the transition is to the spiritual being, and the offense becomes more exclusively moral, and, as such, is, in its consequences, not only more subtle, but more varied and uncertain, these natural reactions, as they are termed, must of necessity fall greatly short of most of the demands made upon discipline.

Thus, in the case of a child who has carelessly lost his knife, you may insist upon the continuance of the natural consequence,—his deprivation of the privilege of having one. But carry out the assumed intimation of nature when he has failed to acquire the knowledge embraced in a certain lesson, and insist upon his continued deprivation of that knowledge as a just punishment, and the whole is simply absurd. Again, suppose a man to have wasted his fortune in riotous indulgence; and the resultant beggary and disease which are the natural consequences of his folly and vice, may serve as a species of discipline, to correct his false notions of pleasure or propriety, and deter him from a repetition of his wild extravagance and destructive indulgence. But, suppose that he has by a base forgery reduced his friend to beggary; or has by an act of perjury deprived an innocent man of character or liberty; or has with cool calculation robbed an unsuspecting victim of life or limb;—suppose any of these, and what natural consequence can you discover to be, with like certainty and severity, treading upon the heels of his transgression, as an adequate and sure corrective?

Nor will it avail to plead that, in such cases, the wants of discipline may be met by the use of the higher means, such as the withdrawal of confidence, the demand for restitution, or deprivation of personal liberty; for in the case of him who has gone to these extremes of crime, there may be an entire insensibility to the verdict of the public sentiment; restitution may be a simple impossibility; and as for the incarceration of the culprit as an unsafe person, that is not at all a natural consequence; it is altogether an authoritative act, and one of those positive inflictions pronounced by the theorist, as artificial and useless punishments. By the very terms of his theory, then, the progress of the natural reactionist in this direction is estopped.

In this direction, then, the theory of moral discipline, chiefly through the medium of natural reactions, is reprehensible on the ground that it practically ignores radical and fixed distinctions that exist between matter and mind; it quietly, but none the less positively, assumes that natural causes and free causes are confederate on the same basis, are bound by the same chain of consequential necessity, and are to be determined in their practical laws and applications by the same processes of investigation, and reasoning. In all this, it betrays its hearty sympathy with that pretentious modern philosophizing (we cannot dignify it as philosophy) which endows each corpuscle with an atom of intelligence, aggregates their force in a nervous system, culminates the whole in the cineritous matter of the brain, and thus, identifying mind with sublimated nerve force, ends in pure, though covert materialism.

Still further, the theory, as just hinted, thoroughly ignores certain cardinal facts in the nature and operation of the moral powers, which underlie all just and effective application of government to the rational subject. Assuming complacently, as it does, that the intimations of nature in the chain of physical causation are a sufficient guide to the consequential discipline of those higher offenses which are either chiefly or exclusively moral, it practically denies the following fact:

That it is fully within the power of a depraved will to destroy all natural reaction of the moral nature, so that no such moral punishment will be possible within the consciousness of the offender. Thus, a person may, from the influence of evil associations, from the strength of habit, or from the power of a depraved propensity, have come to have the reason so perverted in its apprehension, and the conscience so benumbed in its sensibility, that the commission of crimes of no inconsiderable magnitude, may awaken no inconvenient consciousness whatever. For example, how often do profanity, falsehood, or petty theft, occur "and give no sign" of any painful sense of guilt, shame, or remorse? But in such a case, where is the certain, the graduated, the inexorable consequence, that, as natural reaction, is to serve as punishment?

But suppose the theorist appeals to the external effects of such misdeeds,—their influence to awaken displeasure and produce reprehension, in others. Who does not know that the same causes may have operated to make another,—a parent, a teacher, a friend, any person so situated as to become cognizant of the offense and to be able to visit his displeasure as a natural reaction upon the offender,—who does not know that he may have been made just as insensible to the criminal character of the act, and may have come to be just as much beyond the reach of any painful feelings as a consequence of its commission, as the offender himself? How many persons are entirely unaffected by the utterance of an oath, or a petty falsehood, or the taking of some fraudulent advantage of another. In these cases, where is the chance for that displeasure, or withdrawal of confidence, or censure which as external natural reactions may serve as punishment? "But," says the theorist, "the offender is amenable to public sentiment." Suppose, however, your public sentiment, as it often is, is so far debased as to have no voice of condemnation, then what? There are communities where sabbath-breaking, polygamy or licentiousness, do not shock the public sensibility at all; nay, where the abuses are even justified: where are the natural reactions here?

The truth is, while the *physical* reactions, upon which the whole scheme is so plausibly based, are somewhat certain and constant the world over, the *moral* reactions, whether internal or external, individual or social, are so subject to the contingencies of voluntary action, and are, hence, so variable and uncertain, that it is difficult to see how the attempt could be made to reason conclusively from the former to the latter, with an intelligent or honest purpose.

As a third objection to this theory, we urge this; that its proposed provisions for the correction of offenses fail altogether to distinguish the authoritative from the general, or non-authoritative, in discipline: it wholly excludes the very idea fundamental and necessary to all government; namely, that of proper sovereignty. To present this more clearly, take, for example, the case of one who, having eaten to excess, becomes as a natural consequence violently ill. Now the *philosophical thinker* may, in tracing out the line of causation, discover in the painful result of the excessive indulgence, an indication of the Divine will in favor of temperance as a virtue, and against gluttony as a vice. But not so with the mass of mind. To such mind, the ultimate authority is practically submerged in mere natural causation. The whole occurrence, being bounded within the fixed and every way ordinary circuit of natural laws, is, and we may almost add, can only be, apprehended as a thing in nature, and not at all in an authority or government as beyond and above nature. Hence, the almost universal experience of mankind is, that such occurrences are apprehended as involving simply an error in action, and serving as an admonition to the exercise of higher wisdom or prudence; and not at all, as embracing direct guilt, and demanding atonement and subsequent obedience to rightful sovereignty.

Still further, take the case of a child who has been guilty of falsehood. The natural external reaction by which the offense is to be corrected, is a manifestation of displeasure and of withdrawn confidence in the reliability of his word. But suppose the offense to have come equally under the cognizance of A, the parent, and B, a mere acquaintance. The former holds an authoritative relation to the offender; the latter only a general relation. Yet the reaction is the same in kind in the case of both. How then is this reaction as penalty, to distinguish the authoritative from the non-authoritative; how can it evince the superior rights and responsibilities of the proper sovereignty over those of mere association and general regard for virtue? Hence, so far as the "indication of nature" is concerned, the stranger is as competent to apply the corrective, or the punishment, as the parent. But this is abhorrent to the common sense of mankind, and in direct conflict with the necessary ideas of order and justice.

Lastly, we object to this theory of natural reactions according to these assumed intimations of nature, that it disenables the collective authority of civil government from the proper censure or punishment of offenses against its rightful sovereignty. So far as *individual* expressions of displeasure or manifestation of impaired confidence are concerned, we have seen that while they can not cover the required ground necessary for the recognition or maintenance of the authority, they are still possible. But collect all the individuals in a commonwealth, and require them to be represented in a collective authority or government proper, and where are we to find those direct expressions of look, tone, word or natural action, which can effectively say to the offenders, you have committed an offense; displeasure is felt; confidence is withdrawn? Conceive of the culprit as under a government forbidden to go beyond the limit of these natural consequences and reactions, or any others possible in strict accordance with these assumed intimations of nature, as argued from the primary basis of necessary cause and effect and you conceive of him as in the very realm and paradise of villainy. Conceive of a government so conditioned, and you may as well at once append to the law of its constitution the memorable item added by Luther to the twelve articles drawn up by the rebel fanatics under Munzer: "From this day forth, the honorable Council shall be powerless,—its functions shall be to do nothing,—it shall sit as an idol or as a log,—the commune shall chew its meat for it, and it shall be bound hand and foot."

The truth is, the system of nature can only comprehend and consider the being under her administration, as simply *creature:* government must look farther, and hold him under her control and discipline, as *subject.* Under the former, the only conception of that which lies back of, and is installed above, being, is that of superior agency, as *author:* under the latter, it is distinctly that of supreme power, as *authority.* Under the former, therefore, the inflictions are necessarily causal, or consequential: under the latter, they must be positive and penal. Hence, it will be seen that government proper is not the mere natural or constitutional concurrence of creative power and product, cause and effect. It is rather a distinct positive institution, not in conflict with nature, but rising clearly and legitimately above nature; adapted to the higher wants of associated moral beings, and providing for the attainment of ends which nature can not reach. Of this character precisely are civil governments, and as such, they must both for their own manifestation and support, be privileged to employ positive inflictions,—those very "inflictions of pain" which the theory stigmatizes as "artificial and unnecessary," and of which judicial condemnation, civil disabilities, "imprisonment or other restraint," are clear and well-defined examples, all plausible pretense to the contrary notwithstanding. Government is an artificial symbol of the collective sense and will of the community, and it must symbolize its own sense and will to a greater or less extent, by corresponding artificial means. Hence, we urge that the theory of natural reactions is objectionable as practically, in its proper consummation, subversive of civil government.

Without going into a specific application of these facts, it will be seen generally that, inasmuch as these defects in the theory are radical, the assumed superiority of its application to the moral discipline of the child in the school, is wholly fallacious. Under all the fair-seeming philosophy and ingenious reasonings of its popular advocate, there lies a broad substratum of error in both premises and inferences. This error should not be allowed to escape the notice of the teacher. Left unconscious of its presence and nature, he will, not only be in danger of being diverted from the true theory of government, but he will be disenabled to make the wisest use of such just suggestions as the theory really contains.

But there is another species of error current in society, and largely affecting the views of educational reforms. It is not to be found so formally developed in theory as the foregoing; but is, perhaps, more widely and dangerously operative in fact. Superficially, its relation to the scheme of natural reactions, may not be readily apparent. But, substantially, the originating and animating principle is the same in both. What that principle is, and how it leads to the two results, may be seen as follows. Given a consciousness in man of subjection to a divine moral government, and of incurred guilt deserving of condign punishment, the anxious problem to be solved, is, how to escape a just subjection to positive pains and penalties, beyond the present state of being. Now, very clearly, establish the principle that, under a system of moral discipline among men, all the so-called artificial punishments are unnecessary and unjust: or set up the claim that the authoritative infliction of positive pain, or the use of discipline for any other than reformatory purposes, is inhumane, or, at least, inconsistent with perfect benevolence, and the case is apparently gained. Having thus shut up human government within the narrow range of these mere natural consequences of transgression, and to the mere amiable ends of humane individual reformation, there is but a step from that to the application of the same laws and bounds to the moral government of God, the result of which, if successful, will be obvious.

It becomes then important that this (for want of a better term) *humanitarian scheme* of discipline should be carefully examined. The substance of its outcry against its antagonistic system of government and discipline, is that these inflictions of pain are unphilosophical, and inhumane, vindictive rather than reformatory.

With reference to the question of philosophical consistency, we urge the following considerations. First, the infliction of disciplinary pain is the very thing directly sustained by the indications of nature. In more express terms, the supreme authority in nature everywhere inflicts pain for violations of his demands. True, he does it through the medium of what are called natural laws. But that neither makes the infliction less productive of pain, or less an act of the authority. It only makes it the clearer that, rooted as this painful species of corrective discipline is in the very substratum of nature, its general application under contingent modifications, is not arbitrary nor accidental: it is fundamental and necessary. It shows that the right to inflict disciplinary pain is inherent in all just authority, and that authoritative subjection to such penal infliction is a necessary contingency of all actual transgression.

Nor does the more manifest connection of these painful inflictions in nature with the physical side of being, invalidate the argument. God, in nature, no more inflicts pain for the mere physical results, than does man in society. It is done always as a natural and necessary means to a moral end. The blow struck upon the body, in the case of him who, trampling on the laws of temperance, suffers the pangs of indigestion or the horrors of delirium-tremens, is intended to react upon the soul, which cannot otherwise be reached so well. The outcry of nature in the pain endured is not against the hand which grasped the means of excess, nor the mouth which took in the forbidden elements, nor the stomach which received and endeavored to appropriate them; but it is raised against the sinful spirit which demanded the base subservience of these instruments in its bodily nature, to its sensual desires and depraved will. And thus the divine authority in nature stands as a prototype for the human authority in society, in its struggle to repress the evil and preserve the good for the great ends of the common weal.

Nor is it any just counter-plea, that, in nature, it is God who disciplines by pain, while under civil or social law, it is only usurping man. In nature, God has, for the necessary stability of being itself, maintained himself in immediate presence and active authority. But in human society, he has, for the sake of conferred free agency, and the development of voluntary capacity, responsibility and power, withdrawn himself, as it were, from the immediate control, and imposed its exercise, with all its prerogatives and liabilities, upon the human agency itself. Proper human government is, in this sense, a delegated vicegerent of God himself; and it is thus that "the powers that be," whether domestic, scholastic, civil, or ecclesiastical, "are ordained of God." And that such authorities can not discipline by natural laws, as does God in nature, is no argument that they must not administer correction by means of what are stigmatized as "artificial inflictions of pain." The prerogative of ruling is not delegated without the right to the means of discipline; and those means, as has already been seen, involve the positive reaching of the refractory spirit, through the avenues of the bodily organism, and in just such ways as are practicable and effective, whether in accordance with the ordinary laws of nature or not. Indeed, it is not yet in proof, that even the Divine Ruler, in dealing with the more exclusive forms of moral delinquency, has restricted himself to the narrow range of corrective means in simple cause and effect, as he does in the case of the violation of physical laws.

In the second place, as to the plea of inhumanity, which is sometimes urged in objection, it is equally fallacious. The withholding of painful inflictions is not necessarily humane, for it is not clear to any observing and candid mind, that pain is necessarily an evil. Nay, the natural reactionist himself, and in accordance with the common-sense of mankind, admits the benevolent utility of pain in its physical relations, as a necessary means to a merciful end: in other words, it is, in the perfect circle of related being and action, an absolute good. Not less distinctly has it, in all human government, been accepted as the same, and both under the same general law, and for the same general reason. Furthermore, if in nature, where only the preservation of individual being is the cardinal end to be attained, the infliction of pain is a necessary good, much more, may it be reasonably argued, is it both just and true in the society or the state, where a broader and more comprehensive being than that of the mere individual is concerned, and higher and more imperative interests than that of mere existence, are at stake.

It is a significant fact that these objections against he infliction of pain are due in good part to certain errors which characterize these humanitarian schemists, in general. One of these is, that, with a vision narrowed by false sympathy with suffering, they see with effective sharpness, only the suffering individual, while all the broad surrounding circle of related life and interest is lost in vague imperception. Or, if they at all perceive the vital nature and claims of society as a whole, they have, by beginning with the study of the individual sufferer under law, so impaired the habit and grasp of the apprehension, that when it has even worked up and out to the surrounding breadth of the social or civil organism, they behold it only as a thing reduced and remote. They have bent their gaze upon it, only through the inverted glass. If they would but reverse the process; if they would but begin with the greater interests of the organic whole, with the majesty and responsibility of government as the sole conservator of those interests, and thence descend to the proper claims of the individual offender, they would obtain better and broader conceptions of the nature and prerogatives of discipline; they would discover how much greater the whole is than any of its parts, how much more important to be avoided are the pangs of dissolute or dissolving society, than the pains of the individual transgressor who has fallen into the hands of human justice.

With reference to the remaining error,—that of assuming the office of governmental discipline to be primarily and chiefly *reformatory*,—there occurs an inversion of the order of things, no less transparent than in the former case. Indeed a perversely upside down philosophy seems to be the peculiar penchant of these theorizers. Now the reformation of the guilty may, and should somewhere, be an object sought; but rather within the sphere of individual philanthropy than governmental control. The philanthropic element in government, so far as it has a place, must concern itself rather with the general welfare. Hence, to all true government, the first and highest end, is the twofold preservation of the loyal and innocent: first, their preservation as a body politic, intact and secure from the encroachments of the disloyal and vicious; and secondly, their preservation generally from any endangered loss of their own purity and rectitude, as induced by the baleful presence among them of uncurbed example and crimes "unwhipped of justice." The former, it secures by the restraints and disabilities it imposes upon transgressors, and the latter by the inflicted penalties and pains which stand as a perpetual warning to those who have not yet fallen. And we are bold to say, further, that under no true theory of government, can any other than this first and highest end be *directly* proposed; the reformatory end, where it is sought, being so properly, only as a means to the better preservation of the innocent. This it effects by securing their more thorough protection against any further trespass upon their rights by the criminal as once brought to justice and through that, if reformed, restored to positive rectitude.

The application of these broad and comprehensive principles to the use of disciplinary penalties and pains in our schools, as it regards both their utility and natural consistency, is henceforth so clear that we might venture to leave its further consideration to the sound sense of the teacher himself. And yet, we doubt not there will arise in some minds, more tender in feeling than vigorous in thought, the painfully present and pressing question, "Is there, then, no escape from the necessity of employing means of correction so seemingly pitiless and repulsive?"

To this question, we can only answer frankly, no, not until there shall appear in the present state, some new and nobler incarnation of the human spirit with both a regenerated moral nature and a restored perfection of the physical being. So long as man shall continue to exist as a free moral agent, controlled, nevertheless, by a depraved will, and bound in subjection to a material organism; so long it cannot be otherwise, than that, transgressing the higher laws of the spiritual essence within him, he must in some part, for both his own good and that of society, be reined in and driven back from evil doing, by those stern mandates which can only send their living utterances to the soul, through the roused sensibilities of the bodily nature.

The only question, then, which the practical teacher can raise with just reasonableness, is, how can the necessity for the use of these penal inflictions in the school, be reduced to its minimum? This question admits of a more hopeful and happy answer. That answer embraces several practical suggestions.

First. The necessity for the use of penal inflictions in the school can be largely reduced by the careful institution of such a wise and noble order in both arrangement and management, as will, as has already been shown, materially diminish the occasions for transgression, and infuse into the minds of the pupils, a deeper interest and a higher ambition.

Secondly. It may be further reduced by the institution of such exact and effective discipline,—to be fully discussed hereafter,—as will create a prevailing conviction through all its ranks, of the inevitable certainty of detection and just punishment.

Thirdly. The last and crowning means of completing this reduction,—means, alas, too seldom and too feebly employed,—is to be found in the earnest and prominent use of moral instruction in the school; not the mere incidental enunciation of a stale and lifeless ethics,—an ethics discharged of all religious principle, a mere moral cadaver with no divine indwelling and energizing spirit,—but the steady and systematic pressing upon the minds and hearts of the pupils, of those great laws and obligations which, as both moral and religious, are the sole foundation for all pure and perfected character.

This, we are well aware, is broadly broaching the much-mooted question, whether or not, moral instruction should be introduced into schools under the control of the state, as a fixed part of its educational system,—a question the solution of which we regard as neither doubtful nor difficult. That solution, however, is possible, only under the condition that a just view be taken of the end to be sought by the state in establishing a system of popular education. For what the state must seek as its end, determines what the state must do with moral instruction as a means to that end.

Let it then be understood at the outset, that inasmuch as government is instituted, not by the individual, but by the community; and inasmuch as it is established, not for the individual benefit, but for the public good, its entire province and prerogative must be limited by its responsibility to the commonwealth, for the common weal. Hence, government must be made to look municipally,—if we may be allowed the word,—at the state, and not individually at the man; it must be moved by an economical regard for the good of the state, and not by a mere humane concern for the person; it must act to the one comprehensive end, the conservation and advancement of the state, and not for the simple, prior or prominent object of benefiting of the individual. That these secondary objects concerning the mere individual man, may be, and, under any proper administration of government, must be attained, is freely granted; but it is as firmly maintained, that they are not, and never may be, a proper end or direct object of government as such. The first, sole, proper and direct object of the state, then, must be its own conservation and advancement, its own perpetuity, its own prosperity,—these are its objects of concern, its ends of action.

Hence, not at all for the simple direct sake of any person or persons as such; not at all for his or their advantage, other than as the merest consequent of its legitimate action, may any proper government provide schools and instruction for the people. Only to *this* end may it do that,—that there may be possible in the state, that highest and purest exercise of political rights among the people, which will ensure in the state the wisest constitution, the ablest administration, and the most enduring permanence of government, and through these, the true dignity, stability and prosperity of the state itself. In other words, only to the end of its own conservation and advancement, may the state ever establish or maintain a system of public instruction.

Here, then, the question, always pertinent, becomes actually vital; is mere intellectual or scientific culture enough to meet the conditions of the case; is that sufficient to render a state system of public instruction either competent to the attainment of the desired end, or consistent with it? Give the people such culture only, and will that ensure in them, and from them, such combined intelligence, virtue and loyalty, as will secure the state, for all time, against its most dangerous enemies, popular ignorance, social corruption, and political abandonment. Will such a culture make a people both intelligent and virtuous, and as virtuous as intelligent,—this is the question, and a vital one it is.

What now is the inevitable answer to this question? Let us see. What says history? All history teaches us, that popular advancement in the arts and sciences, without a corresponding growth in morality and religion, has been always and only an increased refinement in individual and national wickedness, a more skilful and subtle abuse of power, and a change of the mere form of civil destruction, from external crush and demolition, to a secret and subtle, yet sure sap and subversion.

And what says philosophy? All philosophy teaches, that, for every increase of power in the subjected object, there must be a corresponding augmentation of strength in the controlling agent, and that every advance in individual knowledge, is an augmentation of power, for which there can be no corresponding increase of control, other than that found in a corresponding growth and ascendancy of moral principle.

And what says simple common sense? Common sense urges, that it is the fact that in all enlightened countries and communities, intellectual and moral culture are, in some way or other, so associated or run parallel, that it is almost impossible to dissever them for the purpose of exemplification and comparison; and that this fact alone is enough to establish the existence of a relation between them, at once so natural and necessary, that to ignore it either in theory or practice, and so to dissever moral instruction from intellectual or scientific culture, is simply to make an educational system stultify itself.

Without appealing to specific examples, and without pressing the argument from principles further, it must be seen from what has been advanced, that the original question ought never to have been entertained at all; and that the only consistent form in which it can present itself, is rather this, ought moral instruction ever to be neglected or even subordinated in our public schools? What position, or what prominence should be assigned to moral instruction? may be discussed: that it should have some place and importance, is a foregone conclusion.

There are those, however, who will argue, that observation by no means shows, that the lack of this distinct moral culture in our schools is productive of that uncurbed and therefore destructive intelligence to which reference has been made. The answer to this objection is immediately and conclusively this, that the non-occurrence of that dangerous result is not due to the non-existence of a natural cause for it; but to the existence of important and, to a certain extent, redeeming influences operating on our youth, outside of the schools, and accidentally affording them a certain proportion of the lacking moral culture.

Others may urge, that, even if the moral culture were not thus incidentally secured, the laws would afford the state an adequate protection against this unprincipled or demoralized intelligence. To this it is sufficient to answer, that, not only is there outside of the exact letter of the laws, a wide margin for the most vicious and dangerous exercise of such intelligence, but there is in this very intelligence, and simply because it is corrupt, a power equal to the most triumphant evasion, if not the actual defiance of the laws.

As to those other objections, urged, perhaps, sometimes honestly, but intelligently perhaps never, that this necessary moral instruction can better be given elsewhere, and therefore should be, or that its introduction into our schools will make them sectarian;

it is sufficient to say, that they do not commend themselves enough to the simplest common sense, to claim either a specific notice or a formal refutation. When it shall be shown that it is possible, not to say profitable, to dissever the intellectual and moral faculties in their exercise and development, in this manner; or when it shall appear that ethics, by being, for the sake of convenience, considered apart from mental science, becomes a body of sectarian dogmas, rather than a system of universal principles; in other words, when it shall become clear, that we are to build the most wisely and successfully, by first laying up the brick, and then elsewhere, and by other hands, inserting the mortar; or when it shall have become manifest, that to lay the brick with the mortar, contemporaneously and conjunctively, is to interfere with the rights of both builder and owner, and actually to destroy the catholic excellence of the masonry;—when this shall be, the time for a formal notice of those objections may have come: come before it can not; and till it can, we dismiss them.

Of the exclusive *Moral Suasion Scheme*, so much harped upon by certain shallow theorists, no distinct notice will be taken here, for the reasons, that it is substantially identical in spirit and philosophy with those already considered; taken by itself, it is a mere castle in the air; and if it needs to be refuted at all, it is sufficiently met by the general principles herein urged at large.

# CHAPTER XI.

## GENERAL ELEMENTS CONTINUED—DISCIPLINE—PENAL CORRECTION, OR PUNISHMENT.

Punishment defined—*Its necessary elements*—Authoritative infliction—Act of proper authority—Infliction of an actual suffering—*Process through which effective*—Enlightens the intellect—Arouses the sensibilities—Moves the will—Infliction must be for the support of law, and for the general welfare—*Punishments classified as Privative and Positive*—Defined—Privative distinguished, as Primitive and Retractive—Right to punish by deprivation sustained—Consequent superiority of conditional rewards—Necessity for positive punishments—*Positive punishments defined*—Relation to the privative—Positive classified as Privative, Coercive and Compulsive—*Coercive described—Essential points to be secured*—Actual abandonment of the wrong—Correction of its evil results—Reparation to the government as such—Voluntariness in the whole—*Coercive classified*, as reprimands, loss of privilege, restraint or confinement, corporal punishment, and final exclusion—*General Rules for infliction*—Positive detection must precede—Punishment must be well considered—Must be thorough—Administered with deliberateness—Must be public—*Objections to publicity considered*—Spring from false sympathy or pride—Publicity necessary to the full effect of the discipline—Proper infliction of punishment not brutalizing—The infliction of the punishment to be followed by moral efforts—Evil of neglecting these—*Specific methods*—For correlative rewards and punishments—For public reprimands—For bodily restraint—Objectionable restraints—Particular consideration of detention after school—Method for corporal punishment—Objectionable inflictions—*Compulsive correction*—Nature and use illustrated—Grounds of its reasonableness—Objection to involuntariness answered—*Final exclusion*—Occasion of its existence—Must be held as a last resort—Is less a common necessity than is supposed—Specific method—Must be followed by reclamatory efforts—Summary abandonment of offenders a social vice.

PROCEEDING to the proper discussion of penal correction, we define punishment to be,—as it is accepted in the common sense of mankind,—the authoritative infliction, by some properly constituted sovereignty, of some species of pain or suffering upon offenders, because of their wilful violations of lawful requirement, and for the sake of sustaining the majesty of government, and securing the common weal.

In the thorough consideration of the several elements embraced in the definition, it will be observed, first, that punishment must be an authoritative infliction, as opposed to mere consequential results. In other words, for reasons already discussed at length, consequences are not to be accepted as, in any proper sense, punishments.

Again, the infliction must be the act of a properly constituted authority. Proceeding from any other source than such authority, it loses all legality and, in losing its legality, it becomes simply an abuse or, if you will, an outrage. Thus, suppose the child committing some act in known violation of parental law, to be caught and chastised by a passer-by; or a public offender to be seized and subjected to summary retribution by the private citizen, and in neither case would the act be held to be legitimate, or the infliction be counted as punishment. Nay, both of these self-constituted ministers of justice, would be themselves held as transgressors. Nor, indeed, is this all, the act must be that of the proper authority, and no other. Thus if, for example, the parent chastises the child for some violation of school regulations not at all embraced in his own rules or directions, or if, in a higher field, one state authority should inflict penalties for crimes committed within the jurisdiction, or against the laws of another commonwealth, the act would, in both cases, be one of usurpation or tyranny.

Punishment must, furthermore, involve the infliction of something actually counted by the offender as an evil; and as such it must be capacitated to occasion painful restraint or actual suffering. For reasons already noticed as existing in the depraved condition and vicious power of the will, if government be stopped short of this extreme of its prerogative in infliction, its penal inflictions are, in the majority of cases, reduced to a sham and a failure. The susceptibilities of the culprit are, of course, not to determine the nature or the measure of the infliction; but, whatever the government shall adjudge it to be, it must be a something real to the offender, and probably sufficient to reach his will effectively. This, however, is not to take ground that, in individual cases, in which it may fail to be thus effective, it is to be forborne; for government has other ends in its infliction, other than that of the mere correction of the offender. The deterring of the yet innocent, from the commission of similar crimes, may be itself a sufficient ground for the infliction, even when the offender is already clearly hardened beyond the reach of its influence.

The process through which the punishment is to reach and affect either the guilty or the innocent, in order that the ends of discipline may be attained, is as follows. In the first place, it is designed to bring the intellect to a consciousness of the reality and the magnitude of the offense, by presenting to it a positive symbol of the views and feelings of the offended sovereignty. Its language is to this effect; in the measure of the care taken to bring you to condign punishment, and in the measure of the pains inflicted upon you, behold the measure of that wrong which you have inflicted upon pure rectitude, and of that outrage which you have committed against the majesty of law.

Secondly. It is designed to awaken in the sensibility, a distinct feeling of the reality and heinousness of the offense committed. This it effects, partly through the foregoing influence to enlighten the intellect, and partly through pressing upon the culprit, in a sense of the pains he bears, a feeling of the loss or the evil he himself incurs, and of the necessary folly or turpitude of the act which was an adequate cause for the infliction of such suffering.

Thirdly. Through the intellect and the sensibilities as already affected, it is designed to reach the will, presenting to it motives, from either conviction, desire or fear, calculated to restrain or reverse its evil purposes, and thus operating to prevent, not only the repetition of the evil act for which the punishment is inflicted, but also the commission of others for which it may be justly demanded.

The deterring effect of punishment upon the innocent, is reached through much the same process, differing only in this, that the operation is one of observation rather than experience. It is, in their case, the more hopeful, inasmuch as there is yet no actual guilt to cloud the apprehension, to warp the judgment or benumb the feelings. Hence, the suffering, though only witnessed, sheds a clearer light upon the offended majesty of the law, upon the magnitude of the offense, and upon the bitterness of transgression in its individual consequences.

Finally. The punishment must be inflicted for no merely vindictive or even reformatory ends. Its grand object is, directly, the sustaining of law, and through that, the ultimate preservation of the common welfare. Whenever it degenerates from this, and is made to compass individual or inferior ends alone, the punishment becomes less condemnatory of the culprit, than of the authority which applies it.

Passing now to the specific consideration of punishments, we classify them as of two general species: *Privative* and *Positive.*

Under privative punishment, we include every authoritative deprivation of rights, privileges or honors, of which the pupil has, by his misdemeanors, wrought just forfeiture. Of these punishments, it is proper to remark that they embrace all of the so-called natural reactions that are really valuable; and their natural restriction to this head, is itself a proof of the insufficiency of those reactions as a sole means of moral discipline. These punishments, hence, form a sort of connecting link between purely consequential evils and proper punishments.

These privative punishments may be considered as of two kinds; *Primitive,* or the subtraction of such rights or privileges as may, either naturally or by the action of some antecedent authority, have been conferred upon the pupil: and *Retractive*, or the resumption by the teacher of such privileges or honors as may have been authoritatively conferred by him, upon the pupil, either as specific rewards or otherwise.

As illustrative of these, may be cited, the depriving of the pupil of the right to a recess or play spell; of the privilege of holding some favorite seat, or some post of honor in a class; or of the possession of some badge of distinction or token of the teacher's approval and esteem. Others will naturally occur to the thoughtful teacher, either as originally suggested, or as naturally indicated by the peculiar method of reward adopted in his own system of discipline.

Of the right of the teacher to inflict such deprivation, there can hardly be any question. As the absolute conservator of those rights, and author of those privileges or honors, the teacher must as truly possess a negative, as well as a positive, control over them. He must have as truly the power to say, when the welfare of the school demands it, these shall not be, as to declare, they shall be. Furthermore, all rights are guaranteed and all privileges are conferred only on the assumed ground that they are to be consistently held and employed. Everywhere, under proper government, the malicious use of these rights or privileges to the disadvantage of others or the damage of the sovereignty itself, is naturally held to result in either their partial or complete forfeiture. Resting, as they necessarily do, upon a specific merit or worthiness, as soon as that gives place to its opposite specific demerit or unworthiness, they must fall to the ground for the mere want of foundation. Certainly, the existence of character or conduct which would have precluded their creation, must prohibit their continuance. And to this law of resumption there can be no exception, save only in those cases in which either unavoidably or unwisely they have been, by the authority itself, made permanent or irrevocable.

Herein, then, will be discovered a peculiar evil of bestowing permanent gifts as rewards of merit, instead of resumable privileges, marks of favor or honorable distinctions, already urged as of superior consistency and excellence. Bestow upon the pupil such an absolute gift or prize, and, inasmuch as it cannot be resumed, the authority cuts itself off from the opportunity of indicating its displeasure at subsequent transgression, in one of the most effective ways possible, and also from the power to hold the subject steadily to the principle of continued and progressive worthiness as the true law of excellence, in opposition to that of mere temporary or desultory goodness. Very clearly, any action on the part of the teacher which, as a needless finality, limits his power to retain a disciplinary hold upon his pupils, so doubly important as both a stimulus and a restraint, must be, to say the least, exceedingly unwise.

Hence, the teacher can not be too careful in all disciplinary action of this kind, not only to give his preference to resumable rewards, but also to make the school fully understand that they are held subject to such retraction in case of just forfeiture; and that their sole object is not the mere temporary approval of specific acts, but rather the public evincing of a desire to secure that permanent excellence of character of which these acts appear as the natural and steady outworking. The feeling sought to be aroused should be distinctly and invariably this; these rewards were given, not because this was done, but because there was evinced a constant disposition to do it; and so soon as that disposition is wanting, the right to hold them will be just as truly gone as would be the right to receive them. Wherever, also, this principle of conditionality, or this reserved right of retraction is understood, so that its exercise does not take the pupil by surprise, the resuming of the conferred favor more powerfully sets forth the equity of the teacher's administration than did the original bestowment; and for the reason that the latter was a grace rather than a duty, and was a natural occasion of satisfaction on both sides; but the former is an act of duty alone, and, as productive of mutual pain, would naturally be shunned, but for the pressing claims of higher obligation.

But it will be seen from the foregoing, that these privative punishments are necessarily limited in their application to the smaller number of offenses, and those of the more venial character. To meet all its wants, and to be able to reach effectively the more hardened offenders, and the more flagitious acts of criminality, the government of the school must be empowered to go beyond mere negative punishment; it must have access to those which are positive, and which produce, not merely deprivation and discomfort, but which occasion actual suffering, either bodily or mental.

By positive punishments, or punishments proper, are to be understood all those actual inflictions by the constituted authority, which subject the pupil to pain either bodily or mental, and which are needful for the correction of wrong, and for the maintaining of the teacher's sovereignty as the conservator of the school.

The transition from privative to positive punishments is not abrupt. The one rather passes into the other by gradation. Hence, privative punishments may assume much the character of positive inflictions. For example, let the act of deprivation be a simple act, and let it occasion no other feeling than a clear consciousness of the loss incurred, and the punishment is purely privative. But couple the act of deprivation with circumstances which give it the force of a public censure, or a distinct degradation, and cause the feelings occasioned by it to be those of mortification or remorse, and the punishment becomes properly positive. Beyond its bearing upon the following classification, this fact possesses a practical importance, as indicating to the teacher a means of giving effective force to punishments otherwise purely privative, and, as such not unfrequently found to be powerless.

Positive punishments may be classified as of three kinds; *Privative, Coercive* and *Compulsive.* The first of these has been indicated with sufficient clearness under the preceding head. Its further consideration will consequently be waived altogether.

Coercive punishments may be concisely described, as such inflictions of pain, either bodily or mental, as acting upon the will through the sense, the intellect and the feelings, induce a voluntary abandonment of the wrong-doing for which discipline is instituted, and, as far as is practicable, a proper correction of the evils it has occasioned, whether they be individual or general.

Upon four points herein mentioned, particular stress must be laid. First. There must be the actual abandonment of the wrong-doing. This is opposed to any merely partial correction of the evil course in question. There may be cases in which this partial correction is better than nothing; in which that may even have to be accepted as practically all that, under the circumstances, can be attained. But the government of the school is false to the claims of its own dignity, and of the general welfare, as well as to the true interest of the offender, if it rests satisfied with the attainment of any such end. To be content with this, except upon practical compulsion, is to make itself, in one sense, a "*particeps criminis*" in whatever of the wrong-doing lies beyond that corrected. This is clearly illustrated in civil affairs, in the neglect of the state to restrain altogether the public sale of noxious drinks, instead of contenting itself with a system of restrictive licenses.

Secondly. There must be the proper correction of the evils occasioned by the wrong-doing. Abandonment without reparation, is mere external amendment. It contains no evidence that the real root of the transgression has been reached. It is perfectly consistent with pure hypocrisy. For the government of the school to countenance this last, even indirectly, is a vice. In the disciplining of offenders by punishment, then, no pains must be spared to point out the possible modes of making proper reparation, and to bring the offender to the full and resolute undertaking of that, perhaps, self-sacrificing, but yet necessary work. We greatly fear, however, that teachers generally, either from a failure to apprehend its primary importance, or from indisposition to undertake the necessary moral effort, fail to do anything of the kind. Such a failure is, so far as it goes, a positive pronunciation against their fitness to govern.

Thirdly. The reparation must just as distinctly embrace the wrong done to the government of the school, as that inflicted upon any of its individual members. Too commonly the offending member of the school attains no other idea of his act than that embraced in its relation to an individual, either some fellow-pupil, if it is a personal offense, or if not, then the teacher alone. He reaches no conception of its character beyond and above everything individual, as an offense against the whole school either as such, or as represented in its government. And yet this last is the vital point. In no organized community, can crime be crime, only or chiefly against the individual. Like a blow struck against any part of a compact body, it vibrates through the whole; and by just so much as that body stretches out on every side, by just so much do its vibrations tremble along successive waves of concentric relation, more or less sensibly affecting the whole. It is the ignorant or the studious oversight of this principle, which inspires the pseudo-humanity of that dangerous class whose sympathy for public criminals is, at the present day, infecting and debasing the popular notions of justice. Let the teacher, then, bear this in mind, and see to it, that in the school, this higher idea of the relation of offenses is understood and felt, and the consequent reparation demanded and made.

Lastly. Let not the voluntary element be overlooked or dispensed with. Amendment which is strictly forced, is sometimes all that can be reached. Even as such, it is better than none. It externally sustains the majesty of law, and shuts off the evil example. Sophistry sometimes pleads against this principle, the analogies of nature, as in the case of disease or danger, where mere external improvement may be itself injurious. But it is a lying philosophy which reasons thus from the physical to the moral. Better is that reasoning which, appealing to the case of evils like those of licentiousness or drunkenness, profanity or sabbath-breaking, finds that though, in their secret hiding-places, they are beyond the reach of the law, yet, in their very seclusion, they attest the virtue and the power of the law, and are forced to forego the baleful exercise of a wide-spread influence and an unblushing example.

Nevertheless, generally, and especially in those sacred precincts,—the family, the school, and the church, that correction which lays the ax "at the root of the tree," is better, and is to be studiously sought, Here, higher and holier aims than those of mere legality, must predominate. In these, then, authority must not rest content until, with its appliances and influences, it has reached the heart and secured that that, in its voluntary obedience to the claims of pure rectitude, shall "magnify the law and make it honorable." And the lesson herein taught the teacher is this; that while, in the use of legitimate punishments he more immediately coerces the offending will, he is not to rest satisfied, until coercion has become transfigured in true and permanent submission. Great concern, painful severity, and much benevolent and pains-taking afterwork may this entail upon him. But it is the law of his office, and let him cheerfully accept its issues.

Passing from these considerations bearing on our definition of coercive punishment, we observe that in its several species, it may consist of these general forms of infliction, namely: *public reprimands* either with or without temporary exclusion from rights and privileges; subjection to *personal restraint* or inconvenience; *bodily chastisement*, or corporal punishment proper; and *final exclusion* from the privileges and precincts of the school. The specific nature, restriction and application of the several kinds of punishment will, for the sake of convenience be considered together, under their respective heads.

It will, however, be first incumbent on us to attend

carefully to those general principles which must govern the teacher, in the use of all the several species of coercive punishments. These principles are, to a qualified extent, applicable to all the foregoing kinds of punishment; but they are more especially considered here with reference to those which, as positively coercive, are more important in their nature, and more serious in their contingencies.

First. Whatever punishment it is proposed to inflict, it must be preceded by positive detection or proper investigation. Without this, there can, of course, be no certainty that the teacher's decision is righteous, and the punishment just. Of the necessity of these, little need be said. They are vital to the interests of all concerned, from the government, down. Neither must unjust punishment be inflicted, nor must punishment be unjustly inflicted. To this there is no alternative.

And yet, it is not unfrequently the case that the latter wrong is perpetrated by the teacher. How often,—shame, that it must be said!—does the blow fall upon the mere victim of mischief, rather than upon the real, though concealed offender! For example, how often does a day pass in our schools, without witnessing such justice as this? A pupil naturally impulsive and brimful of giggle, is purposely set a-laughing by some cool-headed, long-faced rogue in his neighborhood, who carefully screens himself from the teacher's observation. Sequel, under these 'second Daniels come to judgment',—the helpless laugher is punished, sometimes regardless of his defense, and the mischief maker goes scot-free. It is simply a falsifying of terms, to call this government.

Secondly. All such punishments must be well considered, and with sharp reference, not only to their nature and application, but also to their possible results. This involves the exercise of special care that no material injury, either bodily or mental, shall result to the pupil. It also demands that the teacher shall have taken a just measure, not only of the true merits of the case, but also of the possible demands of the infliction upon his own strength or firmness. Nothing can be more unfortunate, than for the teacher to attempt the infliction of punishment, and to discover at length, that he has not rightly estimated the refractoriness to be subdued. He will either come out himself half-conquered, or if ultimately the victor, only such, at the expense of a painfully unexpected conflict. Of the two evils of inconsiderateness, it is doubtful which is the worst, the infliction of punishment unduly severe, or that pitiably insufficient or half-successfully resisted.

Thirdly. Punishment must be thorough and effective. It must be no paltering sham. Once well-considered and rightly begun, it must go through to the bitter end. For example, if the pupil is to be subjected to detention after school, for the performance of some neglected duty, let that detention go on inexorably till the work is done, even if it runs out of the daylight into the evening shadows. This particular point is pressed with great earnestness, be cause it is believed that no species of punishment is more common in our schools than this of detention, and that none can be found more commonly a practical failure. And it is little to its credit, that it is unconsciously chosen because it favors an escape from the use of severer but more effective punishments, and because it admits of some ultimate evasion of its own real demands and just extension. It is no more to its credit, that its failure is due either to the teacher's want of firmness in carrying it out, or to his weak willingness to escape the pressure of its own inconvenience upon himself.

If corporal punishment is to be applied, the same general principle holds good. All the proper preliminary steps having been taken, the wise and just penalty must be inflicted, and until the desired submission is secured. Half-way punishment is a fatal blunder. It, not only fails of the true end, but aggravates the assailed evil. Two blows may only toughen the refractoriness, when ten would reduce it to tenderness and submission. Half-complete punishment is, furthermore, false mercy. Ten blows may secure a finality, when two would only prepare the way for twenty in the future. A most pitiable conclusion of administered discipline is that which compels the teacher to exclaim within his heart:

"We have scotched the snake; not killed it."

Fourthly. The punishment must be administered with due deliberateness and resolution. This involves three points; proper preparation, deliberateness in application, and resolution in the manner of carrying it out. It is equally unfortunate for the teacher to undertake to inflict punishment without full preparation for possible contingencies; to proceed to the work in haste or passionate heat; or to evince in its prosecution, anything like hesitation or half-regret.

Hence, if a lengthy and persistent detention of the offender is to be instituted, let the parent be, if possible, duly notified so that no undue anxiety will be occasioned at home; let everything necessary to the cool carrying out of the teacher's purpose be provided at the school, and then let him proceed with calm and imperturbable patience and firmness to the end. Or if corporal punishment is to be inflicted, and the case bids fair to be a severe one, let the parent be notified or even consulted and made to feel the just demands of the case; let the proper appliances be provided beforehand, and then let the whole, however painful, be carried through with immovable coolness and steadiness, to the very end. With reference to the second point especially, let no teacher resort to such pitiful devices (sometimes even ostentatiously practiced,) as that of punishing impromptu, and sending pupils, on the instant, to cut the necessary rod for the occasion. It is the next vice to that of displaying a whip always, to use a heraldic phrase, "rampant gardant."

Fifthly. With regard to publicity, the general law can only be: as is the offense, so must be the correction. Given a purely private offense, if such can be, one exerting no public influence and susceptible of private correction, and the institution of open investigation or the public infliction of punishment, must carry on its face the appearance of either an indiscretion or an abuse. But on the same principle, an open offense, affecting the general welfare, and exerting a public influence, must, with few exceptions, be as publicly investigated and corrected. Hence, generally, there must be no discipline in secret, for offenses committed upon the house-top. And the law applies equally to the various species of punishment, reprimands, restraint, chastisement and expulsion.

We are aware that strong ground is sometimes taken against this publicity. That ground, however, is not tenable. The secret occasion for taking it is itself significant. Sometimes it is little less than a false sympathy for the personal pride of the offender. But if he had not self-respect enough to forbear the commission of the evil act, what claim has he to so sensitive a regard for his reputation under the infliction of the just penalty? Is not his truest, and, under the circumstances, only possible honor, that of manfully acknowledging the wrong and submitting to the full demands of justice? Sometimes, again, the objection to the public infliction of punishment, is either a similar regard for parental pride, or a concern with reference to parental vindictiveness. If it be the former, the answer is as before; the true con servation of family honor is to be found only in the thorough and manly endorsement of the full claims of justice, and the unflinching acceptance of whatever

is necessary to a complete and final correction of the evil. So far as the second motive is concerned, it is unworthy in the teacher to regard it. Let him do justice though the heavens fall.

Still further, the objections too often rest, really, though unconsciously, upon the mere reformatory notion of discipline, which has already been seen to be erroneous. If the administration of discipline is for the preservation of the innocent, no less than for the correction of the guilty manifestly, the pains and penalties incurred as the result of wrong-doing, must be as public as the offense. Shut them up from the observing eye of the commonwealth, and how are its members to learn that "the way of transgressors is hard?" The very "intimations of nature," more often than otherwise, sustain the general principle that, to secure the widest and best influence, the evil consequences of wrong-doing must, sooner or later, become public. Indeed, nature sometimes visits even secret transgression, with open punishment.

With regard to the public infliction of corporal punishment, the cry is sometimes raised, that it is reprehensible, because brutalizing. To this we reply, that the conclusion is based upon a mere assumption. It is not the proper infliction of this species of punishment, that is brutalizing; it is only its abuse. Let the infliction of such punishment be characterized by undue frequency, by needless roughness or excess, or by fierce passion, and doubtless it will, in some part, go to harden and brutalize the nature. But so does the sight of human suffering and sorrow, when they come to be pressed too frequently upon our sensibilities or are inseparably bound up with groveling and depraved associations. Even the death of the human being, when crowded upon the soul under the sweep of the pestilence or the clash of the battle field, or when it glares out from the drunken carousal or the bed of vice and rottenness,—even that otherwise, tender and soul-subduing spectacle may, under such circumstances, exert only a benumbing and debasing influence. But who cries out and demands that nature and society should, therefore, fling the pall of isolation and secrecy over its legitimate occurrence?

There is, however, another grave oversight committed by those who pronounce thus summarily against public punishment in the school. In their anxiety about the immediate, they ignore the ultimate. They fail to inquire whether in this proposed subtraction from punishment, of one of its most effective elements of power as a means of general prevention, the way is not opened for a practical demoralization of the school, as it regards its notions of crime and its retributions, that is itself brutalization in fact, if not in the accepted form. Is he who, through a false pity, pride or fear, withdraws from active influence upon the school, the highest possible warning and safeguard against transgression, doing any less to brutalize its moral sensibility, than is done by him who, perhaps too rudely, shocks that sensibility to allow of its most wholesome reaction? We urge, then, that the objection has no valid force whatever against public punishment as properly administered;

that is, justly, deliberately, thoroughly, and with due pains to secure the subsequent moral results.

Lastly. Whatever punishment is inflicted, the infliction must by no means be accepted as the end of the teacher's opportunity and responsibility. Hardly could a graver mistake be committed. As well might the physician who has by powerful remedies broken the fever, suspend all further treatment of the case. Mere coercion is not the highest end. That is rather persuasion. But coercion is often the necessary preparative for persuasion. Negotiations and amicable arrangements are often impracticable until after a satisfactory trial of arms. Punishments, then, are sometimes chiefly effective as opening the way for the unimpeded application of moral influences. Hence, they should be regarded by the teacher, rather as the rough ladder leading to the only hopeful landing place of moral suasion. Let him, then, see to it that he does not rest content with merely having reached that landing place, instead of zealously pressing up the new and nobler ascent which the former has just rendered practicable. Every infliction of coercive discipline must, then, be carefully followed up and supplemented by sound suggestions and friendly influences, until, if possible, to the subjugation of the will, there has been added the winning of the heart.

And this subsequent use of moral means rises in its imperative claims, just in proportion to the immediate severity or aggravating circumstances of the punishment inflicted. Certainly, the more critical the case, and the more violent the treatment, the more pressing the need for the watchful and unwearied application of the subsequent restoratives. He, then, who fails to perceive this last responsibility, or who lacks either the patience or the firmness to press forward in its discharge to the complete result, practically sounds a retreat in the midst of a half-won battle, and accepts the issue of a substantial defeat. And this is the fatal error of most of the discipline administered in our schools. To this alone, is chargeable much of the need of frequent punishment, much of its failure to prove effective, and much of its alleged brutalizing tendency. Let teachers ponder this well.

It may perhaps be objected by some, that all this is calculated to render the administration of discipline in the school, too complicated and laborious. We answer, not at all, if all this is necessary to its consistency, efficiency, and most benign success. Furthermore, the more of a real, pains-taking labor it is, the less likely will the teacher be to enter upon the work of disciplining offenses hastily or for trivial causes. The grand law of the whole argument is summed up in this indisputably just maxim; less frequency but greater thoroughness.

Beyond these general rules, there are certain specific points bearing on these various kinds of punishment that claim attention.

First. Correlative rewards and punishments should rest upon similar bases. If you bestow a reward for a specific excellence, you may punish by retracting the reward, but only for delinquency in the same direction. Thus, you may punish for bad scholarship by resuming a reward bestowed for good scholarship, but not at all by retracting one conferred for good behavior. The last would be a practical injustice.

Secondly. Public reprimands should set forth clearly the personal unworthiness and the public injuriousness of the act censured, and should, as the case may be, be more or less pointed and severe. But they should never be sarcastic or vituperative. No true force is gained by such means, and they seriously impair the teacher's dignity and dispassionateness of manner in the administration of discipline. Care should be taken to guard the school against the error of summing up the censure in the act of its pronunciation. It must be understood to hold good until, upon amendment, the offender is formally released therefrom. In the meantime, while he is not to be treated unkindly, he is to be held as standing in disfavor. In this direction, some accompanying restriction of privilege will be seen to be of service, inasmuch as it affords a sensible and abiding symbol of the existing censure.

Thirdly. Bodily restraint or confinement as to either position or place must be simply such; it must not be conjoined with contemptible, alarming, or mischievous adjuncts. Stand the offender upon the floor in noticeable isolation from his fellows, if need be but do not stoop to those abominations practiced of old time, such as adorning him with leather spectacles, split sticks, or a fool's cap, or loading him with billets of wood, or forcing him to stand with his finger upon some crack in the floor,—to him, in a very literal sense, the "crack of doom." These are not only needless, but also base and even cowardly devices. We say cowardly, for more often than otherwise, they are chosen because they are a means of dodging the infliction of corporal punishment, or because those upon whom they are imposed are either unable to resist, or dare not in any way protest against the indignity. So too, with regard to separate confinement, avoid immuring the offender in some filthy or dark closet or apartment. It is not well, for any purpose of correction, to attack a pupil's constitutional courage, or his acquired habits of neatness. The reasons are obvious.

We have already noticed somewhat particularly, the use of detention after school as a punishment. That the current method pursued with regard to it, is radically defective and needs to be reformed altogether, must be apparent to the thoughtful teacher. Instead of resorting to it with foolish frequency, conducting it so that it is sure to be as great an annoyance to the teacher as it is to the pupil, and cutting it summarily short at the occurrence of the first possible excuse for so doing, how much better for a course to be pursued, somewhat as follows. Having a just occasion for a thorough detention of a delinquent pupil, let the teacher close his school, send notice of the detention to the parents, if he has not apprized them of it beforehand, and then calmly stating to the offender precisely what he intends and expects, let him set himself quietly about some apparently consistent and earnest employment, and without concern or uneasiness, await the end. Sooner than stop short of its full attainment, let him, if need be, bring forward both lunch and lights, share them pleasantly with his prisoner, and go on as before. A cool preparation and persistence like this, will almost invariably bring the culprit to terms. When this point has been properly attained, let the teacher lay aside the stern character of the ruler, and as a friend calmly and kindly confer with the offender upon the evil nature of the course he has pursued, and exhort him to new and better things. Then let him put up his work, close the school-house, and, if practicable, accompany the pupil home, by the way appearing only as the friend, and seeming to be utterly oblivious of what has just passed. His presence will keep the pupil thoughtful and under restraint until the period for any passionate outbreak has passed, and his forbearing silence as to the discipline will tend to awaken grateful regard. And, subsequently, let nothing be said about the affair, to the school. It is not necessary. The details of the struggle and the result will find their own utterance, and with comments quite calculated to impress upon its members, the wisdom of prompt obedience. To some teachers, we doubt not, all this will seem like pure extravagance. But what a pity it is, that in the use of punishment, in both the family and the school, there is not more of the extravagance of thoroughness, and less of the extravagance of idle frequency and stupid failure.

Fourthly. With regard to chastisement or corporal

punishment proper, it is premised that we here contemplate only the legitimate and divinely established use of the rod. There have been found not a few who, without any warrant either rational or revealed, have gone beyond this and hit upon implements and appliances that might have made the users thereof exclaim:

> "Come sceling night,
> Scarf up the tender eye of pitiful day."

These were they who, finding a hard, rough-hand in readiness, brandished it like Talus' iron flail about the ears and head of the pitiful culprit to the endangering of his very brains; who, possessing a sinewy arm, grasped the helpless victim and, wrenching him from his seat, spun him around like a demon-driven top, in indescribable gyrations upon the mid-floor, and perhaps ended with dashing him down more like a billet than a human being; or who, clutching the massive ferrule, either hurled it like Jove's thunderbolt, at doomed heads in the distance, or, seizing the tender and half-knit hand, beat out with quick remorseless blows the fiery grain of pain, if not of penitence, upon the sad threshing-floor of the quivering palm.

For such punishments there is no stint of condemnation. Irrational and base, they might produce fear, but could create no reverence or regard for government. Indiscriminate and unsparing, they alike crushed the innocent and weak, and exasperated the robust and daring. Blind and dead to the presence and office-work of the understanding and the conscience, they brutalized the feelings, and often beat down all that was sweetest and noblest in the child's nature. It is to be hoped that these are already numbered with the things that were.

With regard to corporal punishment in its proper form as already indicated, much the same course is to be pursued as in the case of restraint or confinement. Whatever of antecedent preparation, of careful explanation, of calm deliberateness, of cool and thorough persistence, and of subsequent moral effort, was needed there, is still more necessary here. But it must all be natural and real, not pretentious or with a studied attempt at effect. Any display of preparations, or tantalizing delay of proceedings, or pompous solemnity of manner, intended to alarm the offender or overawe the school, is worse than weak and ridiculous; it's "villainous, and shows a pitiful ambition in the fool that uses it."

From this, it will be seen that, for obvious reasons, no hasty infliction of punishment is here contemplated. Still it is not denied that cases may arise in which summary punishment must be inflicted; as, for example, when the offender is of a character likely to be strengthened in resistance by delay; when there is a prevailing impression that the teacher's deliberateness is caused by a temporizing fear to punish; or when, from lack of physical power, he must take his antagonist at an advantage. Here, it may be necessary for the stream to "be quick and violent." But these are the exceptional cases, and are to be avoided if possible. The teacher must be his own judge as to the real occurrence of any of these contingencies. In case he accepts one of them as instant, let the blow be sudden and decisive, and only sudden that it may be decisive.

It is sometimes both proper and necessary in the administration of discipline, in the school, to go beyond proper coercion, and make use of *sheer compulsion.* That is, the teacher, instead of bringing the pupil by coercive measures to the voluntary performance of the required act, may apply sheer force and, whether he wills or not wills, may compel him to do it. This species of discipline is quite restricted in its application, and is, only under certain contingencies, and in a modified sense, punishment. But being a disciplinary corrective so far as it goes; tending to inculcate the necessity of submission to the higher power; and not unfrequently causing the pain of feeling ignominiously overcome and justly compelled to submit, it is not improper to consider it under the head of punishments.

The nature and occasion for such a species of infliction may be made clearer by illustration. Take, in the first instance, a very young pupil, who has yet no adequate idea of superior power as in authority over him, and who may be hardly mature enough to comprehend the just claims of authority as rightly constituted. Suppose such an incipient representative of our ungovernable democracy to set himself up precociously as one of the sovereigns,—a by no means rare occurrence in either the family or the school. He is, for example, directed to take a certain seat, or, perhaps, to sit down somewhere, and refuses to obey. Here it may be both proper and sufficient for the teacher to take him and, by the simple exercise of force, compel him to take the prescribed place. A similar emergency may arise in the case of an older pupil who has been too exclusively controlled by force at home, or who, in the overweening sense of his own strength, doubts the teacher's possession of the power to master him, and to compel him to submit. Here, as before, the teacher may with perfect consistency resort to simple compulsion; he may, by the mere exercise of superior strength, force the delinquent to perform the required act,—the act of course as in the former case, being one of a kind properly within reach of force.

While on general principles, or if too largely employed, such a species of discipline may seem objectionable, it is within the range above indicated, quite reasonable. It is not always desirable, as in the first case supposed, to inflict corporal punishment on the extremely young. Nay, in many cases there is no need of applying the rod at all; the thoroughly attained consciousness that the teacher has ample power to enforce his demands, being quite sufficient to prevent further attempts at resistance. Beyond this, there are minds, not only juvenile but adult, in which the primary idea of supremacy is simply that of superior power. This is, of course, not the truest idea, nor the one ultimately to be established. But wherever it prevails, the capacity and the rectitude of the authority as resting on this basis alone, must be practically demonstrated, otherwise the way is not open for the effective development of the higher basis of the authority as properly constituted and as essential to the general welfare. Hence, satisfy the rebellious subject, that the power exists and will be unhesitatingly applied, and one important point,—to him the one first important point,—has been gained. His apprehension, cleared as to the question of power, will be more open to the force of other and higher considerations, into the proper appreciation of which he will speedily grow.

If it be objected that in such cases the submission secured is destitute of any voluntary character and is so far defective; it is sufficient to reply, that under the force of the conviction already gained that resistance is futile, the subsequent obedience will become voluntary, and that, while it is not voluntary upon the best or ultimate basis, yet the tendency of all voluntary obedience is toward a growing recognition of the simple rightfulness of authority and of the worthiness of pure rectitude. One of the worst effects of unconquered insubordination is, not that it establishes the will in its rebellion, but that it works a growing paralysis of the judgment and the reason, so that the offender becomes incapable of discovering the true relations of himself and his evil conduct, and of apprehending the nature and the claims of proper rectitude.

The specific rules for the application of this species of discipline, both immediate and subsequent, being the same as in the case of the other kinds of punishment, their consideration here is unnecessary.

With regard to *final exclusion* as a means of correction, it is to be remarked at the outset, that so far as the great body of our public schools are concerned, but little need be said of it in this place, since the prerogative of applying it, is lodged quite exclusively in the hands of the higher authorities, the teacher having little to do in the premises, beyond the mere making of the proper representation as to its necessity. In certain private schools, however, which are the sole property of the teacher, it may be otherwise. Here, the whole power lying in the hands of the teacher, he may have the right to exclude, just as truly as to inflict any other species of punishment. In still another class of schools generally assumed as of a higher order,—in this direction what they are only because of the higher pride or prejudice of the patrons,—the prerogative of exclusion passes wholly into the hands of the teacher, and becomes common and necessary, simply because he is practically precluded from the use of its only substitute and alternative, corporal punishment. On these accounts, it is proper to bestow upon this species of correction, a somewhat careful consideration.

First, then, final exclusion, which is a punishment only under the same limitation which marked the last species, must always be held as a last resort and to be accepted as a necessity, only when all other and better appliances, faithfully applied, have proved utterly futile. And for the two reasons, first, that it not unfrequently cuts the teacher off from the power to benefit or save the offender; and, secondly, because it involves a practical confession of failure on the part of the government of the school, to secure the best and noblest ends of discipline, just as the amputation of a diseased limb is an acknowledgement of the failure and further powerlessness of the proper curative agency. It is, in short, a practical defeat, since whatever victory it may secure, it is not the one sought by the authority: the result is not one of proper and wholesome subjugation; it is the conquest of extermination. Hence, no true teacher will have recourse to it, except he is reduced to it as an absolute and somewhat humiliating necessity.

Secondly. Excepting perhaps in those schools in which corporal punishment is forbidden, the occasions for its use are less common, than is often supposed. It is hardly to be doubted that it is often accepted as imperative, either because the teacher lacks real force in the use of other means of discipline; because he is of too hasty or arbitrary a temperament; or because he is indisposed to undertake patiently and resolutely, the perhaps lengthy and painful struggle necessary to a victory through the use of other and better means. We have in mind two cases occurring in our own early experience, which we can now clearly trace to the first of these causes, immaturity and lack of thorough acquaintance with the work to be done. We recall also a later case of a most marked character, in which a seemingly hopeless young man was, through the use of the proper patience and tact, reduced to perfect control and won to a real and most friendly regard. And yet this very young man was, by his very next teacher, and for no greater insubordination, summarily excluded from the school, with certainly no better results to the latter, and to the entire destruction of that teacher's influence over him. In this case, the course pursued was due to no lack of power or experience, for both were of a superior order, but to an arbitrariness of temper growing out of an excessive sensibility to the claims of pure justice. We doubt not a careful review of their own experience would bring the conviction of most teachers to this same self-judgment.

Thirdly. When exclusion has become a true necessity, if it be public, it is to be administered according to the same general rules already suggested under the head of coercive punishments. Its specific method is the same with that of public censure. If the exclusion is to be private, as is most commonly the case in those schools in which it takes the place of corporal punishment, its form is so anomalous, that its specific method must be determined altogether by the judgment of the teacher, as guided by the particular circumstances of the case.

Lastly. When exclusion has been resorted to, let the teacher by no means accept it as necessarily a finality. Possibly, he may yet in some way be able to reach the offender for the purpose of reformatory effort. If any such way be open, let him seek out the excluded member, and privately press upon him the unworthiness of sitting down either stubbornly or stolidly under the burden of the inflicted disgrace; open to his mind the practicability of reclaiming his position and redeeming his character; and urge upon him the inherent nobleness of a resolute effort at amendment. When the teacher becomes reasonably assured that these considerations are properly felt, and that reparation and reformation will be heartily attempted, let him take measures to secure the reversal of the decree of exclusion, and effect the restoration of the offender to his former place. In some cases it may be well, with the private consent of the proper authorities, to reinstate him quietly upon trial, reserving the formal restoration to such a time as may have sufficed to evince his sincerity and probability of success in the direction of permanent amendment. If the teacher is successful in these endeavors, his victory is signal and cannot fail to sustain powerfully both the vigor and the benevolence of his administration. Still we insist that the better victory is that won, as previously counseled, before and without exclusion.

The overlooking of this last grand principle is not confined to the precincts of the school; it is one too painfully common throughout society, to which fact the teacher is doubtless largely indebted for his own tendency in this direction. To the thoughtful mind, there will readily occur the sorrowful spectacle of many a difficult and abortive attempt at the reclamation of the fallen who have been summarily excluded by society from its pale, and abandoned to their fate. And the conviction can hardly be escaped that had they been seized upon with the same resolution and benevolence, while they were yet within sight of the lost Eden of blessing, and painfully alive to their present degradation and impending ruin, the moment of imminent and priceless opportunity would have been won, and they would have been found despairingly eager to snatch at the feeblest chance of redemption. But no; the sublime and touching lesson taught by the Great Teacher in the case of the adulterous woman, is lost upon the higher virtue and severer rectitude of human society; and so, multitudes of those, originally the noblest and the most lovely, are consigned to a doom which makes the pitying soul sicken and cry out with mingled indignation and anguish.

It must not be understood, however, that in pressing these considerations, the ground is taken that this noble reformatory effort is, in either society or the school, the proper work of government as such. It should be heartily countenanced and seconded by government: but is not to be authoritatively undertaken by it. It belongs properly within the province of individual or associated philanthropy.

# CHAPTER XII.

## APPLICATION OF PRINCIPLES TO SPECIFIC SCHEMES OF DISCIPLINE AND TO DEPARTMENTAL SCHOOLS.

Occasion for examining specific schemes—*Self-government method*—General objections—Self-government in the school of two kinds,—partial and complete—*Objections to the first*—Practically an imposition—*Objections to the second*—Still a delusion—Overburdens the teacher—Destroys true ideas of government—Distracts the pupil's attention—Tends to dissatisfaction—*Self-reporting scheme*—General nature—Restricted use allowed—*Objections to the scheme*—Teacher evades his own duty—Impairs the pupil's moral sense—Destructive of faith in the teacher's rule—*Demerit mark scheme*—Its features—Subdivided into Pure Merit Scheme, Mixed Form, and Pure Demerit Scheme—*Merit scheme*—*Proper method characterized*—Its practical difficulties—*Mixed form*—General objections—To be treated as a demerit scheme—*Peculiar features of the pure demerit method*—*Evils of the method*—Based on the false principle of depression—Child apt to be left in ignorance of its real significance—Tempts the teacher to neglect to inform him—Leads to minute rules—Fails to evince the real relation of offense and punishment—Too liable to irregular, hasty, and unjust marking—Peculiar difficulty resulting from the use of two rolls, one of scholarship, and one of standing—Only proper use to be made of rolls of standing—*The application of the demerit mark scheme to higher schools*—Its difficulties—Sometimes, nevertheless, a necessity—Specific rules for its use—*Proper government for adult schools, that of influence*—Its obstacles and its aids—*Departmental schools*—Classified as Lower and Higher—Kinds distinguished—Differences in organization—Theoretical and current—*Specific rules for government in the lower species*—Subordinate should be the ruler in his own field—Should govern in harmony with the general method of the school—Principal should not make the subordinate a mere cipher—Should, in punishing, only act as an executive agent for the subordinate—*General directions for the higher order of departmental schools*—Offenses of two kinds; class offenses, general offenses—Proper method of adjudicating them.

Before leaving the subject of discipline entirely, it is not improper that some attention should be given to certain specific schemes, sometimes devised for its administration, and to the particular application of the foregoing principles to those higher schools whose peculiar wants have not thus far in the discussion been especially noticed. It is true that the general principles already laid down might seem a sufficient guide to the truth in those directions. But there are, nevertheless, points of particular importance or difficulty involved, which may escape the notice of the practical teacher, or which, if they occur to him, may not be so clearly accompanied by their proper solution, as to prevent doubt and embarrasment.

As a further reason for turning the attention in this direction, at this stage of the discussion, we urge that these schemes of discipline, and the difficulties of the schools referred to, are intimately related to the vexed question of the "to be or not to be" of corporal punishment,—the former, indeed, having their unsuspected but real origin in a desire to escape the necessity of using it, and the latter, substantially arising from obstacles, either natural or merely notional, thrown in the way of its employment, and not unfrequently amounting to its practical prohibition. And these facts with regard to the origin of the matters in question, and which we believe have seldom occurred to our educators, have here a peculiar significance, and deserve to be kept constantly in mind during the progress of the discussion, since they are, to some extent, the secret key to the real nature of the schemes of discipline now to be examined.

Of these schemes, that of *Self-Government* comes first in order. So far as its relation to the fundamental principles of school government is concerned, this scheme has already been briefly noticed, and its radical errors suggested. That it disregards the law of its derivation as originating in parental government; that it practically assumes the pupil to be capacitated for the exercise of such functions, and sufficiently disposed to render obedience, to be entrusted with the sovereign power; and that it recognizes in the teacher the right to transfer the performance of his own chief duty or any important part of it, to others; —that it does anything of this, is enough of itself to settle the character of its claims.

There are, however, other considerations that pronounce against it. Self-government in the school must be of one of two kinds; it must be either informal and partial or somewhat systematic and complete; that is, it must be summed up in incidental and apparent references of questions and measures to the voice of the school for their decision and execution; or it must attempt something of a formal organization of the school as a body politic, with power to detect, decide and perhaps even discipline offenders.

Now of these two methods, it has already been seen that the first is practically an imposition on the simple faith of the pupil; for he exercises only a seeming, not a real power. The teacher either influences and guides the decisions and consequent action, or he stands in instant readiness to interfere and to counteract the measures of the school, whenever they are likely to conflict with his own convictions of justice or necessity. Like the priest behind the miraculous image, he stands concealed behind the whole democratic machine, and practically determines its movements. Whether such a scheme is really worthy of the teacher's own sound judgment or just integrity; whether it is really a peculiar benevolence to the pupils themselves; or whether it can be expected long to work well or to accomplish any very important ends; or whether it will not speedily be discovered to be precisely the mere sham it is, let the sober-thinking teacher judge for himself.

But suppose that the second form is the one chosen; how will the case stand? To begin with, no such formal democracy can be consistently practicable except in those schools in which the pupils are somewhat advanced in maturity and knowledge. Without the presence among the pupils, of a certain sound judgment and manly self-control, the real power and the actual labor must remain, as in the former case, with the teacher alone; ostensibly a mere "primus inter pares," he is, after all, absolutely imperator. The whole scheme is thus eviscerated of any true reality or popular independence. But this necessary restriction of this system of school government to the maturer class of pupils, at once, decides the question as to its general adaptability or usefulness.

Again, the work of governing, which, as having to

be carried on conjointly with the work of instruction, needs to be as simple as possible, is, under this scheme, necessarily complicated with much new and really cumbrous machinery,—machinery, too, largely subject in its movements, to the notions of the multitude, and, therefore, additionally perplexing from its inherent uncertainty and need of constant watch and control. Now he must be a veritable Atlas, who can properly sustain himself amidst the multifarious duties and burdens of the school, with this new world of a scholastic democracy upon his shoulders. It is certainly competent for us to urge that he who can do this and properly carry out his scheme of self-government, is amply able to govern successfully upon the truer and simpler basis of pure absolutism, and consequently has no need of the scheme at all; and it is positively certain that he who cannot govern wisely and well upon this latter basis, is necessarily unequal to the use and perfection of any scheme of popular self-government in the school, and should, therefore, never attempt it.

Still further, the natural tendency of the scheme must be to pervert the pupil's ideas of the nature of true government, to lower his conceptions of the just majesty of law, and to lay the foundation for restlessness under any other control than that of his own will. For, is it not an error to, in any way inculcate the idea that government must necessarily originate in the will of the governed, however inferior in capacity, condition or virtue they may be? Can it other than eventually belittle government and abase law, to transfer the lawgivership from the higher responsibility and capacity of the teacher, and bring it down to the level of an investment in the child's sovereignty? Should not he who is to be governed, be able to look up with reverence to, and with faith in, authority as enthroned in superior power, wisdom and goodness? But can the child thus look up to, and believe in himself or in a government thus begotten of, and bounded by, himself? Now as to the other question, —that of the influence of such schemes in the school to engender future restlessness under authoritative restraint, and general insubordination,—we are inclined to the opinion that a salutary lesson may be learned from the necessity of our late tremendous struggle, to the preservation of the national unity and the integrity of its government, and to the awakening of the people to a just sense of the vital importance of undivided loyalty, reverence for constituted authority, and self-sacrificing obedience to law.

But once more, finally. In whatever shape the scheme of popular self-government in the school may be put forward, it is subject to these other practical evils. Just so far as the details of government are imposed upon the pupil, their influence must be to divert his attention from that undivided interest and application necessary to his best progress in study. Still further, its tendency must be to create in him an over-critical propensity in judging of the proper acts of the teacher, and, from the habit of debating matters of general moment in his own mind, and of expecting to have a choice as to their decision, to induce in him a disposition to be dissatisfied with even the conclusion reached through the general suffrages of the body politic. Every one knows how easily a question, quietly decided at once for a class or a school, by the proper authority, becomes, when thrown open for general discussion and popular decision, an occasion for difference, contention, and ultimate dissatisfaction. Hence, the weakness and folly of teachers who are forever ready to resort to a public vote in the school, for the decision of matters of any real importance.

Closely related to this scheme of self-government, is the *Self-Reporting Scheme*, a partial method, employed generally in combination with some other fancied system of discipline such as that of popular sovereignty or that of demerit marks. It differs from the former scheme chiefly in that it devolves upon the pupil, not so much the prerogatives of legislation and execution, as that of self-judgment. Its marked feature is, that it allows or requires him to report to the teacher the measure of his own merit or demerit, according to his own judgment. It sometimes even goes to the ridiculous extreme of devolving upon him the determination of the reward or the penalty to be attached.

Now, the teacher may, in his private conferences with the pupil, endeavor to draw from him his view of his own merit or demerit, not at all as a basis of judgment, but only that, if his view be correct, the pupil may be made to feel that his own reason and conscience are to have a voice with regard to his conduct, either "accusing or excusing;" or, if he has judged improperly, that the teacher may be able to show him his error, and thus enlighten and guide him in his apprehension of truth and his convictions of desert.

So, too, as merely an incidental act, not at all as a matter of regular or frequent occurrence, the teacher may, when he knows the precise facts in the case, even publicly call for a pupil's opinion as to his own effort or behavior; not that this opinion may serve, in any part, as a basis for his own judgment in the premises, but that, by correcting its error kindly and without personal reference, he may impress upon the school their liability to misjudge both as to the character of their own conduct and the provisions of his government, and may thus give them moral instruction of a most practical and important nature.

But, employed in any other way, or pursued to any extent as part of a scheme of discipline, the method under consideration is both stupidly ingenious and transparently vicious. For, first, if this opinion of the pupil as to his own merit or demerit is sought as a basis for the teacher's judgment, the thing is false in its first principles. As ruler in the school, and knowing what to establish as law, what are you next to know but when, where and how to apply discipline for the support of law? To read the pupil's character, to discover his merits, to detect his misdemeanors, and to divine the proper means for stimulus or correction,—this is the teacher's art of governing, most "express and admirable." As such, we hold that he has no right to throw it upon the pupil, either in earnest or in mere pretense. If he does the former, he impeaches either his own capacity or faithfulness; if he does the latter, he imposes upon the simple faith of the pupil.

In the second place, the direct tendency of this species of practice is to blunt the moral sense of the pupil, and to induce deception and falsehood. Nor is it of any avail to argue the contrary. Let the pupil suppose that you do in any part rest upon his decision, and how powerful is the stimulus to make out a fair case for himself, even though at the ultimate expense of the truth! Even suppose that he may start, and for a time continue honest, how long under such temptation, will he be able to retain a keen sense of the difference between the exact truth and a self-interested misrepresentation of facts? Go beyond the child in the school, and apply the same practice to every John Doe and Richard Roe in our courts of justice, and how long would it be before every honest man would be compelled to exclaim with deeper feeling and graver cause than did Falstaff; "Lord! how this world is given to lying!" But is it to be supposed that the heedless boy who does not so much discriminate between right and wrong, as between birch and not birch,—is it to be supposed that he will be proof against the temptation thus thrown in his way? We say to the teacher, with the profoundest feeling, before you thus call upon the child to report for or against himself, see to it that you first soberly repeat to yourself the prayer, "Lead us not into temptation."

In the third place, there is another evil incident to the use of this scheme, if not certain to accompany it. Suppose that the teacher, while making use of the pupil's self-reporting statement, does not accept it without qualification, as a basis of judgment, but corrects it by his own knowledge. Here, the *trust* of the first act is practically supplanted by the *distrust* of the second act, and how long will it be, before the pupil will penetrate to this secret of your strategy? But you may depend upon it, that just so soon as he becomes satisfied that you go back of his untrusted word, after the trusted facts, the fair fabric of your whole scheme will dissolve like the frail frost-work of the night under the morning sun, and, what is worse, with it will vanish the pupil's better estimate of your character as worthy of his admiration and confidence. The fact is, in dealing with the young, no truth is more distinct and vital than that there is no safe half-way between distrust and faith.

We pass now to the consideration of the last of these specific schemes which involve a practical attempt to escape the use of penal infliction in the correction of offenses. This scheme, which is a sort of double-entry affair, and, in its way, collects and presents the debits and credits of the pupil's dealing in the school, will perhaps be most readily recognized as "*The Demerit Mark System.*" This title, however, belongs properly to one of its extreme phases; for a system of discipline through a record of standing, may involve three species; namely, that of *Pure Merit;* the *Mixed Form;* and the *Pure Demerit System.*

The *merit scheme* should be marked by the following characteristics. It should start with a certain average standard of character, or sum of merit, assumed as common to all the members of the school. This starting point, however, should never be zero. That would be like compelling an inexperienced man to commence a difficult business without capital; to begin the building of a house without even foundation or site. On the contrary, every pupil should be made to feel that he possesses some actual merit that is appreciated, and that appears on the roll of standing, fairly credited to him. This gives him a hopeful foundation upon which to build; an encouraging accumulation to which he may add, the natural stimulus nowhere so necessary as in the creation of character, and above all, in its formation and improvement among the young.

Proceeding upon this assumed basis of merit, the teacher should carefully add to the credit of the pupil, upon his roll, the sum of everything worthily done *beyond* the regular order, or done *above* a mere average within it. That it should rise above a mere average in performance, is clear, since that alone indicates no real advance from the starting point; and that whatever is done beyond the regular order should be credited entire, rests upon the fact that it is just so far an advance beyond mere ordinary merit.

But no notice whatever is to be taken of acts of

*demerit:* it is foreign to the entire principle and spirit of the scheme. Your object is to develop merit by encouragement. So far as you do that, you are, not only discountenancing, but really supplanting demerit, and in a really more effective manner, because it is indirect and unobserved. Hence, it is of vital importance that the pupil's attention should be studiously kept fastened solely upon the more hopeful prospect,—that of increasing merit, or growing excellence. The same law holds good here, that obtains in the case of generous approval and encouragement as opposed to depressing criticism and habitual censure, of which notice has elsewhere been taken.

Of the general correctness of this scheme, there can be no doubt. We suspect, however, that it is rarely, if ever, practically adopted. And, probably, for the reason that it is attended with the following difficulties: it is more congenial to human nature to interest itself in the faults of others than in their excellences; it is really easier to detect and to measure the former satisfactorily to one's self than it is to properly discern and estimate the latter; and, lastly, in the work of deciding upon the character and measure of a wrong, passion affords a powerful aid (we say nothing of its worthiness) which is not present or available when one has to sit in judgment upon a just or virtuous action. How far these difficulties should be suffered to have weight with the intelligent and earnest teacher, we leave for him to decide.

Of the *mixed form* of the marking system, it is difficult to speak satisfactorily. In its general method, it of course includes a recognition in the roll of standing, of both merit and demerit. But this very fact subjects it to grave exception. From what has just been urged, it will be seen that so far as it is a demerit scheme, it is necessarily false in principle, and unhappy in its tendencies. Besides this, it will be equally apparent that the combination of the two methods involves a practical incongruity in the whole, which is objectionable; and further, if both the merit and demerit elements are equally developed, the scheme is rendered altogether too complicated to secure a just attention and application. A perhaps worse evil than even these is the fact that, for reasons already suggested, the demerit element will like Pharaoh's kine, lean and ill-favored, practically devour the rest, and without becoming itself the fairer or the better for the operation; that is to say, in the minds of both teacher and pupils, the demerit marking will come eventually to assume the chief, if not the sole importance and interest.

The facts, just noticed, show this mixed form of the marking scheme to be so nearly related to that of *pure demerit*, that we shall, proceed to the consideration of that, at once. The attention will first be directed to its characteristics as applied to schools for the younger class of pupils, in which the use of punishment is not wholly discarded. The method here pursued is substantially the following. The slips and misdemeanors of the pupil, sometimes even those of a minute and trivial character, are carefully noted, and, by means of a set of symbols, charged to his account upon a class roll. Sometimes, as a sort of refinement upon its already complicated provisions, a weekly bill of the accumulating wickedness is made out upon a card, and transmitted to the parent for his examination and endorsement, generally with no accompanying explanation of its mysterious symbols or provisions. When the pupil has, in due process of time, either exhausted the patience of the teacher, or run up an amount regarded as sufficiently flagrant, the account is balanced by inflicting the actual punishment, ostensibly for the last transgression, though perhaps really for the sum total.

Now, to all this, there are certainly grave objections. First. The whole scheme is based on the false principle already suggested,—that of censure rather than approval; of depression rather than stimulus and encouragement.

Secondly. It is quite possible for the child to fail altogether of obtaining a clear idea of the real provisions of the scheme and of the symbols employed in marking the charges against him. Indeed, we have known the scheme to be employed with no decent, not to say adequate, pains on the part of the teacher, to explain it to him, so that he might understand his true position under discipline, and the real purport of the entries made against him. We have known a little fellow to be left so lost in its luminous provisions, that he represented himself as having "got a deportment," the precise nature of which disaster he was unable to state. We have seen another sorely puzzled about what he called "a minus extra," when he knew no more of the meaning of minus and extra, than he did of Minos and Rhadamanthus. We have overheard still another, who was dubiously balancing himself upon the curb-stone after school, complaining to his companion that he had been marked by his teacher, and without his knowing for what.

Now, it is an imperative rule in all discipline of children, that they should be made to know unmistakably both the nature of their fault and the significance and justice of the penalty. But in the scheme under consideration, it is easy to see how painfully this very knowledge may be wanting. Nor is it any excuse to urge that, in such cases as the above, its absence is chargeable to the neglect of the teacher rather than to the viciousness of the scheme itself.

For thirdly. We charge that it is in the very nature of the scheme to induce this gross neglect. Removed from the necessity of immediately inflicting punishment, the registry of the charge which might justify it comes to be unconsciously regarded as a mere matter of marking down a certain symbol, and, hence, the inevitable tendency is to do the whole informally, and with no feeling sense of its real bearing upon the pupil, and, consequently, with no effort to impress upon him, its disciplinary nature and importance. It is not strange, then, that teachers who employ this method, rarely follow up the use of demerit marks with those subsequent moral applications which are so essential to all just and wholesome discipline.

Fourthly. In the same direction lies another evil.

For the same reasons as in the preceding case, the teacher is subjected to the constant temptation to mark for trivial offenses, and will consequently multiply minute rules to meet such offenses, and to justify the recorded censure. Yet, as has already been seen, all such minute requisitions and inflictions are a contradiction of the fundamental principles of all good government, and a trespass upon the first elements of the child's nature. Their direct tendency is either to keep the pupil under a petty and perpetual harassment, or to blunt the fineness of his moral sensibility.

Still further, from this minuteness in requisition, and informality in attaching penalties, the pupil is trained to a feeling of contempt, not only for the punishment, but for the actual transgression, and so comes to entertain a low idea of the importance of law, and of the force of moral responsibility. Yet nothing can be clearer than, that discipline which does not, in the apprehension of the subject, magnify the law and make it honorable; which does not set in clearer light the evil of transgression; and which does not sharpen the sense of responsibility, is just so far demoralizing and vicious. And that all this is really the practical result of the use of this marking scheme in juvenile schools, we believe the experience of every observing teacher will attest.

Fifthly. In case the pupil is finally punished, there arise these other evils. If he is punished simply for the last offense for which he is marked, inasmuch as no reason may appear for his not being punished for the others which preceded, either the teacher will seem unjust for not having inflicted punishment for the others; or if they did not deserve it, then he will seem unjust in inflicting it for the last. If, however, he is punished for the sum total which, since the teacher cannot well keep out of mind the entire result of his marking, is likely to be practically the fact, the pupil will fail to get any just idea of the relation existing between transgression and penalty. What he was marked for,—the actual fault,—he has forgotten. What he has in mind is simply the marks either separately or in their sum. Hence, associating the penalty only with what he immediately knows, he apprehends himself as punished for the so many marks. Yet, he is neither likely to discover any real criminality in the existence of so many marks against him, nor is he capable of perpetrating such an abstraction as to apprehend the sum total of the marks as a fixed symbol of the accumulated wickedness for which he is punished.

Finally. Nothing can be clearer than that there can be no certainty of the exercise of cool and evenhanded justice in affixing the marks of demerit to the pupil's standing. Where there are several teachers, as in a departmental school, no two teachers can be expected to form the same precise judgment as to the character of the same act, or as to its proper measure of demerit. In one room or class, the pupil will be marked severely, and in another, lightly for the same offense. Besides this, even in the case of the single teacher, there is every probability that he will mark differently, at different times, for the same act. At one time, it will appear to him, and from the better condition of his judgment and feelings, quite justly, as comparatively trivial and unworthy of notice. At another, when he is harassed with the pressure of his other duties, or vexed with some unexpected complication of affairs, or, perhaps, simply ill or out of temper, down will go upon his roll a singeing token of his displeasure in the shape of a ten or a twenty, —we have even known a teacher call out to an offender in the class, "I give you eighty demerits for conversation,"—the only effect of which was to set him at a ludicrous calculation of the particular per cent. effect of the operation upon his standing. A system open to such flagrant abuses, is certainly "more honored in the breach than the observance."

There is another difficulty sometimes experienced in connection with this marking method which is altogether peculiar. By a refinement in details, the scheme is made to embrace two distinct rolls of standing, one for scholarship and the other for good behavior. Now in theory, it is not only right that conduct should be recognized in the marking, but it should stand foremost as the basis of merit or demerit. This principle has been fully presented in connection with the subject of rewards. And yet, here arises the difficulty. It is found that when two rolls are thus employed, not only does not the marking for conduct enlist the first interest; but, if the standing on the scholarship roll is low, a high standing on the conduct roll is a cause of uneasiness.

Both the nature and the philosophy of the fact may be seen from an illustration. Let A stand on the scholarship roll at 2, on a scale whose maximum is 10, and at the same time stand at 8, on the conduct roll. A is then one of the best boys in the school, but one of the poorest scholars. Now what is the inference on the part of pupil and parents? Simply this, A is one of the poorest scholars, not because he is a bad boy, but because *he is dull and stupid,* his very goodness serving as a proof that he has done the best he can. Now the conduct roll, by evincing his goodness, comes to stand as proof of his dullness; for, without it, it might have been inferred that A was smart enough, but had been negligent. The evident tendency of all this must be not only to destroy the disciplinary utility of the conduct roll, but really to induce bad behavior in poor students.

Now, unreasonable as this view of things may be, it is unavoidable. It grows out of the fact that men respect ability more than goodness. Hence, in their apprehension, ability, like charity, covers a multitude of sins. It is out of this, that there arises the tendency of teachers to mark lightly and with reluctance, the offense of a good scholar; while, for the same offense committed by the luckless scape-goat of the class, they will slap down on the roll promptly and with a grim sort of satisfaction, the full charge of demerit. For the same reason, the parent will evince far greater complacency under the charge that his boy is a rogue, than is possible under the implication that he is a lackbrain. Whatever complaint you may make of his behavior, give him the credit of being the best scholar in the class, and you salve the wound effectually. The scholarship gratifies the parent's pride; the roguery he complacently disposes of as "wild oats,"—a grain which we fear is getting to be the rule rather than the exception, among our youth. But assure the parent as warmly as you will, that, while the boy is one of the dullest of scholars, he is a very model of good conduct, and in nine cases out of ten you will inflict a, perhaps concealed, but yet mortal wound.

The influence of all this to complicate the marking system, and destroy its effectiveness, needs no further illustration.

With regard, now, to the use of the demerit mark scheme in schools for pupils of a maturer class, the reflecting teacher will at once see that many of the objections, just urged against it, hold equally good in this higher field. It is here, just as truly as before, opposed to the true theory of discipline,—that of elevation or encouragement; and it is quite as certain to be irregular, capricious, and even unrighteous in its application. There will, of course, from the greater maturity of the pupils, be less room for ignorance or misapprehension as to its provisions and their immediate bearing on the offenses in question. But that very maturity, and the capacity it gives to comprehend thus much, will also enable them to detect more easily its errors. It thus ensures the certainty that, unless the scheme be employed with a masterly skill, it will come to be held in still deeper contempt than was possible in the case of younger pupils. And it cannot but be seen that this contempt must be the more certain and aggravated from the simple fact that the teacher is powerless to supplement its weakness, by the sterner sanctions of penal infliction.

Here, then, arises the all-important question, "What is the teacher in these higher schools to do? He may not make use of penal inflictions; if he is not to employ this marking scheme of discipline, what resource has he?" To this we answer, first, "Necessity knows no law." Bad as the demerit mark scheme is, he may have to employ it. But if he does resort to it, let him, in the light of the foregoing considerations, correct its common defects as far as he can. Let him employ its symbols *solely as private memoranda* which may serve as a basis for a just knowledge in laboring with the pupil in private, and for a righteous judgment in determining the propriety of final exclusion. Let thorough dispassionateness characterize all his marking, and, if he can not otherwise secure this, let him never mark at the instant nor upon the immediate impulse. If he be indisposed or irritated, he had better not mark at all; let not both teacher and pupil suffer at once for the infirmities of human nature.

And, lastly, let him never announce the marking to the pupil in public: it is an error in principle, and an abomination in practice, which is only calculated to react in either exasperation or contempt, upon the discipline itself. Let not the teacher, even in his private conferences with the pupil, mention it in form; this is hardly less mischievous than the other. The roll is the teacher's private guide; the pupil has no more right of access to it than he has to his "Daily Memorandum." The teacher's final decision as to the pupil's standing embraces general facts beyond the reach of the roll. If, now, he previously announces the pupil's standing according to the mere roll marks, his subsequent judgment is cut off from modification; or, if modified, is likely to be disputed by the pupil. Once more, announce the standing according to the roll marks with any degree of frequency, and the pupil will soon be taught to study merely for the mark standing, and not at all for the higher ends of duty and self-conscious worthiness. He becomes a mere mercenary laborer, as in the case of prizes.

The truth is, all that should come to the knowledge of the pupil is the substantial character of his conduct, as it lies in the teacher's mind, and as positively defined by his record. This may, and should, be as distinctly set before the pupil, as is needful to secure in him a just knowledge of his delinquency and duty, and to afford a sufficient ground for the presentation of those moral considerations which are, in his case, the only real means of correction.

This last thought naturally suggests the second answer to the main question. And that is, that just in proportion as the pupil advances toward maturity of age and capacity, the government of the school must pass from the lower to the higher species. The government of mere force must necessarily expire at an early period. The government of authority endures longer. It may indeed be regarded as holding some important place throughout the whole of the pupil's career in the school; latterly, not as the chief means or reliance, but rather as a sustaining element in the use of the higher species. In the last stage, the government of influence enters the field as the chief, and often sole means of hopeful and effective control in the school. He, therefore, who, in the government of adult pupils, cannot skilfully and succesfully apply its provisions, will sooner or later be driven to an unconditional surrender of his prerogatives as ruler. To this, there is but one alternative, and that too seldom practicable among us; namely, the establishment of a purely military rule.

The resort to the government of influence in our higher schools, unsupported, as to a great extent it must be, by the direct sanctions of positive authority, will undoubtedly be attended with some difficulties. But, inasmuch as those difficulties are only such as always attend the proper management and control of men, they are no just cause for discouragement. Nay, rather, the field thus opened to the true teacher should be one of especial ambition, since here only is it that his highest executive skill, his truest practical greatness as a man, is to be developed or evinced.

And, further, in this transition from the lower to this higher species of government in the school, there are, with the increased difficulties, some peculiar attending advantages. That very maturity which compels a resort to influence, renders the pupil more accessible to its effective use. He can now better understand and appreciate the genial good will which brings the teacher into closer association with him as a companion and friend. He can more clearly comprehend the nature and force of the reasonings by which his true interest and obligation are enforced upon his conscience. And his moral susceptibilities, though often sadly blunted, are yet, if properly approached and wrought upon, better adapted to substantial and permanent effects, than is to be expected in the case of younger pupils. If, with these facts before him, the teacher is still incapable of applying himself patiently and resolutely to the use of this higher species of control, he is fitter to be governed than to govern.

There are certain points connected with the government of *departmental schools*, which, while not necessarily involved in this connection, may be more conveniently noticed here than elsewhere. We shall therefore give them such attention as their general importance demands, though necessarily in brief.

By departmental schools we mean such as are under the conduct of a number of teachers, principal and subordinate, and as consequently appear in several divisions, either more or less distinctly organized. They are of two kinds; those of a lower order, in which the several teachers are not held as constituting a faculty proper, in which the division of the school is not one of specific departments, and in which the pupils, during the school hours, are held to a fixed and common place of study; and those of the higher order, in which the departments are organized on the basis of specialties in instruction or distinct courses of study, in which the teachers or professors form a proper faculty, and in which the pupils are congregated only in class rooms and for the purpose of recitation. These last are departmental schools proper.

With regard to the first or lower order of divided schools, there are some practical difficulties bearing upon their government, which it is not easy to reach. For example, the attainment of the most thorough supervision of the several pupils, the greater simplification of the discipline, and the more direct and effective individualizing of cases under treatment, would suggest the somewhat equal distribution of the pupils in different study-rooms under the different teachers, and the consequent equalization of the respective shares of the latter in the instruction and government. On the other hand, convenience in the movements of the pupils and the change of classes, economy in the provision of school rooms, and the difficulty of securing the proper governmental capacity in all the teachers, to which may be added the public hostility to the infliction of the severer punishments except by the highest authority,—all these demand the general congregation of the pupils in one study-room, and the devolving of their general government chiefly upon one teacher, the others being restricted to the simple charge and control of classes in recitation.

We shall enter into no discussion of the relative merits of these two forms, since it is a question of organization rather than government, and since its decision must rest, not upon theories, but upon the practical facts involved. But, inasmuch as the latter species of organization is the one more commonly adopted, and so far appears to be practically accepted as the best possible under the circumstances, we shall confine ourselves to its exclusive consideration.

So far now, as, under this organization, the general government of the school as devolving upon the teacher permanently in charge of the study-room, is concerned, the principles of the art as herein set forth are of direct application, and constitute of themselves a sufficient guide. But there are specific questions that may arise with regard to the duties and prerogatives of subordinates, merely in charge of classes in recitation, that require a more definite solution. The following considerations are, therefore, urged as chiefly important in the premises.

First. So far as the teacher has the privilege of governing his class, he should be guided by the principles of school government in general as herein set forth; and, so far as he can, within his limited field and with his restricted powers, he should faithfully endeavor to carry them out. This is essential to the welfare of his class as, for the time being, the body politic, and to the maintenance of his authority as ruler for the time being.

Secondly. He should, nevertheless, endeavor, even though at the sacrifice of some personal convictions, to govern in substantial accordance with the general method established for the whole school. This is necessary that there may be no clash between departments, no failure on the part of each department to supplement and sustain the rest, and no occasion for invidious comparisons of individual departments or teachers. The work of providing such a general method and of harmonizing its specific application by the several teachers, should be one of the first and chief objects of concern on the part of the proper principal.

Thirdly. Great pains should be taken by the principal not to denude the individual teacher of disciplinary power so completely that he becomes, as is too commonly the case, a mere puppet before his class. A supervision which destroys the independence of a subordinate, or an absorption of power which reduces him to a mere cipher, is narrow in policy and eventually destructive in practice. Reduce the class-teacher to the mere privilege or duty of reporting offenses,—a practice peculiarly incident to the extended use of the marking system,—and you impair the teacher's sense of personal responsibility; you encourage him to neglect the duty of laboring individually with offenders, and you offer a premium upon the exercise among his pupils, of a thorough and contemptuous disregard for his position and authority.

Hence, so far as may be practicable, he should be empowered to investigate, decide, and discipline within his own sphere, subject only to the general restriction suggested under the second head. If, further, it may be, for any cause, necessary to withhold from him the right to inflict punishment, let it be done only with reference to the severer penalties which, as bearing more directly upon the delicate sensibilities of the public, may endanger the peace or safety of the school authorities. And, in inflicting those punishments at the instance of the subordinate, let the principal, by all means, do it in the proper field and immediate presence of the subordinate, and *substantially under his direction*, so that, to the eye of the class, the latter shall practically stand forth as the authoritative ruler in his own department. In no other way is it possible for the principal to preserve the self-respect of the subordinate or hold him steadily to his proper responsibility; in no other way can he hold the class firmly to the exercise of a respectful regard for the position and authority of the subordinate, or a uniform obedience to the general order of the school.

Of those higher departmental schools, in which there is a properly organized faculty and no fixed congregation of the pupils, during the school session, in a common study-room, little need be said. The offenses here are of course restricted to those committed against the proper order of the recitation room, and those committed outside against the general order of the school.

Of these, the former fall exclusively under the jurisdiction of the teacher or professor proper, and should, in accordance with the foregoing rules for the lower schools, be adjudged and disciplined by him alone, except in case of reference or appeal to the faculty entire. For obvious reasons elsewhere suggested, such discipline should be always in substantial conformity with the general order agreed upon for the whole school.

Those general offenses which bear upon the government of the school at large, should, as a matter of course, be properly considered and adjudged by the faculty as such. Only in this way can organic unity in oversight, responsibility, effort, and influence be secured throughout the whole corps. This, however, is by no means to relieve the individual teacher from his obligation to make direct personal effort for the correction of offenses of which he is cognizant; nor is it to detract from the sovereign prerogative of the principal to have a voice and power over and above the will of the faculty, when in the exercise of a superior sagacity, it may seem necessary to transcend that will. Generally, however, when there is in the superior officer, the proper executive capacity, such a necessity will seldom occur. The exercise of what should be, in a principal, a characteristic good sense and tact, will usually succeed in commanding the reasonable acquiescence and support of all, without the need of overruling any.

# CHAPTER XIII.

## SCHOOL GOVERNMENT—GENERAL RESUMÉ OF ITS SPECIES; THEIR CHARACTERISTICS, AND THE QUALIFICATIONS REQUISITE TO THEIR ADMINISTRATION.

Species classified, as those of Force, Authority, and Influence—General elements, means, ideas, and ends, severally stated—*Relative order and importance of the species considered*—Government of force, inferior, restricted, and insufficient alone—That of authority higher—Needs to be supplemented by the others—That of influence, superior—Insufficient alone, in a depraved moral system—Government must combine all three species—Qualifications, why reconsidered, or stated anew—*Qualifications for the use of force*—Strength, promptitude, and resolution—These severally considered—*Qualifications for the exercise of control*—Good bodily presence—Includes physical exterior and mien or carriage—Power of these—Gross defects to which they are opposed—Illustration of the power of these qualifications—*Intellectual qualifications—Sound judgment*—Its importance—Its elements, accurate perception of facts, ready apprehension of just method of treatment—Method of culture—*Imperturbable temper*—Evils of a lack of this—Faults sure to be aggravated unless thoroughly corrected—False apologies for indulgence in hasty temper—*Intelligent persistency*—Not mere blind stubbornness—Importance of rational persistency—*Qualifications for the use of the government of influence—Genial nature*—Necessity to the existence of sympathy and love between teacher and pupil—*Logical skill*—Restriction in the use of reasoning with the pupil—Proper use—*Personal goodness*—Not a weak easiness or indulgence—But positive worthiness, the result of self-conquest—Base character sure of ultimate detection and defeat—*Tact*—Its nature—Relation to good sense—Its utility—Means of development—*Persistence*—As distinguished from authoritative persistence—*Power of retraction*—Difficulty of retracting successfully—*Rules for retraction*—Not every error needs correction—Even important errors, when observed, not always to be corrected—Folly of petty apologies and constant retraction—Government must simply evince power and willingness to correct when best—Retraction to be made frankly, but unostentatiously—*Suggested facts—Difference of female qualifications*—Woman's lack of the stronger physical and intellectual qualities—Her superiority in the more delicate moral qualifications—Error of those who demand mere masculine vigor in the woman as teacher—*Differences in power and qualification among men*—All have not, and cannot acquire, the same—*Exclusive forms of government objectionable*—The best form that the man can best apply—Government summed up, not in the measures, but the spirit of the man.

WE are now prepared for our closing work, a comprehensive resumé of school government considered with reference to its *general species*, their characteristics, and the *qualifications* requisite to their successful administration.

From the preceding discussion, it has been seen that the government of the school is practically of three general species: 1st, that of *Force;* 2d, that of *Authority;* and 3d, that of *Love.*

The general elements of effect in these species respectively are, in the first, mere physical capacity, or *Strength;* in the second, *Power,* either bodily or mental; and in the third, *Influence,* both intellectual and moral.

The general means employed in each respectively are, in the first, *Compulsion;* in the second, *Requisitions* or *Mandates,* either with or without reasonings or penal inflictions; and in the third, *Persuasion,* either argumentative or pathetic.

The general idea entertained of the subject, under each respectively, is as follows: under the government of force, he is regarded as a mere unreasoning creature; under that of authority, he is held as an intelligent subject; and under that of love, he is looked upon as not only an intelligent subject, but as capacitated for the exercise of a true and loving loyalty.

The ultimate supremacy attained in the successful administration of the three general species respectively, is of different kinds corresponding. In the first, the supremacy is that of mere *Mastery;* in the second, it is that of *Sovereign Control,* or *Lordship;* and in the third, it is that of *Moral Supremacy.*

This analysis at once reveals the relative importance of these species of government in the school, to be precisely that of the order in which they have just been presented, beginning with the lowest and ending with the highest.

The government of mere force, resulting only in physical mastery, however just in its place, or complete in its success, stands necessarily lowest in the scale. It is inferior in its governing idea, in the means it employs, and in the ends attained. Furthermore, although necessary and useful within its prescribed limits, it is insufficient of itself; it is unable and unfit to stand alone; and if made the sole or chief reliance, must even be pronounced to be the necessary resource of mere incompetence to govern, and to be, in its essential character, base and despotic.

Far higher in the scale stands the government of authoritative power, or true control. It is nobler in the idea cherished both of itself and of its subjects, more comprehensive in its capabilities and means, and more effective and salutary in its results. Yet even this species can hardly be considered as, in itself, sufficient or complete. Without the co-operation of the first, it may sometimes fail for lack of material power to command universal obedience. Without the full alliance of the last species, the government of love, it must often stop short of evincing the highest elements of excellence, and must fail to attain the truest and noblest results. It is, of itself, adequate to the preservation of substantial order and organic harmony and prosperity. But it cannot reach that perfect crown of all governmental success in the school, the thorough and benign transformation of character, and the permanent alliance of its subjects in the cause of its own perpetuation and perfection.

The last, the government of influence, or true supremacy, is, in its individual character, whether we look at its controlling idea, its specific appliances or its ultimate achievements, doubtless the purest and best. Still, it must not be forgotten, that, taken as an exclusive mode, even this species of government is not without its defects. In a perfect moral system, yet unvitiated by the introduction of depraved passions and a disloyal will, it might, perhaps, be able to stand and rule alone. But where the opposite characteristics are prevalent; where the subjects of moral government are, not only imperfect in apprehension, but depraved in nature; where there are endless counteracting notions, desires, examples, and influences, it stands in reason, that the case is different. Here, it lacks the grand element which is alone able to secure free scope and fair play for the exercise of its own better appliances, and which only can guaranty it either safety or success. Able it may be, when the way is clear, to secure the desired transformation of character, and substantial order as consequent; but it is not unfailingly competent to make that way clear when once it has been obstructed. It may indeed go down upon the realm of a corrupted nature, and

> "Tempt with wand'ring feet
> The dark, unbottomed, infinite abyss;"

but it can give no sure pledge that it will not at the last be driven,

> "Bootless home, and weather-beaten back,"

Generous then may be the nature which espouses its cause, and seeks to rely on it alone; but it is neither well informed nor practically wise. Hence, we are forced to accept the general conclusion, that in the school, as indeed elsewhere, the system of government chosen and administered must be eclectic rather than partial or exclusive: it must range freely through all three of the foregoing species, and, employing them in their proper order and proportion, must perfect itself in a just alliance and harmonious co-operation of the whole. A just apprehension of the validity and force of this conclusion would go far toward the effective correction of the too current tendency to assume the sufficiency and exclusive lawfulness of the various schemes, of natural reactions, moral suasion, and reformatory discipline,—schemes, in themselves considered, not destitute of individual excellencies, but which, as commonly taught and urged, are only deceptive and dangerous.

We are now prepared to notice the *qualifications* requisite to the successful administration of the government of the school, as set forth in this analysis. In doing this, we shall follow the order of the foregoing analysis as the most convenient, and as susceptible of presenting each class in the better light of its relations and comparative importance. Some of these will doubtless occur to the reader, as having been suggested in the previous discussion. These, however, cannot be entirely excluded here, without impairing the general classification and losing the benefit of such additional light as may be thrown upon them. But the notice taken of them will, for the reason just suggested, be comparatively brief.

Others will be presented, not because the attainment of them is possible in the case of every teacher, nor because the effort toward such attainment is obligatory on those naturally deficient; but because they properly have their place in the complete scheme of qualifications; because they are suggestive of directions in which important culture and improvement may be sought; and because the mention of them will evince the greater advantage and responsibility of those who have been, by a beneficent nature, thus nobly endowed. Let the earnest teacher, then, be upon his guard against being discouraged by the early discovery of his natural or constitutional lack of any of these particular qualifications; and be equally careful not to form a hasty estimate of their value, upon the unfair basis of a partial or ill-digested examination of the entire scheme. Our object is to explore faithfully the whole field before us, that, so far as it may be possible, every one may be able to find something clearly adapted to his own individual necessities or responsibilities.

To proceed, then, the qualifications requisite to the successful administration of the first species of government, that of mere force, are few and simple, being primarily, mere physical strength; and, secondarily, when the former is inadequate alone, alertness, or promptitude in action. Every one knows how potent an element this last is in a trial of strength, in which the parties are unequally matched, and how often it is itself sufficient to secure the victory. In cases in which both of these elements of mastery are either wanting or are inadequate to the task imposed upon them, there is no resource except

> "The mind and spirit remains
> Invincible."

The higher strength must be found in aroused and determined resolution. Every one conversant with human conflict knows how possible it is for such resolution to reduplicate, for the time being, even the physical powers. Indeed, here, as well as in the higher fields of struggle, it is often true that the measure of the will is the measure of the ability.

The qualifications favoring the happy administration of the second and higher species of government, that of control, or proper sovereignty, are more varied and deserving of a fuller consideration. They are, first, a good physical exterior or bodily presence. This includes several distinct elements, such as size, just proportions, proper solidity of frame, an eye keen and penetrating or clear and commanding, and a voice full, distinct, and naturally authoritative. Milton recognizes the general principle when he says of Adam:

> "His large, fair front and eye sublime declared
> Absolute rule."

As has been intimated, however, these qualities are not always at command; nor is he to be judged necessarily incompetent, who may be wanting in them. Still it must be patent to every observing mind, that, other things being equal, he who possessing these, looks

> "Every inch a king,"

will, at once, command a respectful attention and a prompt obedience, which will be denied to a person of feeble or insignificant appearance, and which the latter must first conquer by the force of a subsequent development of hidden and unsuspected power, before he can confidently and surely claim them.

Secondly. A becoming or noble mien, or carriage of one's self, is important, and, aside from the general reason,—its bearing upon the government,—because it is a direct symbol of the inward spirit which certainly has some just claim to a fitting outward representation; because it is to a good degree susceptible of development in every person of any force of character; and because, in some of its elements, Americans are notoriously and culpably deficient. This quality embraces the several elements; erectness of form; self-possessed steadiness in movement and certainty in action; unembarrassed directness of look and address; and a deliberate and unfaltering utterance.

The faults to which these are opposed are an unnatural and unhealthy stoop, and careless or lounging postures,—both matters of the merest habit, and simply inexcusable; undue haste or fitful irregularity in movement, either original or acquired; clumsy and imperfect action in doing things, not uncommonly the result of conscious incompetence; a lowering, downcast, or averted look, either the product of constitutional timidity or mere *mauvais honte;* a hesitating or bungling style of address, quite generally the just retribution of our common disloyalty to the study of our noble "mother tongue;" and a thick, feeble, or vulgar utterance, sometimes natural, but more often the base birth of the abominable neglect in our schools, of the noble art of reading. "From such withdraw thyself," if thou art either an earnest teacher or indeed but half a man. Contentment with them is a vice.

Of the utility of this grand qualification, we urge nothing beyond its self-evident claims, except by way of brief practical illustration. Let, for example, a command be issued, and with a cool, self-possessed mien, and a direct and confident look and tone, and who does not know that it carries with it, a clear conviction to the mind addressed, not merely of the necessity of obedience, but also of its own inherent rectitude. "Confidence," says Tupper, "was bearer of the palm because it looked like conviction of desert." So too, what skillful teacher has not witnessed the simple and effective power of a sudden pause, profound silence, and a steady and penetrating look fastened upon some thoughtless and disturbing member of the little commonwealth? Looks, like gestures, are often mightier than words, and their right and effective use might well be more frequently a subject of study among our teachers. In practical dealing with human nature, it is a cardinal maxim; that manner is more vital than even matter.

But nothing here urged is to be accepted as countenancing a mere studied pompousness or pretentiousness of manner. Simple affectation or pretence in the teacher is a vice of no insignificant dimensions. But a properly cultivated or a naturally noble manner is quite another thing, and is both legitimate and desirable.

Passing, thirdly, to the higher and more exclusively intellectual qualities, the first to be noticed is sound judgment or, in common phraseology, good common sense. This is of the utmost importance. It is for the teacher, (as indeed for every man who has to deal with human affairs,) the touchstone of practical character and endowment: it is the master attribute. No other good qualities which he may possess, can counterbalance any especial deficiency in this direction. The best designs and the fairest plans may be hopelessly marred or foiled, by the simple lack, on the part of the teacher, of good common sense. With it, those even intrinsically defective may count upon a reasonable success.

Its elements are few and simple, being, first, a prompt and accurate perception of the facts in the case, and, secondly, a ready intuitive apprehension of their just relations to the probable treatment demanded. They may be summed up, in a rapid and transparent survey of the whole field of the specific fact or measure concerned, irrespective of mere personal prepossessions or considerations. It involves really the power of wholly discharging the observer himself, from the view taken, and of looking at things in their own nature and relations exclusively. In the lack of this power, lies the real secret of the failure of many persons to evince sound judgment or common sense. They cannot, in their judgments, get out of, away from, and above themselves. Hence, self-conceited and egotistical minds must always be wanting in this quality.

Good judgment or common sense is usually, to a great extent, a native endowment. Its attainment, when it is not native, is a matter of some difficulty; in some cases, it is seemingly impossible. Yet teachers should guard against too readily accepting this last as the fact in their own case. For the quality may be, to an important degree, either acquired or cultivated.

The proper means to be employed in that direction are simple and within reach. They are first, a well-balanced culture of the intellect generally; secondly, the habit of hearty association with others; thirdly, the constant practice of close observation both of men and things; and lastly, the thoughtful and continued study of one's own experience. The last is, of itself, in many cases sufficient. Indeed the universal value attached to experience is really due to the fact that it produces, not merely enlarged knowledge, but enlarged common sense. And these means, so simple and accessible, can neither be too highly esteemed, nor too assiduously employed. Teachers are, we fear, too prone, either from original indisposition to self-culture, or from entire preoccupation with books, to neglect them. But the error is a fatal one. Sooner or later, the price must be paid and to the uttermost farthing. Hence, (to vary the maxim); "caveat doctor;" let the teacher beware.

Fourthly. Let the teacher either possess, or fully acquire a cool and imperturbable temper. Of the practical and pressing importance of this qualification, little need be said. Easy excitability or hasty violence are, of necessity, dangerous elements in the government of the school. Their tendency to weaken the teacher's influence; to impair the accuracy of his judgment; to complicate his administration of discipline; to occasion positive injustice; and to stimulate and strengthen both by example and direct collision, the fiercer passions of his pupils, is unmistakable.

Furthermore, these faults cannot remain stationary. Unless effectually subdued, they must grow in frequency of exhibition and in power. The school will afford a thousand petty occasions for the aggravation of the one, and the stimulation of the other to unseemly and destructive outbreaks. Correction is, then, the only safety. It is idle to plead that the teacher is *naturally hasty*, or to rely upon that shallowest of all subterfuges that it will soon be learned that it "is his way." As to the first, he has no right as teacher to leave so public a fault uncorrected; and for the second, let him remember that he rules among those, who, in their yet unsophisticated views of consistency, are not likely to feel the force of the apology. There is no evading of this grand principle; he who cannot or will not control himself, is not fit to control others.

Lastly, under this second species of government, we notice as a requisite qualification, intelligent stability of will, or persistency of purpose. We say distinctly, *intelligent persistency;* for simple blind pertinacity, or mere stubbornness is itself an infirmity, of which can come but little good, and if any, that only by chance. The famous, and often nauseatingly reiterated maxim; "perseverance conquers all things;" is true only with limitations. Perseverance may possess this power, but only when it is rational, that is, when it is inspired and guided by proper knowledge and sound judgment. An ass may be conceived as kicking with the characteristic stubbornness of his race, against, for example, the Hoosic mountain, till "the crack of doom;" but it does not therefore follow that he will eventually, by the mere virtue of his perseverance, either buffet back its iron walls, or conquer for himself a successful subterranean passage to its farther slope.

But of an intelligent, a rational persistency, all may be promised that is possible. Hence, let the teacher either have or acquire this important characteristic. He will have large and constant occasion for its exercise, as has elsewhere been shown. If he is naturally deficient, he may do more to correct the evil than many suppose. It is quite possible for him, by the simple practice of carefully considering beforehand the work he proposes to undertake, by repeatedly and firmly bringing himself back from any irresolute lapsing therefrom, and by renewedly girding himself up to the unflinching endeavor,—it is quite possible through the use of those means, to almost recreate the will. And a firm will is a power in the school.

Of the qualifications calculated to insure success in the administration of the third, and last species of government in the school, that of influence, or moral supremacy, the first in order is a *genial nature.*

Influence can only be secured and exerted where there is a certain amount of mutual attraction; and attraction involves mutual modifications, different, perhaps, in degree, but yet similar in kind. To obtain this power over the pupil, the teacher must be able to arouse and enlist in his own behalf the more genial side of the pupil's nature. The only direct means of effecting this is to disclose and apply the genial elements of his own nature. Certainly, if he be of a cold or distant temper; if he stands aloof from the most susceptible and sunny of all natures,—that of the child; or if he approaches it, but with no near and sympathizing contact, with no warm and radiant sunshine from his own heart, he cannot expect to bring the child out from his isolation, distance, timidity, or antagonism, into the realm and atmosphere of influence and regard. Unrelenting rigidity and frost have no business to look for the evoking of a bland and blooming spring.

The importance, then, of the teacher's careful cultivation of a pleasant and kindly address, if he has it not by nature; of his unbending himself at the proper times, from his sterner moods and duties, to seek a proper companionship with his pupils, and of his careful exhibition of a just but lively sympathy with them in their little joys and sorrows, becomes again not less apparent than it has been already elsewhere seen to be.

Secondly. Under this general head, *logical ability* or skill must be included as a qualification of no slight value. We embrace in this, not only a capacity to discover consistent reasons for things required, but also proper skill in presenting them to the mind to be influenced. In the exercise of authority proper, the teacher has need, for his own sake as legislator and ruler, to be a clear and self-consistent thinker. But, as has elsewhere been hinted, his logical conclusions, are not, under that species of government, except to a very limited and guarded extent, to be applied directly to the understanding of the subject. Requirements and decisions are, by the very nature of authority, to be generally unargued. But, under the rule of influence, it is often quite otherwise. Whenever the pupil is in a proper frame of mind; is somewhat effectively drawn to the teacher by an incipient or substantial regard; and is already measurably prepared to yield obedience for its own sake, the way is open for the generous unfolding to him of the reasons which reveal the justice or benevolence of the claims laid upon him, and the dignity and beauty, not merely of obedience, but of hearty cooperation. And when this can be done, it is an element of the purest power.

Here, then, the teacher who possesses this logical ability or skill will have a most important advantage over those not thus endowed or qualified. And it is in this direction, that that system of professional training which, despising a mere martinet drill in formal rules and methods, seeks to develop in the teacher the power of acute, vigorous and independent thought, at once reveals its just superiority. Let no teacher in process of professional training be content with any other. To do so is simply slavish and suicidal. Mastery of form, avails him, only when the forms apply. Power to think makes him master of the entire position, at the very time of his need, and precisely as he needs it.

A third qualification for the attainment and exercise of influence is *personal goodness;* not a mere inconsiderate or weak goodishness, but that clear, strong, positive, rational worthiness which is more especially the product of pure self-conquest. He is, for the use of this moral influence, the most truly and effectively pure, and good who, whatever may have been his original defects of notion or character, has hunted them out and dethroned them; and who has, for the sake of his own virtue, installed in their stead, traits and principles both admirable and sure-founded. Here, it is quite possible for the last to become signally the first. Constitutional amiability is, of course, lovely; but acquired worthiness is the most mighty, and the most to be revered.

But, whether it be constitutional or acquired, the worthiness must be. Base character may by self-concealment and artifice, attain and wield a potent influence. But that influence is uncertain. There is always lying under it the dangerous powder-heap, to which some unexpected revelation of the hidden deformity may apply the igniting spark and fatally explode the whole of the seemingly fair fabric. To command a true and abiding influence, there must be that near approach of character to character; that direct contact of thought, feeling, and sympathy, which renders no-one permanently safe and sure, who cannot, in the full assurance of conscious rectitude say, and with a better principle and purpose than did the subtle Iago:

> "I will wear my heart upon my sleeve
> For daws to peck at."

In the fourth place, and pre-eminently, the teacher must possess *tact*. This quality, so often incomprehensible to those who are destitute of it, is really no mystery. Tact is simply good sense skilfully operative. Between the two, the difference is that good sense is internal; tact external: good sense is reflective; tact applicative: good sense is the subject matter; tact is its just delivery. Indeed, the two are but necessary parts of a perfect practical duality of powers. Good sense and tact are the two contiguous plates in the one electrical combination,—the one on the negative, the other on the positive side of the circuit, but both equally necessary to the evolution of the required force. Hence, tact is indispensable to the attainment and exercise of true and effective influence. Tact is the golden groove along which you glide unperceived to the very gate of the human heart: tact is the cunning sap by which you press your way beneath its stubborn outworks to the inner citadel: tact is the master key that commands all its complicated locks, and gives you entrance to its secret vaults and hiding places. Were every other power denied the teacher, tact might still avail to win an important success.

The close relation just shown to exist between good sense and tact, will suggest the fact that much the same laws are true of the existence or the acquisition of the latter, as prevail in the case of the former. The difficulties to be encountered in the work of acquiring it, and the means to be employed in the prosecution of that work, are substantially identical with those already noticed under the head of good sense. They need not then be repeated.

Much the same may be said of the last quality to

be considered under this head; namely, *persistence.* Essential to the highest success in the administration of the preceding forms of government, it certainly can be none the less so here. Indeed, the attainment of important ends through the use of purely moral means, or through influence and persuasion, is generally a more circuitous, tardy, and complicated operation, than could be the attainment of the same results through the use of mere authority. Its path, like

> "That, on which blessing comes and goes, doth follow
> The river's course, the valley's playful windings,
> Curves round the corn-field and the hill of vines,
> Honoring the holy bounds of property;
> And thus secure, though late, leads to its end."

But this very circuitousness, this very regard for the rights of human feeling and imperfection, and this pure reliance upon peaceful, but indirect and slow-paced measures, renders the demand for patient persistence the more imperative.

There is, however, this difference between the persistency of this last species of government, and that of the two former, which it is instructive to notice. The steadiness of purpose involved in the exercise of either force or authority, is, like all the attributes of those two forms of government, more positive and outstanding. It stands forth with unconcealed arms and unrolled banners of battle, on the very edge of the first onset. In pressing the milder plans and purposes of influence, it must be none the less present, but more quiet and undemonstrative. It lies, rather in abeyance, like a concealed but ready and powerful reserve. Its presence, if at once revealed, would only betray the whole projected movement to the hostile pupil, and would only tend to put him upon his guard, and stiffen his resistance. Hence, it should be rather unconsciously felt than immediately seen. It should rather shine out steadily in the quiet progress of the patient effort, than appear

> "Before the cloudy van,
> On the rough edge of battle ere it join."

One more general qualification, belonging equally to all the various species of government enumerated, remains to be noticed, and we have done. This is the *power of retraction,* or the capacity to correct and atone for the errors which may have occurred in the teacher's administration of the government of the school. It is doubtless true in principle that errors should not be committed, especially those of a grave or far-reaching character. But inasmuch as the teacher is not infallible, and is, moreover, hedged about by difficulties both complicated and constant, "it must needs be that offenses come;" and, looking at the pain and peril incident upon the attempt to retrace the false steps taken, we may also add, "but woe to that man by whom the offense cometh." He will sooner or later learn the truth of the ancient saying:

> "Facilis decensus Averni;
> Sed revocare gradum, superasque evadere ad auras,
> Hoc opus, hic labor est."

In case, then, the hard necessity of refraction seems to be pressed upon the teacher, let him accept the issue fairly, and observe the following maxims. First. Not every error needs correction. Some may not have been observed by the pupils, and others may be altogether of minor importance. Here, the attempt at correction will only reveal errors before unsuspected, or will unfortunately exaggerate the importance of those discovered. The evils thus induced will more than counterbalance the good proposed in the attempted retraction. The true course in such a case is for the teacher to stand quietly still upon his reserved rights, and leave the error to the natural correction of his subsequent administration of affairs.

Secondly. Even where the errors may have been observed, or may possess some grave importance, the teacher is not to regard himself as scrupulously bound to make public amends for every one. One of the most pitiable of weaknesses in him who governs, is that of ostentatiously engaging in the punctilious correction of his own short-comings, by perpetual declarations and petty apologies. Nothing can be more foreign to the evincing of true governmental capacity; nothing more destructive to confidence in the government, and esteem for it. Its folly may be seen in the fact that it is the product of either a pitiful timidity in ruling, or as pitiful a conceit of superior rectitude. It is as if the teacher should confess that he dare not steadily press forward to the attainment of the greater objects in view, undaunted by temporary failures; or as if he should be constantly crying out, "Behold the marvel of my unfailing and fearless conscientiousness." The whole is a vice, only inferior to sheer vanity or obsequiousness.

What is wanted in the teacher as governor, is not the correction of every noticeable fault, but the evincing of complete power and willingness to correct them, when, in his higher judgment, that is truly demanded by the general welfare. Evince this power and willingness, and the uncorrected errors will not only, not materially impair his authority or influence, but they will not unfrequently, by their very incorrection, suggest to tho pupil the possibility of higher capacity and superior reasons, unknown to himself, but determining the teacher's course. The tendency of this will naturally be to strengthen the general confidence in, not only his ability, but even his rectitude.

When correction is clearly just and necessary, let the retraction be frankly and fearlessly made, but without any needless comment or display, and above all, without personal reference, elaborate regrets, or unmanly whining. Let the teacher show that he still stands strong in conscious rectitude, and unimpaired in manly self-respect. Let him remember that what might be due between man and man, in the correction of faults, is not to the same extent demanded between government and subject. The broader claims, the far more difficult responsibilities, and the higher necessities of government as involving the welfare of the whole, are, in some part, an apology for its incidental failures. The preservation of its authoritative dignity and power are too vital to the general interests of the whole commonwealth, to be subjected to the needless humiliation of minute confessions and demure contrition. Let, then, enough appear in formal retraction to shed a clear and satisfactory light upon the subsequent amendment in governing, and, for the rest, let this latter correction be the sole reliance. The maxim of government in the correction of faults must be; not words without deeds, but deeds rather than words.

The power to institute such wise and successful retraction, it will be now seen, is one of rare combination and great importance. It involves a happy and effective blending of all the more important intellectual and moral qualifications which have just been set forth. Fortunate is he who finds this master combination instant in his nature, or solidly built up in his acquired endowments.

In two directions, the foregoing considerations as to the qualification of the teacher, suggest facts demanding a passing notice. It will doubtless have occurred to some, that of the qualifications demanded, there are those that are neither so native to woman, nor so easily to be acquired by her; as, for example, those of physical strength, commanding presence and authoritative voice, and logical breadth and power. It is, however, by no means necessary that she should either possess or seek to acquire these, at least in their more masculine or manly phase. She possesses, to a more eminent degree and excellence than man can boast, others that more than counterbalance any loss accruing from want of these. In

> "Those graceful acts,
> Those thousands decencies, that daily flow
> From all her words and actions,"

she is possessed of a power for the successful administration of that highest species of supremacy,—the supremacy of loving influence, which not unfrequently, in its proper sphere, puts to shame man's more stern and positive capabilities, sometimes, even conquers them outright. Indeed, in her sharpness of perception; her instantaneous certainty of intuition, sometimes amounting to even a prophetic instinct; her facile adaptation; her winning grace; her subtle tact; and her pure and noble sympathies, she is, in this field of direction and control, without a peer. Let her, then, cultivate others so far as she may without disloyalty to her sex; but let her rely rather upon these her own pre-eminent and altogether sufficient endowments.

In this direction may be seen, at a glance, the stupidity of those who either possess or affect a conviction of the superiority in the woman as teacher, of the more masculine traits of strength, courage, and so-called energy. They either fail to possess, or they foolishly ignore the knowledge of the highest, sweetest and most effective endowments of the sex. We say to such,

> "There are more things in heaven and earth,
> Than are dreamt of in your philosophy."

Hence, a hundred times greater importance is to be attached to the quiet, all pervading and sweetly transforming influence of her, who in the school room moves on serenely from day to day, in all her pure proprieties and loving efforts, unconsciously both blessed and blessing, than can be attributed to the sturdy vigor and storming energy of those who either unthinkingly or unblushingly sacrifice the sweeter and more benign elements of their better nature, upon the altar of a masculine ambition.

It may, furthermore, occur to some that, after all that may be done by teachers in the way of personal and professional culture and acquirements, there will still exist unavoidable individual differences in qualification, which must seriously affect them in their administration of the various species of government herein set forth; and which may even preclude the possibility of the highest success in either as an exclusive form. One lesson taught by this is that of a necessary eclecticism in the choice of means and methods, which has already been touched upon.

It remains, however, to suggest here, another important and concluding principle. There is, doubtless, a purest and best form of government. But as all are not adapted to be controlled by this theoretically superior form; so are all no more adapted to its exercise. This superior scheme of government should, beyond question, be so far understood and aspired to, as will secure its presence in the thought, as an inspiring and informing influence toward the steady improvement of the method necessarily chosen. But it is not imperative, nay, it may be simply a folly to aspire to its exclusive use and realization. The particular qualifications of some teachers may, not only render this an impossibility, but may render an attempt in that direction, only a source of constant embarrassment and failure in that especial province in which, though inferior, a signal success awaits them. All attempts, then, at imposing a one best and exclusive form of governing upon the teacher, are simply absurd and tyrannous.

The general law in this direction, has been tersely and truly expressed by Pope:

> "For forms of government let fools contest,
> Whate'er is best administered is best."

The substance of it is this: some government is better than none, and government is as truly relative to the capacity of the ruler, as to the condition of the subject. The wise teacher, then, while carefully availing himself of the offered aid of all, will rely chiefly upon that species of government for which he intelligently discovers himself to be the best adapted. "The government of the school," said an able teacher to us once, "is summed up, not so much in the measures, as in the spirit of the man." But that clear and commanding spirit is possible, and can be free and effective, only in that field where he who rules is consciously at home. David was mightier with his sling and stone than he could have been, girt with all the panoply of Saul, and he had both the good sense to know it and the courage to avow it. Let the teachers learn from his example.

Nor let them learn from it only this one lesson. It is instinct with even nobler truth. Beyond his judicious preference for his own well-approved, though unpretending weapons; beyond his modest, but self-respectful reliance upon his own self-developed powers; beyond his prompt, but unostentatious acceptance of the duty and the trial providentially imposed upon him; beyond that imperturbable coolness and calmness which stamped him every inch a man, as well as a hero;—beyond all this, let the true teacher discover, and ponder well, that lesson of simple unwavering faith in a divine guidance and support, which he, in his conflicts with ignorance and insubordination, needs not less than did David in his memorable combat with the giant of Gath; and may he, in his time of need, both seek and find that guidance and support, and through them, come off conqueror indeed.

# THE NATIONAL SERIES OF READERS.

*COMPLETE IN TWO INDEPENDENT PARTS.*

## I.
## THE NATIONAL READERS.

By PARKER & WATSON.

| | | | |
|---|---|---|---|
| No. 1.—National Primer, | . . . . . | *64 pp., 16mo,* | $0 25 |
| No. 2.—National First Reader, | . . . | *128 pp., 16mo,* | 38 |
| No. 3.—National Second Reader, | . . | *224 pp., 16mo,* | 63 |
| No. 4.—National Third Reader, | . . | *288 pp., 12mo,* | 1 00 |
| No. 5.—National Fourth Reader, | . . | *432 pp., 12mo,* | 1 50 |
| No. 6.—National Fifth Reader, | . . | *600 pp., 12mo,* | 1 88 |
| National Elementary Speller, | . . . | *160 pp., 16mo,* | 25 |
| National Pronouncing Speller, | . . . | *188 pp., 12mo,* | 50 |

## II.
## THE INDEPENDENT READERS.

By J. MADISON WATSON.

| | | | |
|---|---|---|---|
| The Independent First Reader, | . . | *80 pp., 16mo,* | 25 |
| The Independent Second Reader, | . | *160 pp., 16mo,* | 50 |
| The Independent Third Reader, | . . | *240 pp., 16mo,* | 75 |
| The Independent Fourth Reader, | . . | *264 pp., 12mo,* | 1 00 |
| The Independent Fifth Reader, | . . | *336 pp., 12mo,* | 1 25 |
| The Independent Sixth Reader, | . . | *474 pp., 12mo,* | 1 50 |
| The Independent Child's Speller (Script), | | *80 pp., 16mo,* | 25 |
| The Independent Youth's Speller (Script), | | *168 pp., 12mo,* | 50 |
| The Independent Spelling Book, | . . | *160 pp., 16mo,* | 25 |

***** The Readers constitute two complete and entirely distinct series, either of which is adequate to every want of the best schools. The Spellers may accompany either Series.**

# PARKER & WATSON'S NATIONAL READERS.

The salient features of these works which have combined to render them so popular may be briefly recapitulated as follows:

1. **THE WORD-BUILDING SYSTEM.**—This famous progressive method for young children originated and was copyrighted with these books. It constitutes a process with which the beginner with *words* of one letter is gradually introduced to additional lists formed by prefixing or affixing single letters. and is thus led almost insensibly to the mastery of the more difficult constructions. This is one of the most striking modern improvements in methods of teaching.

2. **TREATMENT OF PRONUNCIATION.**—The wants of the youngest scholars in this department are not overlooked. It may be said that from the first lesson the student by this method need never be at a loss for a prompt and accurate rendering of every word encountered.

3. **ARTICULATION AND ORTHOEPY** are considered of primary importance.

4. **PUNCTUATION** is inculcated by a series of interesting *reading lessons*, the simple perusal of which suffices to fix its principles indelibly upon the mind.

5. **ELOCUTION.** Each of the higher Readers (3d, 4th and 5th) contains elaborate, scholarly, and thoroughly practical treatises on elocution. This feature alone has secured for the series many of its warmest friends.

6. **THE SELECTIONS** are the crowning glory of the series. Without exception it may be said that no volumes of the same size and character contain a collection so diversified, judicious, and artistic as this. It embraces the choicest gems of English literature, so arranged as to afford the reader ample exercise in every department of style. So acceptable has the taste of the authors in this department proved, not only to the educational public but to the reading community at large, that thousands of copies of the Fourth and Fifth Readers have found their way into public and private libraries throughout the country, where they are in constant use as manuals of literature, for reference as well as perusal.

7. **ARRANGEMENT.** The exercises are so arranged as to present constantly alternating practice in the different styles of composition, while observing a definite plan of progression or gradation throughout the whole. In the higher books the articles are placed in formal sections and classified topically, thus concentrating the interest and inculcating a principle of association likely to prove valuable in subsequent general reading.

8. **NOTES AND BIOGRAPHICAL SKETCHES.** These are full and adequate to every want. The biographical sketches present in pleasing style the history of every author laid under contribution.

9. **ILLUSTRATIONS.** These are plentiful, almost profuse, and of the highest character of art. They are found in every volume of the series as far as and including the Third Reader.

10. **THE GRADATION** is perfect. Each volume overlaps its companion preceding or following in the series, so that the scholar, in passing from one to another, is only conscious, by the presence of the new book, of the transition.

11. **THE PRICE** is reasonable. The National Readers contain more matter than any other series in the same number of volumes published. Considering their completeness and thoroughness they are much the cheapest in the market.

12. **BINDING.** By the use of a material and process known only to themselves, in common with all the publications of this house, the National Readers are warranted to outlast any with which they may be compared—the ratio of relative durability being in their favor as two to one.

# WATSON'S INDEPENDENT READERS.

**This Series** is designed to meet a general demand for smaller and cheaper books than the National Series proper, and to serve as well for intermediate volumes of the National Readers in large graded schools requiring more books than one ordinary series will supply.

**Beauty.** The most casual observer is at once impressed with the unparalleled mechanical beauty of the Independent Readers. The Publishers believe that the æsthetic tastes of children may receive no small degree of cultivation from their very earliest school books, to say nothing of the importance of making study attractive by all such artificial aids that are legitimate. In accordance with this view, not less than $25,000 was expended in their preparation before publishing, with a result which entitles them to be considered "The Perfection of Common School Books."

**Selections.** They contain, of course, none but entirely new selections. These are arranged according to a strictly progressive and novel method of developing the elementary sounds in order in the lower numbers, and in all, with a view to topics and general literary style. The mind is thus led in fixed channels to proficiency in every branch of good reading, and the evil results of 'scattering' as practised by most school-book authors, avoided.

**The Illustrations,** as may be inferred from what has been said, are elegant beyond comparison. They are profuse in every number of the series from the lowest to the highest. This is the only series published of which this is true.

**The Type** is semi-phonetic, the invention of Prof. Watson. By it every letter having more than one sound is clearly distinguished in all its variations without in any way mutilating or disguising the normal form of the letter.

**Elocution** is taught by prefatory treatises of constantly advancing grade and completeness in each volume, which are illustrated by wood-cuts in the lower books, and by black-board diagrams in the higher. Prof. Watson is the first to introduce Practical Illustrations and Black-board Diagrams for teaching this branch.

**Foot Notes** on every page afford all the incidental instruction which the teacher is usually required to impart. Indices of words refer the pupil to the place of their first use and definition. The Biographies of Authors and others are in every sense excellent.

**Economy.** Although the number of pages in each volume is fixed at the minimum, for the purpose recited above, the utmost amount of matter available without overcrowding is obtained in the space. The pages are much wider and larger than those of any competitor and contain *twenty per cent* more matter than any other series of the same type and number of pages.

**All the Great Features.** Besides the above all the popular features of the National Readers are retained except the Word-Building system. The latter gives place to an entirely new method of progressive development, based upon some of the best features of the Word System, Phonetics and Object Lessons.

# NATIONAL READERS.

## ORIGINAL AND "INDEPENDENT" SERIES.

### SPECIMEN TESTIMONIALS.

*From* D. H. HARRIS, *Supt. Public Schools, Hannibal, Mo.*

The National Series of Readers are now in use in our public schools, and I regard them *the best* that I have ever examined or used.

*From* HON. J. K. JILLSON, *Supt. of Education, State of South Carolina.*

I have carefully examined your new and beautiful Series of Readers known as "The Independent Readers," and do not hesitate to recommend it as the finest and most excellent ever presented to the public.

*From* D. N. ROOK, *Sec. of School Board, Williamsport, Pa.*

I would say that Parker & Watson's Series of Readers and Spellers give the best satisfaction in our schools of any Series of Readers and Spellers that have ever been used. There is nothing published for which we would exchange them

*From* PROF. H. SEELE, *New Braunfels Academy, Texas.*

I recommend the National Readers for four good reasons: (1.) The printing, engraving, and binding is excellent. (2.) They contain choice selections from English Literature. (3.) They inculcate good morals without any sectarian bias. (4.) They are truly *National*, because they teach pure patriotism and not sectional prejudice.

*From* S. FINDLEY, *Supt. Akron Schools, Ohio.*

We use no others, and have no desire to. They give entire satisfaction. We like the freshness and excellence of the selections. We like the biographical notes and the definitions at the foot of the page. We also like the white paper and clear and beautiful type. In short, we do not know where to look for books which would be so satisfactory both to teachers and pupils.

*From* PRES. ROBERT ALLYN, *McKendree College, Ill.*

Since my connection with this college, we have used in our preparatory department the Series of Readers known as the "National Readers," compiled by Parker & Watson, and published by Messrs. A. S. Barnes & Co. They are *excellent;* afford choice selections; contain the right system of elocutionary instruction, and are well printed and bound so as to be serviceable as well as interesting. I can commend them as among the excellent means used by teachers to make their pupils proficient in that noblest of school arts, GOOD READING.

*From* W. T. HARRIS, *Supt. Public Schools, St. Louis, Mo.*

I have to admire these excellent selections in prose and verse, and the careful arrangement which places first what is easy of comprehension, and proceeds gradually to what is difficult. I find the lessons so arranged as to bring together different treatments of the same topic, thereby throwing much light on the pupil's path, and I doubt not adding greatly to his progress. The proper variety of subjects chosen, the concise treatise on elocution, the beautiful typography and substantial binding—all these I find still more admirable than in the former series of National Readers, which I considered *models* in these respects.

*From* H. T. PHILLIPS, Esq., *of the Board of Education, Atlanta, Ga.*

The Board of Education of this city have selected for use in the public schools of Atlanta the entire series of your Independent Readers, together with Steele's Chemistry and Philosophy. As a member of the Board, and of the Committee on Text-books, the subject of Readers was referred to me for examination. I gave a pretty thorough examination to ten (10) different series of Readers, and in endeavoring to arrive at a decision upon the sole question of merit, and entirely independent of any extraneous influence, I very cordially recommended the Independent Series. This verdict was approved by the Committee and adopted by the Board.

*From Report of* REV. W. T. BRANTLY, D.D., *late Professor of Belles Lettres, University of Georgia, on "Text-Books in Reading," before the Teachers' Convention of Georgia, May 4, 1870.*

The *National Series*, by Parker & Watson, is deserving of its high reputation. The Primary Books are suited to the weakest capacity; whilst those more advanced supply instructive illustration on all that is needed to be known in connection with the art.

# WATSON'S CHILD'S SPELLER.

## THE INDEPENDENT CHILD'S SPELLER.

**Price 25 Cents.**

This unique book, published in 1872, is the first to be consistently printed in imitation of writing; that is, it teaches orthography as we use it. It is for the smallest class of learners, who soon become familiarized with words by their forms, and learn to read writing while they spell.

### EXTRACT FROM THE PREFACE.

Success in teaching English orthography is still exceptional, and it must so continue until the principles involved are recognized in practice. Form is foremost: the eye and the hand must be trained to the formation of words; and since spelling is a part of writing, the written form only should be used. The laws of mental association, also—especially those of resemblance, contrast, and contiguity in time and place—should receive such recognition in the construction of the text-book as shall insure, whether consciously or not, their appropriate use and legitimate results. Hence, the spelling-book, properly arranged, is a necessity from the first; and, though primers, readers, and dictionaries may serve as aids, it can have no competent substitute.

Consistently with these views, the words used in the Independent Child's Speller have such original classifications and arrangements in columns—in reference to location, number of letters, vowel sounds, alphabetic equivalents, and consonant terminations—as exhibit most effectively their formation and pronunciation. The vocabulary is strictly confined to the simple and significant monosyllables in common use. He who has mastered these may easily learn how to spell and pronounce words of more than one syllable.

The introduction is an illustrated alphabet in script, containing twenty-six pictures of objects, and their names, commencing both with capitals and small letters. Part First embraces the words of one, two, and three letters; Part Second, the words of four letters; and Part Third, other monosyllables. They are divided into short lists and arranged in columns, the vowels usually in line, so as to exhibit individual characteristics and similarity of formation. The division of words into paragraphs is shown by figures in the columns. Each list is immediately followed by sentences for reading and writing, in which the same words are again presented with irregularities of form and sound. Association is thus employed, memory tested, and definition most satisfactorily taught.

Among the novel and valuable features of the lessons and exercises, probably the most prominent are their adaptedness for young children and their being printed in exact imitation of writing. The author believes that hands large enough to spin a top, drive a hoop, or catch a ball, are not too small to use a crayon, or a slate and pencil; that the child's natural desire to draw and write should not be thwarted, but gratified, encouraged, and wisely directed; and that since the written form is the one actually used in connection with spelling in after-life, the eye and the hand of the child should be trained to that form from the first. He hopes that this little work, designed to precede all other spelling-books and conflict with none, may satisfy the need so universally recognized of a fit introduction to orthography, penmanship, and English composition.

# The National Readers and Spellers.

## THEIR RECORD.

These books have been adopted by the School Boards, or official authority, of the following important States, cities, and towns—in most cases for exclusive use.

**The State of Minnesota.**
**The State of Texas.**
**The State of Missouri.**
**The State of Alabama.**
**The State of North Carolina.**
**The State of Louisiana.**

**New York.**
New York City.
Brooklyn.
Buffalo.
Albany.
Rochester.
Troy.
Syracuse.
Elmira.
&c., &c.

**Pennsylvania.**
Reading.
Lancaster.
Erie.
Scranton.
Carlisle.
Carbondale.
Westchester.
Schuylkill Haven.
Williamsport.
Norristown.
Bellefonte.
Wilkesbarre.
&c., &c.

**New Jersey.**
Newark.
Jersey City.
Paterson.
Trenton.
Camden.
Elizabeth.
New Brunswick.
Phillipsburg.
Orange.
&c., &c.

**Delaware.**
Wilmington.

**D. C.**
Washington.

**Illinois.**
Chicago.
Peoria.
Alton.
Springfield.
Aurora.
Galesburg.
Rockford.
Rock Island.
&c., &c.

**Wisconsin.**
Milwaukee.
Fond du Lac.
Oshkosh.
Janesville.
Racine.
Watertown.
Sheboygan.
La Crosse.
Waukesha.
Kenosha.
&c., &c.

**Michigan.**
Grand Rapids.
Kalamazoo.
Adrian.
Jackson.
Monroe.
Lansing.
&c., &c.

**Ohio.**
Toledo.
Sandusky.
Conneaut.
Chardon.
Hudson.
Canton.
Salem.
&c., &c.

**Indiana.**
New Albany.
Fort Wayne.
Lafayette.
Madison.
Logansport.
Indianapolis.

**Iowa.**
Davenport.
Burlington.
Muscatine.
Mount Pleasant.
&c.

**Nebraska.**
Brownsville.
Lincoln.
&c.

**Oregon.**
Portland.
Salem.
&c.

**Virginia.**
Richmond.
Norfolk.
Petersburg.
Lynchburg.
&c.

**South Carolina.**
Columbia.
Charleston.

**Georgia.**
Savannah.

**Louisiana.**
New Orleans.

**Tennessee.**
Memphis

The *Educational Bulletin* records periodically all new points gained

# SCHOOL-ROOM CARDS.

**Baade's Reading Case,** . . . . . . . . . . .*$10 00

A frame containing movable cards, with arrangement for showing one sentence at a time, capable of 28,000 transpositions.

**Eureka Alphabet Tablet** . . . . . . . . . .*1 50

Presents the alphabet upon the Word Method System, by which the child will learn the alphabet in nine days, and make no small progress in reading and spelling in the same time.

**National School Tablets,** 10 Nos. . . . . . .*8 00

Embrace reading and conversational exercises, object and moral lessons, form, color, &c. A complete set of these large and elegantly illustrated Cards will embellish the school-room more than any other article of furniture.

# READING.

**Fowle's Bible Reader** . . . . . . . . . . . .$1 00

The narrative portions of the Bible, chronologically and topically arranged, judiciously combined with selections from the Psalms, Proverbs, and other portions which inculcate important moral lessons or the great truths of Christianity. The embarrassment and difficulty of reading the Bible itself, by course, as a class exercise, are obviated, and its use made feasible, by this means.

**North Carolina First Reader** . . . . . . . 40

**North Carolina Second Reader** . . . . . . 65

**North Carolina Third Reader** . . . . . . . 1 00

Prepared expressly for the schools of this State, by C. H. Wiley, Superintendent of Common Schools, and F. M. Hubbard, Professor of Literature in the State University.

**Parker's Rhetorical Reader** . . . . . . . . 1 00

Designed to familiarize Readers with the pauses and other marks in general use, and lead them to the practice of modulation and inflection of the voice.

**Introductory Lessons in Reading and Elocution** . . . . . . . . . . . . . . . 75

Of similar character to the foregoing, for less advanced classes.

**High School Literature** . . . . . . . . . . 1 50

Admirable selections from a long list of the world's best writers, for exercise in reading, oratory, and composition. Speeches, dialogues, and model letters represent the latter department.

# ORTHOGRAPHY.

## SMITH'S SERIES

Supplies a speller for every class in graded schools, and comprises the most complete and excellent treatise on English Orthography and its companion branches extant.

**1. Smith's Little Speller . . . . . . . . .$ 20**

First Round in the Ladder of Learning.

**2. Smith's Juvenile Definer . . . . . . . . 45**

Lessons composed of familiar words grouped with reference to similar signification or use, and correctly spelled, accented, and defined.

**3. Smith's Grammar-School Speller . . . . 50**

Familiar words, grouped with reference to the sameness of sound of syllables differently spelled. Also definitions, complete rules for spelling and formation of derivatives, and exercises in false orthography.

**4. Smith's Speller and Definer's Manual . 90**

A complete *School Dictionary* containing 14,000 words, with various other useful matter in the way of Rules and Exercises.

**5. Smith's Etymology**—Small, 75; Complete . 1 25

The first and only Etymology to recognize the *Anglo-Saxon* our *mother tongue;* containing also full lists of derivatives from the Latin, Greek, Gaelic, Swedish, Norman, &c., &c; being, in fact, a complete etymology of the language for schools.

**Sherwood's Writing Speller . . . . . . . 15**

**Sherwood's Speller and Definer . . . . . 15**

**Sherwood's Speller and Pronouncer . . . 15**

The Writing Speller consists of properly ruled and numbered blanks to receive the words dictated by the teacher, with space for remarks and corrections. The other volumes may be used for the dictation or ordinary class exercises.

**Price's English Speller . . . . . . . . . . *15**

A complete spelling-book for all grades, containing more matter than "Webster," manufactured in superior style, and sold at a lower price—consequently the cheapest speller extant.

**Northend's Dictation Exercises . . . . . 65**

Embracing valuable information on a thousand topics, communicated in such a manner as at once to relieve the exercise of spelling of its usual tedium, and combine it with instruction of a general character calculated to profit and amuse.

**Wright's Analytical Orthography . . . . 25**

This standard work is popular, because it teaches the elementary sounds in a plain and philosophical manner, and presents orthography and orthoepy in an easy, uniform system of analysis or parsing.

**Fowle's False Orthography . . . . . . . . 45**

Exercises for correction.

**Page's Normal Chart . . . . . . . . . .*3 75**

The elementary sounds of the language for the school-room walls.

RTHOGRAPHY—Continued.

**:arber's Critical Writing Speller. . . . . 20 cts.**

"The Student's Own Hand-Book of Orthography, Definitions, and Sentences, nsisting of Written Exercises in the Proper Spelling, Meaning, and Use of 'ords." (Published 1873.) This differs from Sherwood's and other Writing ellers in its more comprehensive character. Its blanks are adapted to writing iole sentences instead of detached words, with the proper divisions for number-g, corrections, etc. Such aids as this, like Watson's Child's Speller and Sher-od's Writing Speller, find their *raison d'être* in the postulate that the art of cor-ct spelling is dependent upon written, and not upon spoken language, for its util-, if not for its very existence. Hence the indirectness of purely oral instruction.

# ETYMOLOGY.

**mith's Complete Etymology, . . . . . . . $1 25**

**nith's Condensed Etymology, . . . . . . 75**

:ontaining the Anglo-Saxon, French, Dutch, German, Welsh, Danish, Gothic, edish, Gaelic, Italian, Latin, and Greek Roots, and the English words derived :refrom accurately spelled, accented, and defined.

*From* HON. JNO. G. MCMYNN, *late State Superintendent of Wisconsin.*

wish every teacher in the country had a copy of this work.

*From* PRIN. WM. F. PHELPS, *Minn. State Normal.*

:he book is superb—just what is needed in the department of etymology and :lling.

*From* PROF. C. H. VERRILL, *Pa. State Normal School.*

'he Etymology (Smith's) which we procured of you we like much. It is the :t work for the class-room we have seen.

*From* HON. EDWARD BALLARD, *Supt. of Common Schools, State of Maine.*

:any a teacher who has turned his attention to the derivation of words has oiced in the helps furnished by dictionaries and smaller "hand-books," where taste could be gratified, and the labors of patient students have been available his own improvement. A treatise on this subject, called "A Complete Ety-logy of the English Language," contains very much information in a small space. : author, W. W. Smith, is evidently a lover of this branch of study, and has fur-hed a manual of singular utility for its purpose.

# DICTIONARY.

**ıe Topical Lexicon, . . . . . . . . . . . 1 75**

his work is a School Dictionary, an Etymology, a compilation of synonyms, and :anual of general information. It differs from the ordinary lexicon in being -nged by topics instead of the letters of the alphabet, thus realizing the apparent :dox of a "Readable Dictionary." An unusually valuable school-book.

# ENGLISH GRAMMAR.

## CLARK'S DIAGRAM SYSTEM.

### Clark's Easy Lessons in Language, . . . $0 35

Published 1874. Contains illustrated object-lessons of the most attractive charac. ter, and is couched in language freed as much as possible from the dry technicalities of the science.

### Clark's Brief English Grammar, . . . . . 60

Published 1872. Part I. is adapted to youngest learners, and the whole forms a complete "brief course" in one volume, adequate to the wants of the common school.

### Clark's Normal Grammar, . . . . . . . . . 1 00

Published 1870, and designed to take the place of Prof. Clark's veteran "Practical" Grammar, though the latter is still furnished upon order. The Normal is an entirely new treatise. It is a full exposition of the system as described below with all the most recent improvements. Some of its peculiarities are—A happy blending of SYNTHESES with ANALYSES; thorough Criticisms of common errors in the use of our Language; and important improvements in the Syntax of Sentences and of Phrases.

### Clark's Key to the Diagrams, . . . . . . . 1 0C

### Clark's Analysis of the English Language, . 6(

### Clark's Grammatical Chart, . . . . . . . . *3 7[illegible]

The theory and practice of teaching grammar in American schools is meetin with a thorough revolution from the use of this system. While the old method offer proficiency to the pupil only after much weary plodding and dull memorizing this affords from the inception the advantage of *practical Object Teaching*, addressing the eye by means of illustrative figures; furnishes association to the memory its most powerful aid, and diverts the pupil by taxing his ingenuity. Teacher who are using Clark's Grammar uniformly testify that they and their pupils find the most interesting study of the school course.

Like all great and radical improvements, the system naturally met at first wit much unreasonable opposition. It has not only outlived the greater part of th opposition, but finds many of its warmest admirers among those who could nc at first tolerate so radical an innovation. All it wants is an impartial trial to coi vince the most skeptical of its merit. No one who has fairly and intelligenti tested it in the school-room has ever been known to go back to the old metho A great success is already established, and it is easy to prophecy that the day i not far distant when it will be the *only system of teaching English Grammar.* A the SYSTEM is copyrighted, no other text-books can appropriate this obvious ar great improvement.

---

### Welch's Analysis of the English Sentence, . 1 2

Remarkable for its new and simple classification, its method of treating connc tives, its explanations of the idioms and constructive laws of the language, etc.

# Clark's Diagram English Grammar.

## TESTIMONIALS.

*From* J. A. T. DURNIN, *Principal Dubuque R. C. Academy, Iowa.*

In my opinion, it is well calculated by its system of analysis to develop those rational faculties which in the old systems were rather left to develop themselves, while the memory was overtaxed, and the pupils discouraged.

*From* B. A. COX, *School Commissioner, Warren County, Illinois.*

I have examined 150 teachers in the last year, and those having studied or taught Clark's System have universally stood fifty per cent. better examinations than those having studied other authors.

*From* M. H. B. BURKET, *Principal Masonic Institute, Georgetown, Tennessee.*

I traveled two years amusing myself in instructing (exclusively) Grammar classes with Clark's system. The first class I instructed fifty days, but found that this was more time than was required to impart a theoretical knowledge of the science. During the two years thereafter I instructed classes only *thirty* days each. Invariably I proposed that unless I prepared my classes for a more thorough, minute, and accurate knowledge of English Grammar than that obtained from the ordinary books and in the ordinary way in from one to two years, I would make no charge. I never failed in a solitary case to far exceed the hopes of my classes, and made money and character rapidly as an instructor.

*From* A. B. DOUGLASS, *School Commissioner, Delaware County, New York.*

I have never known a class pursue the study of it under a *live* teacher, that has not succeeded; I have never known it to have an opponent in an educated teacher who had *thoroughly* investigated it; I have never known an *ignorant* teacher to examine it; I have never known a teacher who has used it, to try any other.

*From* J. A. DODGE, *Teacher and Lecturer on English Grammar, Kentucky.*

We are tempted to assert that it foretells the dawn of a brighter age to our mother-tongue. Both pupil and teacher can fare sumptuously upon its contents, however highly they may have prized the manuals into which they may have been initiated, and by which their expressions have been moulded.

*From* W. T. CHAPMAN, *Superintendent Public Schools, Wellington, Ohio.*

I regard Clark's System of Grammar the best published. For teaching the analysis of the English Language, it surpasses any I ever used.

*From* F. S. LYON, *Principal South Norwalk Union School, Connecticut.*

During ten years' experience in teaching, I have used six different authors on the subject of English Grammar. I am fully convinced that Clark's Grammar is better calculated to make thorough grammarians than any other that I have seen.

*From* CATALOGUE OF ROHRER'S COMMERCIAL COLLEGE, *St. Louis, Missouri.*

We do not hesitate to assert, without fear of successful contradiction, that a better knowledge of the English language can be obtained by this system in six weeks than by the old methods in as many months.

*From* A. PICKETT, *President of the State Teachers' Association, Wisconsin.*

A thorough experiment in the use of many approved authors upon the subject of English Grammar has convinced me of the superiority of Clark. When the pupil has completed the course, he is left upon a foundation of *principle*, and not upon the *dictum* of the author.

*From* GEO. F. MCFARLAND, *Prin. McAllisterville Academy, Juniata Co., Penn.*

At the first examination of public-school teachers by the county superintendent, when one of our student teachers commenced analyzing a sentence according to Clark, the superintendent listened in mute astonishment until he had finished, then asked what that meant, and finally, with a very knowing look, said such work wouldn't do here, and asked the applicant to parse the sentence right, and gave the lowest certificates to all who barely mentioned Clark. Afterwards, I presented him with a copy, and the next fall he permitted it to be partially used, while the third of last fall, he openly commended the system, and appointed three of my best teachers to explain it at the two Institutes and one County Convention held since September.

☞ For further testimony of equal force, see the **Publishers' Special Circular, or current numbers of the Educational Bulletin.**

# GEOGRAPHY.

## NATIONAL GEOGRAPHICAL SYSTEM.

### THE SERIES.

| | | |
|---|---|---|
| I. | **Monteith's First Lessons in Geography,** . . . | $ 35 |
| II. | **Monteith's New Manual of Geography,** . . . | 1 10 |
| II. | **McNally's System of Geography,** . . . . . | 2 00 |

INTERMEDIATE OR ALTERNATE VOLUMES.

| | | |
|---|---|---|
| I*. | **Monteith's Introduction to Geography,** . . . . . . | 63 |
| 2*. | **Monteith's Physical and Political Geography,** . . . | 1 88 |

### ACCESSORIES.

| | |
|---|---|
| **Monteith's Wall Maps** 2 sets (see page 15), $*20 00 and | *35 00 |
| **Monteith's Manual of Map-Drawing** (Allen's System) . | 25 |
| **Monteith's Map-Drawing and Object-Lessons,** . . | 75 |
| **Monteith's Map-Drawing Scale,** . . . . . . | *25 |

1. PRACTICAL OBJECT TEACHING. The infant scholar is first introduced to *a picture* whence he may derive notions of the shape of the earth, the phenomena of day and night, the distribution of land and water, and the great natural divisions, which mere words would fail entirely to convey to the untutored mind. Other pictures follow on the same plan, and the child's mind is called upon to grasp no idea without the aid of a pictorial illustration. Carried on to the higher books, this system culminates in Physical Geography, where such matters as climates, ocean currents, the winds, peculiarities of the earth's crust, clouds and rain, are pictorially explained and rendered apparent to the most obtuse. The illustrations used for this purpose belong to the highest grade of art.

2. CLEAR, BEAUTIFUL, AND CORRECT MAPS. In the lower numbers the maps avoid unnecessary detail, while respectively progressive, and affording the pupil new matter for acquisition each time he approaches in the constantly enlarging circle the point of coincidence with previous lessons in the more elementary books. In the Physical and Political Geography the maps embrace many new and striking features. One of the most effective of these is the new plan for displaying on each map the relative sizes of countries not represented, thus obviating much confusion which has arisen from the necessity of presenting maps in the same atlas drawn on different scales. The maps of "McNally" have long been celebrated for their superior beauty and completeness. This is the only school-book in which the attempt to make a *complete* atlas *also clear and distinct*, has been successful. The map *coloring* throughout the series is also noticeable. Delicate and subdued tints take the place of the startling glare of inharmonious colors which too frequently in such treatises dazzle the eyes, distract the attention, and serve to overwhelm the names of towns and the natural features of the landscape.

GEOGRAPHY—Continued.

3. **THE VARIETY OF MAP EXERCISE.** Starting each time from a different basis, the pupil in many instances approaches the same fact no less than *six times*, thus indelibly impressing it upon his memory. At the same time this system is not allowed to become wearisome—the extent of exercise on each subject being graduated by its relative importance or difficulty of acquisition.

4. **THE CHARACTER AND ARRANGEMENT OF THE DESCRIPTIVE TEXT.** The cream of the science has been carefully culled, unimportant matter rejected, elaboration avoided, and a brief and concise manner of presentation cultivated. The orderly consideration of topics has contributed greatly to simplicity. Due attention is paid to the facts in history and astronomy which are inseparably connected with, and important to the proper understanding of geography—and *such only* are admitted on any terms. In a word, the National System teaches geography as a science, pure, simple, and exhaustive.

5. **ALWAYS UP TO THE TIMES.** The authors of these books, editorially speaking, never sleep. No change occurs in the boundaries of countries, or of counties, no new discovery is made, or railroad built, that is not at once noted and recorded, and the next edition of each volume carries to every school-room the new order of things.

6. **SUPERIOR GRADATION.** This is the only series which furnishes an available volume for every possible class in graded schools. It is not contemplated that a pupil must necessarily go through every volume in succession to attain proficiency. On the contrary, *two* will suffice, but *three* are advised; and if the course will admit, the whole series should be pursued. At all events, the books are at hand for selection, and every teacher, of every grade, can find among them one *exactly suited* to his class. The best combination for those who wish to abridge the course consists of Nos. 1, 2, and 3, or where children are somewhat advanced in other studies when they commence geography, Nos. 1*, 2, and 3. Where but *two* books are admissible, Nos. 1* and 2*, or Nos. 2 and 3, are recommended.

7. **FORM OF THE VOLUMES AND MECHANICAL EXECUTION.** The maps and text are no longer unnaturally divorced in accordance with the time-honored practice of making text-books on this subject as inconvenient and expensive as possible. On the contrary, all map questions are to be found on the page opposite the map itself, and each book is complete in one volume. The mechanical execution is unrivalled. Paper and printing are everything that could be desired, and the binding is—A. S. Barnes and Company's.

8. **MAP-DRAWING.** In 1869 the system of Map-Drawing devised by Professor JEROME ALLEN was secured *exclusively* for this series. It derives its claim to originality and usefulness from the introduction of a *fixed unit of measurement* applicable to every Map. The principles being so few, simple and comprehensive, the subject of Map-Drawing is relieved of all practical difficulty. (In Nos. 2, 2*, and 3, and published separately.)

8. **ANALOGOUS OUTLINES.** At the same time with Map-Drawing was also introduced (in No. 2), a new and ingenious variety of Object Lessons, consisting of a comparison of the outlines of countries with familiar objects pictorially represented.

GEOGRAPHY—Continued.

## MONTEITH'S INDEPENDENT COURSE.

**Elementary Geography** (published 1874) . . $0 80

**Comprehensive Geography** (with 103 Maps) . 1 60

☞ These volumes are not revisions of old works—not an addition to any series—but are entirely new productions—each by itself complete, independent, comprehensive, yet simple, brief, cheap, and popular; or, taken together, the most admirable "series" ever offered for a common-school course. They present the following features, skillfully interwoven—the student learning all about one country at a time.

**LOCAL GEOGRAPHY,** or the Use of Maps. Important features of the Maps are the coloring of States as objects, and the ingenious system for laying down a much larger number of names for reference than are found on any other Maps of same size—and without crowding.

**PHYSICAL GEOGRAPHY,** or the Natural Features of the Earth, illustrated by the original and striking ***Relief Maps,*** being bird's-eye views or photographic pictures of the Earth's surface.

**DESCRIPTIVE GEOGRAPHY,** including the Physical; with some account of Governments, and Races, Animals, etc.

**HISTORICAL GEOGRAPHY,** or a brief summary of the salient points of history, explaining the present distribution of nations, origin of geographical names, etc.

**MATHEMATICAL GEOGRAPHY,** including ASTRONOMICAL, which describes the Earth's position and character among planets; also the Zones, Parallels, etc.

**COMPARATIVE GEOGRAPHY,** or a system of analogy, connecting new lessons with the previous ones. Comparative sizes and latitudes are shown on the margin of each Map, and all countries are measured in the "*frame of Kansas.*"

**TOPICAL GEOGRAPHY,** consisting of questions for review, and testing the student's general and specific knowledge of the subject, with suggestions for *Geographical Compositions.*

**ANCIENT GEOGRAPHY.** A section devoted to this subject, with Maps, will be appreciated by teachers. It is seldom taught in our common schools because it has heretofore required the purchase of a separate book.

**GRAPHIC GEOGRAPHY,** or MAP-DRAWING by Allen's "Unit of Measurement" system (now almost universally recognized as without a rival) is introduced throughout the lessons, and not as an appendix.

**CONSTRUCTIVE GEOGRAPHY,** or GLOBE-MAKING. With each book a set of Map Segments is furnished, with which each student may make his own Globe by following the directions given.

**RAILROAD GEOGRAPHY,** with a grand Map illustrating routes of travel in the United States. Also, a "Tour in Europe."

# The National System of Geography,

BY MONTEITH & MCNALLY.

ITS RECORD.

These popular text-books have been adopted, by official authority, for the schools of the following States and Cities—in most cases for *exclusive* and uniform use.

## STATES.

**California, Missouri, Alabama, Tennessee, Texas, Vermont, Iowa, Louisiana, Oregon, Arkansas, Florida, Minnesota, North Carolina, Kansas, Mississippi.**

## CITIES.

New York City, Brooklyn, New Orleans, Buffalo, Richmond, Jersey City, Hartford, Worcester, San Francisco, &c.

Louisville, Newark, Milwaukee, Charleston, Rochester, Mobile, Syracuse, Memphis, Salt Lake City, &c.

Nashville, Utica, Wilmington, Trenton, Norfolk, Norwich, Lockport, Dubuque, Galveston, &c.

Portland, Savannah, Indianapolis, Springfield, Wheeling, Toledo, Bridgeport, St. Paul, Vicksburg, &c.

---

# STANDARD WALL MAPS.

By JAMES MONTEITH.

**Monteith's School Maps,** 8 Numbers, per set *$20 00

The "School Series" includes the Hemispheres (2 Maps), United States, North America, South America, Europe, Asia, Africa.—Price. $2.50 each.

Each Map is 28 x 34 inches, beautifully colored, has the names all laid down, and is substantially mounted on canvas with rollers.

**Monteith's Grand Maps,** 7 Numbers, per set (in locked box) . . . . . . . . . . . . *35 00

The "Grand Series" includes the Hemispheres (1 Map), United States, South America, Europe, Asia, Africa, The World on Mercator's Projection.—Price, $5.00 each. Size 42 x 52 inches, names laid down, colored, mounted, &c., like the School Series.

# Monteith & McNally's National Geographies.

## CRITICAL OPINIONS.

*From* R. A. ADAMS, *Member of Board of Education, New York.*

I have found, by examination of the Book of Supply of our Board, that considerably the largest number of any series now used in our public schools is the National, by Monteith and McNally.

*From* BRO. PATRICK, *Chief Provincial of the Vast Educational Society of the* CHRISTIAN BROTHERS *in the United States.*

Having been convinced for some time past that the series of Geographies in use in our schools were not giving satisfaction, and came far short of meeting our most reasonable expectations, I have felt it my imperative duty to examine into this matter, and see if a remedy could not be found.

Copies of the different Geographies published in this country have been placed at our command for examination. On account of other pressing duties we have not been able to give as much time to the investigation of all these different series as we could have desired; yet we have found enough to convince us that there are many others better than those we are now using; but we cheerfully give our most decided preference, above all others, to the National Series, by Monteith & McNally.

Their easy gradation, their thoroughly practical and independent character, their comprehensive completeness as a full and accurate system, the wise discrimination shown in the selection of the subject matter, the beautiful and copious illustrations, the neat cut type, the general execution of the works, and *other excellencies*, will commend them to the friends of education everywhere.

*From the* "HOME MONTHLY," *Nashville, Tenn.*

MONTEITH'S AND MCNALLY'S GEOGRAPHIES.—Geography is so closely connected with Astronomy, History, Ethnology, and Geology, that it is difficult to define its limits in the construction of a text-book. If the author confines himself strictly to a description of the earth's surface, his book will be dry, meager, and unintelligible to a child. If, on the other hand, he attempts to give information on the cognate sciences, he enters a boundless field, and may wander too far. It seems to us that the authors of the series before us have hit on the happy medium between too much and too little. *The First Lessons*, by applying the system of object-teaching, renders the subject so attractive that a child, just able to read, may become deeply interested in it. The second book of the course enlarges the view, but still keeps to the maps and simple descriptions. Then, in the third book, we have Geography combined with History and Astronomy. A general view of the solar system is presented, so that the pupil may understand the earth's position on the map of the heavens. The first part of the fourth book treats of Physical Geography, and contains a vast amount of knowledge compressed into a small space. It is made bright and attractive by beautiful pictures and suggestive illustrations, on the principle of object-teaching. The maps in the second part of this volume are remarkably clear, and the map exercises are copious and judicious. In the fifth and last volume of the series, the whole subject is reviewed and systematized. This is strictly a Geography. Its maps are beautifully engraved and clearly printed. The map exercises are full and comprehensive. In all these books the maps, questions and descriptions are given in the same volume. In most geographies there are too many details and minute descriptions—more than any child out of purgatory ought to be required to learn. The power of memory is overstrained; there is confusion—no clearly defined idea is formed in the child's mind. But in these books, in brief, pointed descriptions, and constant use of bright, accurate maps, the whole subject is photographed on the mind.

# MATHEMATICS.

# DAVIES' NATIONAL COURSE.

## ARITHMETIC.

| | | | SLATED. |
|---|---|---|---|
| 1. | Davies' Primary Arithmetic, | $ 25 | $ 32 |
| 2. | Davies' Intellectual Arithmetic, | 40 | 48 |
| 3. | Davies' Elements of Written Arithmetic, | 50 | 60 |
| 4. | Davies' Practical Arithmetic, | 90 | 1 00 |
| | Key to Practical Arithmetic, | 90 | |
| 5. | Davies' University Arithmetic, | 1 40 | 1 50 |
| | Key to University Arithmetic, | *1 40 | |

## ALGEBRA.

| | | | |
|---|---|---|---|
| 1. | Davies' New Elementary Algebra, | *1 25 | 1 35 |
| | Key to Elementary Algebra, | *1 25 | |
| 2. | Davies' University Algebra, | 1 50 | 1 60 |
| | Key to University Algebra, | *1 50 | |
| 3. | Davies' New Bourdon's Algebra, | 2 25 | 2 38 |
| | Key to Bourdon's Algebra, | *2 25 | |

## GEOMETRY.

| | | | |
|---|---|---|---|
| 1. | Davies' Elementary Geometry and Trigonometry, | 1 40 | 1 50 |
| 2. | Davies' Legendre's Geometry, | 2 25 | 2 38 |
| 3. | Davies' Analytical Geometry and Calculus, | 2 50 | 2 63 |
| 4. | Davies' Descriptive Geometry, | 2 75 | 2 88 |
| 5. | Davies' New Calculus, | 2 00 | |

## MENSURATION.

| | | | |
|---|---|---|---|
| 1. | Davies' Practical Mathematics and Mensuration, | 1 50 | 1 60 |
| 2. | Davies' Elements of Surveying, | 2 50 | 2 63 |
| 3. | Davies' Shades, Shadows, and Perspective, | 3 75 | 3 88 |

## MATHEMATICAL SCIENCE.

| | |
|---|---|
| Davies' Grammar of Arithmetic, | * 50 |
| Davies' Outlines of Mathematical Science, | *1 00 |
| Davies' Nature and Utility of Mathematics, 8vo, *2 00, 12mo, | *1 50 |
| Davies' Metric System, | *1 50 |
| Davies & Peck's Dictionary of Mathematics, | *5 00 |
| Davies' Foundations Mathematical Science, | * 25 |

MATHEMATICS—Continued.

## ARITHMETICAL EXAMPLES.

**Reuck's Examples in Denominate Numbers** $ 50

**Reuck's Examples in Arithmetic** . . . . . 1 00

These volumes differ from the ordinary arithmetic in their peculiarly *practical* character. They are composed mainly of examples, and afford the most severe and thorough discipline for the mind. While a book which should contain a complete treatise of theory and practice would be too cumbersome for every-day use, the insufficiency of *practical* examples has been a source of complaint.

## HIGHER MATHEMATICS.

**Church's Elements of Calculus** . . . . . . 2 50

**Church's Analytical Geometry** . . . . . . 2 50

**Church's Descriptive Geometry,** with Shades, Shadows, and Perspective . . . . . . . . 4 00

These volumes constitute the "West Point Course" in their several departments.

**Courtenay's Elements of Calculus** . . . . 3 00

A work especially popular at the South.

**Hackley's Trigonometry** . . . . . . . . . . 2 50

With applications to navigation and surveying, nautical and practical geometry and geodesy.

**Peck's Analytical Geometry** . . . . . . . 1 75

**Peck's Practical Calculus** . . . . . . . . . 1 75

## APPLIED MATHEMATICS.

**Peck's Ganot's Popular Physics** . . . . . . 1 75

**Peck's Elements of Mechanics** . . . . . . 2 00

**Peck's Practical Calculus** . . . . . . . . 1 75

**Peck's Analytical Geometry,** . . . . . . . 1 75

Prof. W. G. Peck, of Columbia College, has designed the first of these works for the ordinary wants of schools in the department of Natural Philosophy. The other volumes are the briefest treatises on those subjects now published. Their methods are purely practical, and unembarrassed by the details which rather confuse than simplify science.

## SLATED ARITHMETICS.

This consists of the application of an artificially slated surface to the inner cover of a book, with flap of the same opening outward, so that students may refer to the book and use the slate at one and the same time, and as though the slate were detached. When folded up, the slate preserves examples and memoranda till needed. The material used is as durable as the stone slate. The additional cost of books thus improved is trifling.

# Davies' National Course of Mathematics.

## TESTIMONIALS.

*From* L. VAN BOKKELEN, *State Superintendent Public Instruction, Maryland.*

The series of Arithmetics edited by Prof. Davies, and published by your firm, have been used for many years in the schools of several counties, and the city of Baltimore, and have been approved by teachers and commissioners.

Under the law of 1865, establishing a uniform system of Free Public Schools, these Arithmetics were unanimously adopted by the State Board of Education, after a careful examination, and are now used in all the Public Schools of Maryland.

These facts evidence the high opinion entertained by the School Authorities of the value of the series theoretically and practically.

*From* HORACE WEBSTER, *President of the College of New York.*

The undersigned has examined, with care and thought, several volumes of Davies' Mathematics, and is of the opinion that, as a whole, it is the most complete and best course for Academic and Collegiate instruction, with which he is acquainted.

*From* DAVID N. CAMP, *State Superintendent of Common Schools, Connecticut.*

I have examined Davies' Series of Arithmetics with some care. The language is clear and precise; each principle is thoroughly analyzed, and the whole so arranged as to facilitate the work of instruction. Having observed the satisfaction and success with which the different books have been used by eminent teachers, it gives me pleasure to commend them to others.

*From* J. O. WILSON, *Chairman Committee on Text-Books, Washington, D. C.*

I consider Davies' Arithmetics decidedly superior to any other series, and in this opinion I am sustained, I believe, by the entire Board of Education and Corps of Teachers in this city, where they have been used for several years past.

*From* JOHN L. CAMPBELL, *Professor of Mathematics, Wabash College, Indiana.*

A proper combination of abstract reasoning and practical illustration is the chief excellence in Prof. Davies' Mathematical works. I prefer his Arithmetics, Algebras, Geometry and Trigonometry to all others now in use, and cordially recommend them to all who desire the advancement of sound learning.

*From* MAJOR J. H. WHITTLESEY, *Government Inspector of Military Schools.*

Be assured, I regard the works of Prof. Davies, with which I am acquainted, as by far the best text-books in print on the subjects which they treat. I shall certainly encourage their adoption wherever a word from me may be of any avail.

*From* T. McC. BALLANTINE, *Prof. Mathematics Cumberland College, Kentucky.*

I have long taught Prof. Davies' Course of Mathematics, and I continue to like their working.

*From* JOHN McLEAN BELL, B. A., *Prin. of Lower Canada College.*

I have used Davies' Arithmetical and Mathematical Series as text-books in the schools under my charge for the last six years. These I have found of great efficacy in exciting, invigorating, and concentrating the intellectual faculties of the young.

Each treatise serves as an introduction to the next higher, by the similarity of its reasonings and methods; and the student is carried forward, by easy and gradual steps, over the whole field of mathematical inquiry, and that, too, in a *shorter* time than is usually occupied in mastering a single department. I sincerely and heartily recommend them to the attention of my fellow-teachers in Canada.

*From* D. W. STEELE, *Prin. Philekoian Academy, Cold Springs, Texas.*

I have used Davies' Arithmetics till I know them nearly by heart. A better series of school-books never were published. I have recommended them until they are now used in all this region of country.

---

A large mass of similar "Opinions" may be obtained by addressing the publishers for special circular for Davies' Mathematics. New recommendations are published in current numbers of the *Educational Bulletin.*

# DAVIES' NATIONAL COURSE of MATHEMATICS.

## ITS RECORD.

In claiming for this series the first place among American text-books, of what ever class, the Publishers appeal to the magnificent record which its volumes have earned during the *thirty-five years* of Dr. Charles Davies' mathematical labors. The unremitting exertions of a life-time have placed *the modern series* on the same proud eminence among competitors that each of its predecessors has successively enjoyed in a course of constantly improved editions, now rounded to their perfect fruition—for it seems almost that this science is susceptible of no further demonstration.

During the period alluded to, many authors and editors in this department have started into public notice, and by borrowing ideas and processes original with Dr. Davies, have enjoyed a brief popularity, but are now almost unknown. Many of the series of to-day, built upon a similar basis, and described as "modern books," are destined to a similar fate; while the most far-seeing eye will find it difficult to fix the time, on the basis of any data afforded by their past history, when these books will cease to increase and prosper, and fix a still firmer hold on the affection of every educated American.

One cause of this unparalleled popularity is found in the fact that the enterprise of the author did not cease with the original completion of his books. Always a practical teacher, he has incorporated in his text-books from time to time the advantages of every improvement in methods of teaching, and every advance in science. During all the years in which he has been laboring, he constantly submitted his own theories and those of others to the practical test of the class-room—approving, rejecting, or modifying them as the experience thus obtained might suggest. In this way he has been able to produce an almost perfect series of class-books, in which every department of mathematics has received minute and exhaustive attention.

Nor has he yet retired from the field. Still in the prime of life, and enjoying a ripe experience which no other living mathematician or teacher can emulate, his pen is ever ready to carry on the good work, as the progress of science may demand. Witness his recent exposition of the "Metric System," which received the official endorsement of Congress, by its Committee on Uniform Weights and Measures.

---

Davies' System is the acknowledged National Standard for the United States, for the following reasons:—

1st. It is the basis of instruction in the great national schools at West Point and Annapolis.

2d. It has received the *quasi* endorsement of the National Congress.

3d. It is exclusively used in the public schools of the National Capital.

4th. The officials of the Government use it as authority in all cases involving mathematical questions.

5th. Our great soldiers and sailors commanding the national armies and navies were educated in this system. So have been a majority of eminent scientists in this country. All these refer to "Davies" as authority.

6th. A larger number of American citizens have received their education from this than from any other series.

7th. The series has a larger circulation throughout the whole country than any other, being *extensively used in every State in the Union.*

MATHEMATICS—Continued.

# PECK'S ARITHMETICS.

By the Prof. of Mathematics at Columbia College, New York.

## 1. Peck's First Lessons in Numbers, . . . $0 25

Embracing all that is usually included in what are called Primary and Intellectual Arithmetics; proceeding gradually from object lessons to abstract numbers; developing Addition and Subtraction simultaneously: with other attractive novelties.

## 2. Peck's Manual of Practical Arithmetic, . 50

An excellent "Brief" course, conveying a sufficient knowledge of Arithmetic for ordinary business purposes.

It is thoroughly "practical," because the author believes the Theory cannot be studied with advantage until the pupil has acquired a certain facility in combining numbers, which can only be had by practice.

## 3. Peck's Complete Arithmetic, . . . . . 90

The whole subject—theory and practice—presented within very moderate limits. This author's most remarkable faculty of mathematical treatment is comprehended in three words: System, Conciseness, Lucidity. The directness and simplicity of this work cannot be better expressed than in the words of a correspondent who adopted the book at once, because, as he said, it is "free from that *juggling with numbers*" practiced by many authors.

*From the "Galaxy," New York.*

In the "Complete Arithmetic" each part of the subject is logically developed. First are given the necessary definitions; second, the explanations of such signs (if any) as are used; third, the principles on which the operation depends; fourth, an exemplification of the manner in which the operation is performed, which is so conducted that the reason of the rule which is immediately thereafter deduced is made perfectly plain; after which follow numerous graded examples and corresponding practical problems. All the parts taken together are arranged in logical order. The subject is treated as a whole, and not as if made up of segregated parts. It may seem a simple remark to make that (for example) addition is in principle one and the same everywhere, whether employed upon simple or compound numbers, fractions, etc., the only difference being in the *unit* involved; but the number of persons who understand this practically, compared to the number who have studied arithmetic, is not very great. The student of the "Complete Arithmetic" cannot fail to understand it. All the principles of the science are presented within moderate limits. Superfluity of matter—to supplement defective definitions, to make clear faulty demonstrations and rules expressed either inaccurately or obscurely, to make provision for a multiplicity of cases for which no provision is requisite—has been carefully avoided. The definitions are plain and concise; the principles are stated clearly and accurately; the demonstrations are full and complete; the rules are perspicuous and comprehensive; the illustrative examples are abundant and well fitted to familiarize the student with the application of principles to the problems of science and of every-day life.

☞ The Definitions constitute the power of the book. We have never seen them excelled for clearness and exactness.—*Iowa School Journal.*

# PENMANSHIP.

## Beers' System of Progressive Penmanship.

Per dozen . . . . . . . . . . . . $1 68

This "round hand" system of Penmanship in twelve numbers, commends itself by its simplicity and thoroughness. The first four numbers are primary books. Nos. 5 to 7, advanced books for boys. Nos. 8 to 10, advanced books for girls. Nos. 11 and 12, ornamental penmanship. These books are printed from steel plates (engraved by McLees), and are unexcelled in mechanical execution. Large quantities are annually sold.

## Beers' Slated Copy Slips, per set . . . . . *50

All beginners should practice, for a few weeks, slate exercises, familiarizing them with the form of the letters, the motions of the hand and arm, &c., &c. These copy slips, 32 in number, supply all the copies found in a complete series of writing-books, at a trifling cost.

## Payson, Dunton & Scribner's Copy-B'ks. P. doz., *1 80

The National System of Penmanship, in three distinct series—(1) Common School Series, comprising the first six numbers; (2) Business Series, Nos. 8, 11, and 12; (3) Ladies' Series, Nos. 7, 9, and 10.

## Fulton & Eastman's Chirographic Charts, *3 75

To embellish the school room walls, and furnish class exercise in the elements of Penmanship.

## Payson's Copy-Book Cover, per hundred . *4 00

Protects every page except the one in use, and furnishes "lines" with proper slope for the penman, under. Patented.

## National Steel Pens, Card with all kinds . . . *15

Pronounced by competent judges the perfection of American-made pens, and superior to any foreign article.

| Pen | Price |
|---|---|
| SCHOOL SERIES. | |
| School Pen, per gross, . . | $ 60 |
| Academic Pen, do . . | 63 |
| Fine Pointed Pen, per gross | 70 |
| POPULAR SERIES. | |
| Capitol Pen, per gross, . . | 1 00 |
| do do pr. box of 2 doz. | 25 |
| Bullion Pen (imit. gold) pr. gr. | 75 |
| Ladies' Pen do | 63 |
| Index Pen, per gross . . . | 75 |
| BUSINESS SERIES. | |
| Albata Pen, per gross, . . | 40 |
| Bank Pen, do . . | 70 |
| Empire Pen, do . . | 70 |
| Commercial Pen, per gross . | 60 |
| Express Pen, do . | 75 |
| Falcon Pen, do . | 70 |
| Elastic Pen, do . | 75 |

## Stimpson's Scientific Steel Pen, per gross . *2 00

One forward and two backward arches, ensuring great strength, well-balanced elasticity, evenness of point, and smoothness of execution. One gross in twelve contains a Scientific Gold Pen.

## Stimpson's Ink-Retaining Holder, per doz. . *2 00

A simple apparatus, which does not get out of order, withholds at a single dip as much ink as the pen would otherwise realize from a dozen trips to the inkstand, which it supplies with moderate and easy flow.

## Stimpson's Gold Pen, $3 00; with Ink Retainer *4 50

## Stimpson's Penman's Card, . . . . . . . * 50

One dozen Steel Pens (assorted points) and Patent Ink-retaining Pen holder.

# HISTORY.

**Monteith's Youth's History,** . . . . . . . .$ 75

A History of the United States for beginners. It is arranged upon the catechetical plan, with illustrative maps and engravings, review questions, dates in parentheses (that their study may be optional with the younger class of learners), and interesting Biographical Sketches of all persons who have been prominently identified with the history of our country.

**Willard's United States,** School edition, . . . 1 40
Do. do. University edition, . 2 25

The plan of this standard work is chronologically exhibited in front of the title-page; the Maps and Sketches are found useful assistants to the memory, and dates, usually so difficult to remember, are so systematically arranged as in a great degree to obviate the difficulty. Candor, impartiality, and accuracy, are the distinguishing features of the narrative portion.

**Willard's Universal History,** . . . . . . 2 25

The most valuable features of the "United States" are reproduced in this. The peculiarities of the work are its great conciseness and the prominence given to the chronological order of events. The margin marks each successive era with great distinctness, so that the pupil retains not only the event but its time, and thus fixes the order of history firmly and usefully in his mind. Mrs. Willard's books are constantly revised, and at all times written up to embrace important historical events of recent date.

**Berard's History of England,** . . . . . . 1

By an authoress well known for the success of her History of the United States. The social life of the English people is felicitously interwoven, as in fact, with the civil and military transactions of the realm.

**Ricord's History of Rome,** . . . . . . . . 1 75

Possesses the charm of an attractive romance. The Fables with which this history abounds are introduced in such a way as not to deceive the inexperienced, while adding materially to the value of the work as a reliable index to the character and institutions, as well as the history of the Roman people.

**Hanna's Bible History,** . . . . . . . . . . . 1 25

The only compendium of Bible narrative which affords a connected and chronological view of the important events there recorded, divested of all superfluous detail.

**Summary of History,** Complete . . . . . . . 60
American History, $0 40. French and Eng. Hist. 35

A well proportioned outline of leading events, condensing the substance of the more extensive text-book in common use into a series of statements so brief, that every word may be committed to memory, and yet so comprehensive that it presents an accurate though general view of the whole continuous life of nations.

**Marsh's Ecclesiastical History,** . . . . . 2 00
Questions to ditto, . . . . . . . . . . . . 75

Affording the History of the Church in all ages, with accounts of the pagan world during Biblical periods, and the character, rise, and progress of all Religions, as well as the various sects of the worshipers of Christ. The work is entirely non-sectarian, though strictly catholic.

**Mill's History of the Jews,** . . . . . . . 1 75

HISTORY—Continued.

# BARNES' ONE-TERM HISTORY.

## A Brief History of the United States, . . . $1 50

This is probably the MOST ORIGINAL SCHOOL-BOOK published for many years, in any department. A few of its claims are the following:

1. **Brevity.**—The text is complete for Grammar School or intermediate classes, in 290 12mo pages, large type. It may readily be completed, if desired, in one term of study.

2. **Comprehensiveness.**—Though so brief, this book contains the pith of all the wearying contents of the larger manuals, and a great deal more than the memory usually retains from the latter.

3. **Interest** has been a prime consideration. Small books have heretofore been bare, full of dry statistics, unattractive. This one is charmingly written, replete with anecdote, and brilliant with illustration.

4. **Proportion of Events.**—It is remarkable for the discrimination with which the different portions of our history are presented according to their importance. Thus the older works being already large books when the civil war took place, give it less space than that accorded to the Revolution.

5. **Arrangement.**—In six epochs, entitled respectively, Discovery and Settlement. the Colonies, the Revolution, Growth of States, the Civil War, and Current Events.

6. **Catch Words.**—Each paragraph is preceded by its leading thought in prominent type, standing in the student's mind for the whole paragraph.

7. **Key Notes.**—Analogous with this is the idea of grouping battles, etc., about some central event, which relieves the sameness so common in such descriptions, and renders each distinct by some striking peculiarity of its own.

8. **Foot Notes.**—These are crowded with interesting matter that is not strictly a part of history proper. They may be learned or not, at pleasure. They are certain in any event to be read.

9. **Biographies** of all the leading characters are given in full in foot-notes.

10. **Maps.**—Elegant and distinct Maps from engravings on copper-plate, and beautifully colored, precede each epoch, and contain all the places named.

11. **Questions** are at the back of the book, to compel a more independent use of the text. Both text and questions are so worded that the pupil must give intelligent answers IN HIS OWN WORDS. "Yes" and "No" will not do.

12. **Historical Recreations.**—These are additional questions to test the student's knowledge, in review, as: "What trees are celebrated in our history?" "When did a fog save our army?" "What Presidents died in office?" "When was the Mississippi our western boundary?" "Who said, 'I would rather be right than President?'" etc.

13. **The Illustrations,** about seventy in number, are the work of our best artists and engravers, produced at great expense. They are vivid and interesting, and mostly upon subjects never before illustrated in a school-book.

14. **Dates.**—Only the leading dates are given in the text, and these are so associated as to assist the memory, but at the head of each page is the date of the event first mentioned, and at the close of each epoch a summary of events and dates.

15. **The Philosophy of History** is studiously exhibited—the causes and effects of events being distinctly traced and their interconnection shown.

16. **Impartiality.** —All sectional, partisan, or denominational views are avoided. Facts are stated after a careful comparison of all authorities without the least prejudice or favor.

17. **Index.**—A verbal index at the close of the book perfects it as a work of reference.

It will be observed that the above are all particulars in which School Histories have been signally defective, or altogether wanting. Many other claims to favor it shares in common with its predecessors.

HISTORY—Continued.

**Hunter's Historical Games,** with cards . . . $0 75

An invaluable accompaniment for the text-book, by way of stimulating interest in the Class; affording, at once, Amusement and Instruction.

## SOME TESTIMONIALS FOR BARNES' BRIEF HISTORY.

*From* HON. J. M. MCKENZIE, *Supt. Pub. Inst., Nebraska.*

I have examined your "Brief History of the United States," and like it *real well;* and were I teaching a graded school, I think I should use it as a text-book.

*From* HON. H. B. WILSON, *Supt. Pub. Inst., Minnesota.*

I have read with much interest the "One-Term History of the United States." I am much pleased with it. In my judgment, it contains all of the United States history that the majority of pupils in our common schools can spare time to study.

*From* PRES. EDWARD BROOKS, *Millersville State Normal School, Pa.*

It is a work that will be a favorite with teachers and pupils. Its scope and style especially adapt it for use in our public schools. I cordially commend it to teachers desiring to introduce an interesting and practical text-book upon this subject.

*From* PRES. BARKER, *Buffalo State Normal School, N. Y.*

In the copy of your "Brief History," before me, the important items to be learned in history seem most ingeniously brought out and kept in the foreground. These items are *time, persons, places,* and *events.* It has the appearance of an exceedingly fresh and systematic work. I think I shall put it into my classes

*From* PROF. WM. F. ALLEN, *State Univ. of Wisconsin.*

I think the author of the new "Brief History of the United States" has been very successful in combining brevity with sufficient fullness and interest. *Particularly,* he has avoided the excessive number of names and dates that most histories contain. Two features that I like *very much* are the *anecdotes* at the foot of the page and the "*Historical Recreations*" in the Appendix. The latter, I think, is quite a *new* feature, and the other is *very* well executed.

*From* S. G. WRIGHT, *Assist.-Supt. Pub. Inst., Kansas.*

It is with extreme pleasure we submit our recommendation of the "Brief History of the United States." It meets the needs of young and older children, combining concision with perspicuity, and if "brevity is the soul of wit," this "Brief History" contains not only that well-chosen ingredient, but wisdom sufficient to enlighten those students who are wearily longing for a "new departure" from certain old and uninteresting presentations of fossilized writers. We congratulate a progressive public upon a progressive book.

*From* HON. NEWTON BATEMAN, *Supt. Pub. Inst., Illinois.*

Barnes' One-Term History of the United States is an exceedingly attractive and spirited little book. Its claim to several new and valuable features seems well founded. Under the form of six well-defined Epochs, the History of the United States is traced tersely, yet pithily, from the earliest times to the present day. A good map precedes each epoch, whereby the history and geography of the period may be studied together, *as they always should be.* The syllabus of each paragraph is made to stand in such bold relief, by the use of large, heavy type, as to be of much *mnemonic* value to the student. The book is written in a sprightly and piquant style, the interest never flagging from beginning to end—a rare and difficult achievement in works of this kind.

*From the* "*Chicago Schoolmaster*" (*Editorial*).

A thorough examination of Barnes' Brief History of the United States brings the examiner to the conclusion that it is a superior book in almost every respect. The book is neat in form, and of good material. The type is clear, large, and distinct. The facts and dates are correct. The arrangement of topics is just the thing needed in a history text-book. By this arrangement the pupil can see at once what he is expected to do. The topics are well selected, embracing the leading ideas or principal events of American history. . . . The book as a whole is much superior to any I have examined. So much do I think this, that I have ordered it for my class, and shall use it in my school. (Signed) B. W. BAKER.

**Baker's Brief History of Texas,** . . . . . $1 25

# DRAWING.

## Chapman's American Drawing Book, . . .*$6 00

The standard American text-book and authority in all branches of art. A compilation of art principles. A manual for the amateur, and basis of study for the professional artist. Adapted for schools and private instruction.

CONTENTS.—"Any one who can Learn to Write can Learn to Draw."—Primary Instruction in Drawing.—Rudiments of Drawing the Human Head.—Rudiments in Drawing the Human Figure.—Rudiments of Drawing.—The Elements of Geometry.—Perspective.—Of Studying and Sketching from Nature.—Of Painting.—Etching and Engraving.—Of Modeling.—Of Composition —Advice to the American Art-Student. The work is of course magnificently illustrated with all the original designs.

## Chapman's Elementary Drawing Book, . . 1 50

A Progressive Course of Practical Exercises, or a text-book for the training of the eye and hand. It contains the elements from the larger work, and a copy should be in the hands of every pupil; while a copy of the "American Drawing Book," named above, should be at hand for reference by the class.

## The Little Artist's Portfolio, . . . . . . . . *50

25 Drawing Cards (progressive patterns), 25 Blanks, and a fine Artist's Pencil, all in one neat envelope.

## Clark's Elements of Drawing, . . . . . . *1 00

A complete course in this graceful art, from the first rudiments of outline to the finished sketches of landscape and scenery.

## Fowle's Linear and Perspective Drawing, . *60

For the cultivation of the eye and hand, with copious illustrations and directions for the guidance of the unskilled teacher.

## Monk's Drawing Books—Six Numbers, per set, *2 25

Each book contains *eleven* large patterns, with opposing blanks. No. 1. Elementary Studies. No. 2. Studies of Foliage. No. 3. Landscapes. No. 4. Animals, I. No. 5. Animals, II. No. 6. Marine Views, etc.

## Allen's Map-Drawing, . . . 25 cts.; Scale, 25

This method introduces a new era in Map-Drawing, for the following reasons:—1. It is a system. This is its greatest merit.—2. It is easily understood and taught. —3. The eye is trained to exact measurement by the use of a scale.—4. By no special effort of the memory, distance and comparative size are fixed in the mind.—5. It discards useless construction of lines.—6. It can be taught by any teacher, even though there may have been no previous practice in Map-Drawing.—7. Any pupil old enough to study Geography can learn by this System, in a short time, to draw accurate maps.—8. The System is not the result of theory, but comes directly from the school-room. It has been thoroughly and successfully tested there, with all grades of pupils.—9. It is economical, as it requires no mapping plates. It gives the pupil the ability of rapidly drawing accurate maps.

## Ripley's Map-Drawing, . . . . . . . . . 1 25

Based on the Circle. One of the most efficient aids to the acquirement of a knowledge of Geography is the practice of map-drawing. It is useful for the same reason that the best exercise in orthography is the *writing* of difficult words. Sight comes to the aid of hearing, and a double impression is produced upon the memory. Knowledge becomes less mechanical and more intuitive. The student who has sketched the outlines of a country, and dotted the important places, is little likely to forget either. The impression produced may be compared to that of a traveller who has been over the ground, while more comprehensive and accurate in detail.

# BOOK-KEEPING.

## Folsom's Logical Book-keeping, . . . . . $2 00
## Folsom's Blanks to Book-keeping, . . . . *4 50

This treatise embraces the interesting and important discoveries of Prof. Folsom (of the Albany "Bryant & Stratton College"), the partial enunciation of which in lectures and otherwise has attracted so much attention in circles interested in commercial education.

After studying business phenomena for many years, he has arrived at the positive laws and principles that underlie the whole subject of Accounts; finds that the science is based in *Value* as a generic term; that value divides into *two classes* with varied species; that all the exchanges of values are reducible to nine equations; and that all the results of all these exchanges are limited to *thirteen* in number.

As accounts have been universally taught hitherto, without setting out from a radical analysis or definition of values, the science has been kept in great obscurity, and been made as difficult to impart as to acquire. On the new theory, however, these obstacles are chiefly removed. In reading over the first part of it, in which the governing laws and principles are discussed, a person with ordinary intelligence will obtain a fair conception of the *double entry* process of accounts. But when he comes to study thoroughly these laws and principles as there enunciated, and works out the examples and memoranda which elucidate the *thirteen results* of business, the student will neither fail in readily acquiring the science as it is, nor in becoming able intelligently to apply it in the interpretation of business.

## Smith & Martin's Book-keeping, . . . . . 1 25
## Smith & Martin's Blanks, . . . . . . . . . *60

This work is by a practical teacher and a practical book-keeper. It is of a thoroughly popular class, and will be welcomed by every one who loves to see theory and practice combined in an easy, concise, and methodical form.

The Single Entry portion is well adapted to supply a want felt in nearly all other treatises, which seem to be prepared mainly for the use of wholesale merchants, leaving retailers, mechanics, farmers, etc., who transact the greater portion of the business of the country, without a guide. The work is also commended, on this account, for general use in Young Ladies' Seminaries, where a thorough grounding in the simpler form of accounts will be invaluable to the future housekeepers of the nation.

The treatise on Double Entry Book-keeping combines all the advantages of the most recent methods, with the utmost simplicity of application, thus affording the pupil all the advantages of actual experience in the counting-house, and giving a clear comprehension of the entire subject through a judicious course of mercantile transactions.

The shape of the book is such that the transactions can be presented as in actual practice; and the simplified form of Blanks—three in number—adds greatly to the ease experienced in acquiring the science.

# NATURAL SCIENCE.

## FAMILIAR SCIENCE.

**Norton & Porter's First Book of Science,** . $1 75

By eminent Professors of Yale College. Contains the principles of Natural Philosophy, Astronomy, Chemistry, Physiology, and Geology. Arranged on the Catechetical plan for primary classes and beginners.

**Chambers' Treasury of Knowledge,** . . . . 1 25

Progressive lessons upon—*first*, common things which lie most immediately around us, and first attract the attention of the young mind; *second*, common objects from the Mineral, Animal, and Vegetable kingdoms, manufactured articles, and miscellaneous substances; *third*, a systematic view of Nature under the various sciences. May be used as a Reader or Text-book.

## NATURAL PHILOSOPHY.

**Norton's First Book in Natural Philosophy,** 1 00

By Prof. NORTON, of Yale College. Designed for beginners. Profusely illustrated and arranged on the Catechetical plan.

**Peck's Ganot's Course of Nat. Philosophy,** . 1 75

The standard text-book of France, Americanized and popularized by Prof. PECK, of Columbia College. The most magnificent system of illustration ever adopted in an American school-book is here found. For intermediate classes.

**Peck's Elements of Mechanics,** . . . . . . 2 00

A suitable introduction to Bartlett's higher treatises on Mechanical Philosophy, and adequate in itself for a complete academical course.

**Bartlett's** SYNTHETIC, AND ANALYTIC, **Mechanics,** . each 5 00

**Bartlett's Acoustics and Optics,** . . . . . 3 50

A system of Collegiate Philosophy, by Prof. BARTLETT, of West Point Military Academy.

**Steele's 14 Weeks Course in Philos.** (see p. 34) 1 50

**Steele's Philosophical Apparatus,** . . . . *125 00

Adequate to performing the experiments in the ordinary text-books. The articles will be sold separately, if desired. See special circular for details.

## GEOLOGY.

**Page's Elements of Geology,** . . . . . . . 1 25

A volume of Chambers' Educational Course. Practical, simple, and eminently calculated to make the study interesting.

**Emmons' Manual of Geology,** . . . . . . 1 25

The first Geologist of the country has here produced a work worthy of his reputation.

**Steele's 14 Weeks Course** (see p. 34) . . . . . 1 50

**Steele's Geological Cabinet,** . . . . . . . . *40 00

Containing 125 carefully selected specimens. In four parts. Sold separately, if desired. See circular for details.

# Peck's Ganot's Popular Physics.

## TESTIMONIALS.

*From* PROF. ALONZO COLLIN, *Cornell College, Iowa.*

I am pleased with it. I have decided to introduce it as a text-book.

*From* H. F. JOHNSON, *President Madison College, Sharon, Miss.*

I am pleased with Peck's Ganot, and think it a magnificent book.

*From* PROF. EDWARD BROOKS, *Pennsylvania State Normal School.*

So eminent are its merits, that it will be introduced as the text-book upon elementary physics in this institution.

*From* H. H. LOCKWOOD, *Professor Natural Philosophy U. S. Naval Academy.*

I am so pleased with it that I will probably add it to a course of lectures given to the midshipmen of this school on physics.

*From* GEO. S. MACKIE, *Professor Natural History University of Nashville, Tenn.*

I have decided on the introduction of Peck's Ganot's Philosophy, as I am satisfied that it is the best book for the purposes of my pupils that I have seen, combining simplicity of explanation with elegance of illustration.

*From* W. S. MCRAE, *Superintendent Vevay Public Schools, Indiana.*

Having carefully examined a number of text-books on natural philosophy, I do not hesitate to express my decided opinion in favor of Peck's Ganot. The matter, style, and illustration eminently adapt the work to the popular wants.

*From* REV. SAMUEL MCKINNEY, D.D., *Pres't Austin College, Huntsville, Texas.*

It gives me pleasure to commend it to teachers. I have taught some classes with it as our text, and must say, for simplicity of style and clearness of illustration, I have found nothing as yet published of equal value to the teacher and pupil.

*From* C. V. SPEAR, *Principal Maplewood Institute, Pittsfield, Mass.*

I am much pleased with its ample illustrations by plates, and its clearness and simplicity of statement. It covers the ground usually gone over by our higher classes, and contains many fresh illustrations from life or daily occurrences, and new applications of scientific principles to such.

*From* J. A. BANFIELD, *Superintendent Marshall Public Schools, Michigan.*

I have used Peck's Ganot since 1862, and with increasing pleasure and satisfaction each term. I consider it superior to any other work on physics in its adaptation to our high schools and academies. Its illustrations are superb—better than three times their number of pages of fine print.

*From* A. SCHU[illegible]ER, *Prof. of Mathematics in Baldwin University, Berea, Ohio.*

After a careful examination of Peck's Ganot's Natural Philosophy, and an actual test of its merits as a text-book, I can heartily recommend it as admirably adapted to meet the wants of the grade of students for which it is intended. Its diagrams and illustrations are *unrivaled*. We use it in the Baldwin University.

*From* D. C. VAN NORMAN, *Principal Van Norman Institute, New York.*

The Natural Philosophy of M. Ganot, edited by Prof. Peck, is, in my opinion, the best work of its kind, for the use intended, ever published in this country. Whether regarded in relation to the natural order of the topics, the precision and clearness of its definitions, or the fullness and beauty of its illustrations, it is certainly, I think, an advance.

---

☞ For many similar testimonials, see current numbers of the Illustrated Educational Bulletin.

**NATURAL SCIENCE—Continued.**

## CHEMISTRY.

**Porter's First Book of Chemistry,** . . . . $1 00

**Porter's Principles of Chemistry,** . . . . . 2 00

The above are widely known as the productions of one of the most eminent scientific men of America. The extreme simplicity in the method of presenting the science, while exhaustively treated, has excited universal commendation.

**Darby's Text-Book of Chemistry,** . . . . . 1 75

Purely a Chemistry, divesting the subject of matters comparatively foreign to it (such as heat, light, electricity, etc.), but usually allowed to engross too much attention in ordinary school-books.

**Gregory's Organic Chemistry,** . . . . . . . 2 50

**Gregory's Inorganic Chemistry,** . . . . . . 2 50

The science exhaustively treated. For colleges and medical students.

**Steele's Fourteen Weeks Course,** . . . . . . 1 50

A successful effort to reduce the study to the limits of a *single term*, thereby making feasible its general introduction in institutions of every character. The author's felicity of style and success in making the science pre-eminently *interesting* are peculiarly noticeable features. (See page 34.)

**Steele's Chemical Apparatus,** . . . . . . . *20 00

Adequate to the performance of all the important experiments.

## BOTANY.

**Thinker's First Lessons in Botany,** . . . . 40

For children. The technical terms are largely dispensed with in favor of an easy and familiar style adapted to the smallest learner.

**Wood's Object-Lessons in Botany,** . . . . 1 50

**Wood's American Botanist and Florist,** . . 2 50

**Wood's New Class-Book of Botany,** . . . . 3 50

The standard text-books of the United States in this department. In style they are simple, popular, and lively; in arrangement, easy and natural; in description, graphic and strictly exact. The Tables for Analysis are reduced to a perfect system. More are annually sold than of all others combined.

**Wood's Plant Record,** . . . . . . . . . . . *75

A simple form of Blanks for recording observations in the field.

**Wood's Botanical Apparatus,** . . . . . . . *8 00

A portable Trunk, containing Drying Press, Knife, Trowel, Microscope, and Tweezers, and a copy of Wood's Plant Record—composing a complete outfit for the collector.

**Young's Familiar Lessons,** . . . . . . . . . 2 00

**Darby's Southern Botany,** . . . . . . . . . 2 00

Embracing general Structural and Physiological Botany, with vegetable products and descriptions of Southern plants, and a complete Flora of the Southern States.

# WOOD'S BOTANIES.

## TESTIMONIALS.

*From* PRES. R. B. BURLESON, *Waco University, Texas.*
Wood's Botanies—books that meet every want in their line.

*From* PRIN. J. G. RALSTON, *Norristown Seminary, Pa.*
We find the "Class-Book" entirely satisfactory.

*From* PRES. D. F. BITTLE, *Roanoke College, Va.*
Your text-books on Botany are the best for students.

*From* PROF. W. C. PIERCE, *Baldwin University, Ohio.*
I think his Flora the best we have. His method of analysis is excellent.

*From* PROF. BLAKESLEE, *State Normal School, Potsdam, N.Y.*
It is admirably concise, yet it does not seem to be deficient or obscure. In paper, print, and binding, the book leaves little to be desired.

*From* PRES. J. M. GREGORY, *State Agricultural College, Ill.*
I find myself greatly pleased with the perspicuity, compactness, and completeness of the book (Wood's Botanist and Florist). I shall recommend it freely to my friends.

*From* PROF. A. WINCHELL, *University of Michigan.*
I am free to say that I had been deeply impressed, I may say almost astonished, at the evidences which the work bears of skillful and experienced authorship in his field, and nice and constant adaptation to the wants and conveniences of students of Botany. I pronounce it emphatically an admirable text-book.

*From* PROF. RICHARD OWEN, *University of Indiana.*
I am well pleased with the evidence of philosophical method exhibited in the general arrangement, as well as with the clearness of the explanations, the ready intelligibility of the analytical tables, and the illustrative aid furnished by the numerous and excellent wood-cuts. I design using the work as a text-book with my next class.

*From* PRIN. B. R. ANDERSON, *Columbus Union School, Wisconsin.*
I have examined several works with a view to recommending some good text-book on Botany, but I lay them all aside for "Wood's Botanist and Florist." The arrangement of the book is in my opinion excellent, its style fascinating and attractive, its treatment of the various departments of the science is thorough, and last, but far from unimportant, I like the topical form of the questions to each chapter. It seems to embrace the entire science. In fact, I consider it a complete, attractive, and exhaustive work.

*From* M. A. MARSHALL, *New Haven High School, Conn.*
It has all the excellencies of the well-known Class-Book of Botany by the same author in a smaller book. By a judicious system of condensation, the size of the Flora is reduced one-half, while no species are omitted, and many new ones are added. The descriptions of species are very brief, yet sufficient to identify the plant, and, when taken in connection with the generic description, form a complete description of the plant. The book as a whole will suit the wants of classes better than anything I have yet seen. The adoption of the Botanist and Florist would not require the exclusion of the Class-Book of Botany, as they are so arranged that both might be used by the same class.

*From* PROF. G. H. PERKINS, *University of Vermont and State Agricultural College.*
I can truly say that the more I examine Wood's Class-Book, the better pleased I am with it. In its illustrations, especially of particulars not easily observed by the student, and the clearness and compactness of its statements, as well as in the territory its flora embraces, it appears to me to surpass any other work I know of. The whole science, so far as it can be taught in a college course, is well presented, and rendered unusually easy of comprehension. The mode of analysis is excellent, avoiding as it does to a great extent those microscopic characters which puzzle the beginner, and using those that are obvious as far as possible. I regard the work as a most admirable one, and shall adopt it as a text-book another year.

NATURAL SCIENCE—Continued.

## PHYSIOLOGY.

**Jarvis' Elements of Physiology,** . . . . .$ 75

**Jarvis' Physiology and Laws of Health,** . 1 65

The only books extant which approach this subject with a proper view of the true object of teaching Physiology in schools, viz., that scholars may know how to take care of their own health. In bold contrast with the abstract *Anatomies*, which children learn as they would Greek or Latin (and forget as soon), to *discipline the mind*, are these text-books, using the *science* as a secondary consideration, and only so far as is necessary for the comprehension of the *laws of health*.

**Hamilton's Vegetable & Animal Physiology,** 1 25

The two branches of the science combined in one volume lead the student to a proper comprehension of the Analogies of Nature.

**Steele's Fourteen Weeks Course** (see p. 34), . 1 50

## ASTRONOMY.

**Steele's Fourteen Weeks' Course,** . . . . . 1 50

Reduced to a single term, and better adapted to school use than any work heretofore published. Not written for the information of scientific men, but for the inspiration of youth, the pages are not burdened with a multitude of figures which no memory could possibly retain. The whole subject is presented in a clear and concise form. (See p. 34.)

**Willard's School Astronomy,** . . . . . . 1 00

By means of clear and attractive illustrations, addressing the eye in many cases by analogies, careful definitions of all necessary technical terms, a careful avoidance of verbiage and unimportant matter, particular attention to analysis, and a general adoption of the simplest methods, Mrs. Willard has made the best and most attractive *elementary* Astronomy extant.

**McIntyre's Astronomy and the Globes,** . . . 1 50

A complete treatise for intermediate classes. Highly approved.

**Bartlett's Spherical Astronomy,** . . . . . 5 00

The West Point course, for advanced classes, with applications to the current wants of Navigation, Geography, and Chronology.

## NATURAL HISTORY.

**Carll's Child's Book of Natural History,** . . 0 50

Illustrating the Animal, Vegetable, and Mineral Kingdoms, with application to the Arts. For beginners. Beautifully and copiously illustrated.

## ZOOLOGY.

**Chambers' Elements of Zoology,** . . . . . 1 50

A complete and comprehensive system of Zoology, adapted for academic instruction, presenting a systematic view of the Animal Kingdom as a portion of external Nature.

# Jarvis' Physiology and Laws of Health.

## TESTIMONIALS.

*From* SAMUEL B. MCLANE, *Superintendent Public Schools, Keokuk, Iowa.*

I am glad to see a really good text-book on this much neglected branch. This is clear, concise, accurate, and eminently adapted to the *class-room.*

*From* WILLIAM F. WYERS, *Principal of Academy, West Chester, Pennsylvania*

A thorough examination has satisfied me of its superior claims as a text-book to the attention of teacher and taught. I shall introduce it at once.

*From* H. R. SANFORD, *Principal of East Genesee Conference Seminary, N. Y.*

"Jarvis' Physiology" is received, and fully met our expectations. We immediately adopted it.

*From* ISAAC T. GOODNOW, *State Superintendent of Kansas—published in connection with the "School Law."*

"Jarvis' Physiology," a common-sense, practical work, with just enough of anatomy to understand the physiological portions. The last six pages, on Man's Responsibility for his own health, are worth the price of the book.

*From* D. W. STEVENS, *Superintendent Public Schools, Fall River, Mass.*

I have examined Jarvis' "Physiology and Laws of Health," which you had the kindness to send to me a short time ago. In my judgment it is far the best work of the kind within my knowledge. It has been adopted as a text-book in our public schools.

*From* HENRY G. DENNY, *Chairman Book Committee, Boston, Mass.*

The very excellent "Physiology" of D. Jarvis I had introduced into our High School, where the study had been temporarily dropped, believing it to be by far the best work of the kind that had come under my observation; indeed, the reintroduction of the study was delayed for some months, because Dr. Jarvis' book could not be had, and we were unwilling to take any other.

*From* PROF. A. P. PEABODY, D.D., LL.D., *Harvard University.*

* * I have been in the habit of examining school-books with great care, and I hesitate not to say that, of all the text-books on Physiology which have been given to the public, Dr. Jarvis' deserves the first place on the score of accuracy, thoroughness, method, simplicity of statement, and constant reference to topics of practical interest and utility.

*From* JAMES N. TOWNSEND, *Superintendent Public Schools, Hudson, N. Y.*

Every human being is appointed to take charge of his own body; and of all books written upon this subject, I know of none which will so well prepare one to do this as "Jarvis' Physiology"—that is, in so small a compass of matter. It considers the pure, simple *laws of health* paramount to science; and though the work is thoroughly scientific, it is divested of all cumbrous technicalities, and presents the subject of physical life in a manner and style really charming. It is unquestionably the best text-book on physiology I have ever seen. It is giving great satisfaction in the schools of this city, where it has been adopted as the standard.

*From* L. J. SANFORD, M.D., *Prof. Anatomy and Physiology in Yale College*

Books on human physiology, designed for the use of schools, are more generally a failure perhaps than are school-books on most other subjects.

The great want in this department is met, we think, in the well-written treatise of Dr. Jarvis, entitled "Physiology and Laws of Health." * * The work is not too detailed nor too expansive in any department, and is clear and concise in all. It is not burdened with an excess of anatomical description, nor rendered discursive by many zoological references. Anatomical statements are made to the extent of qualifying the student to attend, understandingly, to an exposition of those functional processes which, collectively, make up health; thus the laws of health are enunciated, and many suggestions are given which, if heeded, will tend to its preservation.

---

☞ For further testimony of similar character, see current numbers of the Illustrated Educational Bulletin.

# NATURAL SCIENCE.

## "FOURTEEN WEEKS" IN EACH BRANCH.

### By J. DORMAN STEELE, A. M.

| | |
|---|---|
| **Steele's 14 Weeks Course in Chemistry** NEW ED. | $1 50 |
| **Steele's 14 Weeks Course in Astronomy** . | 1 50 |
| **Steele's 14 Weeks Course in Philosophy** . | 1 50 |
| **Steele's 14 Weeks Course in Geology.** . | 1 50 |
| **Steele's 14 Weeks Course in Physiology** . | 1 50 |

Our Text-Books in these studies are, as a general thing, dull and uninteresting. They contain from 400 to 600 pages of dry facts and unconnected details. They abound in that which the student cannot learn, much less remember. The pupil commences the study, is confused by the fine print and coarse print, and neither knowing exactly what to learn nor what to hasten over, is crowded through the single term generally assigned to each branch, and frequently comes to the close without a definite and exact idea of a single scientific principle.

Steele's Fourteen Weeks Courses contain only that which every well-informed person should know, while all that which concerns only the professional scientist is omitted. The language is clear, simple, and interesting, and the illustrations bring the subject within the range of home life and daily experience. They give such of the general principles and the prominent facts as a pupil can make familiar as household words within a single term. The type is large and open; there is no fine print to annoy; the cuts are copies of genuine experiments or natural phenomena, and are of fine execution.

In fine, by a system of condensation peculiarly his own, the author reduces each branch to the limits of a single term of study, while sacrificing nothing that is essential, and nothing that is usually retained from the study of the larger manuals in common use. Thus the student has rare opportunity to *economize his time*, or rather to employ that which he has to the best advantage.

A notable feature is the author's charming "style," fortified by an enthusiasm over his subject in which the student will not fail to partake. Believing that Natural Science is full of fascination, he has moulded it into a form that attracts the attention and kindles the enthusiasm of the pupil.

The recent editions contain the author's "Practical Questions" on a plan never before attempted in scientific text-books. These are questions as to the nature and cause of common phenomena, and are not directly answered in the text, the design being to test and promote an intelligent use of the student's knowledge of the foregoing principles.

**Steele's General Key to his Works** . . . . *1 50

This work is mainly composed of Answers to the Practical Questions and Solutions of the Problems in the author's celebrated "Fourteen Weeks Courses" in the several sciences, with many hints to teachers, minor Tables, &c. Should be on every teacher's desk.

# Steele's 14 Weeks in each Science.

## TESTIMONIALS.

*From* L. A. Bikle, *President N. C. College.*

I have not been disappointed. Shall take pleasure in introducing this series.

*From* J. F. Cox, *Prest. Southern Female College, Ga.*

I am much pleased with these books, and expect to introduce them.

*From* J. R. Branham, *Prin. Brownsville Female College, Tenn.*

They are capital little books, and are now in use in our institution.

*From* W. H. Goodale, *Professor Readville Seminary, La.*

We are using your 14 Weeks Course, and are much pleased with them.

*From* W. A. Boles, *Supt. Shelbyville Graded School, Ind.*

They are as entertaining as a story book, and much more improving to the mind.

*From* S. A. Snow, *Principal of High School, Uxbridge, Mass.*

Steele's 14 Weeks Courses in the Sciences are a perfect success.

*From* John W. Doughty, *Newburg Free Academy, N. Y.*

I was prepared to find Prof. Steele's Course both attractive and instructive. My highest expectations have been fully realized.

*From* J. S. Blackwell, *Prest. Ghent College, Ky.*

Prof. Steele's unexampled success in providing for the wants of academic classes, has led me to look forward with high anticipations to his forthcoming issue.

*From* J. F. Cook, *Prest. La Grange College, Mo.*

I am pleased with the neatness of these books and the delightful diction. I have been teaching for years, and have never seen a lovelier little volume than the Astronomy.

*From* M. W. Smith, *Prin. of High School, Morrison, Ill.*

They seem to me to be admirably adapted to the wants of a public school, containing, as they do, a sufficiently comprehensive arrangement of elementary principles to excite a healthy thirst for a more thorough knowledge of those sciences.

*From* J. D. Bartley, *Prin. of High School, Concord, N. H.*

They are just such books as I have looked for, viz., those of interesting style, not cumbersome and filled up with things to be omitted by the pupil, and yet sufficiently full of facts for the purpose of most scholars in these sciences in our high schools; there is nothing but what a pupil of average ability can thoroughly master.

*From* Alonzo Norton Lewis, *Principal of Parker Academy, Conn.*

I consider Steele's Fourteen Weeks Courses in Philosophy, Chemistry, &c., the *best* school-books that have been issued in this country.

As an introduction to the various branches of which they treat, and especially for that numerous class of pupils who have not the time for a more extended course, I consider them *invaluable.*

*From* Edward Brooks, *Prin. State Normal School, Millersville, Pa.*

At the meeting of Normal School Principals, I presented the following resolution, which was unanimously adopted: "*Resolved*, That Steele's 14 Weeks Courses in Natural Philosophy and Astronomy, or an amount equivalent to what is contained in them, be adopted for use in the State Normal Schools of Pennsylvania." The works themselves will be adopted by at least three of the schools, and, I presume, by them all.

# LITERATURE.

**Cleveland's Compendiums** . . . . each, $*2 50

ENGLISH LITERATURE. AMERICAN LITERATURE.
ENGLISH LITERATURE OF THE XIXTH CENTURY.

In these volumes are gathered the cream of the literature of the English speaking people for the school-room and the general reader. Their reputation is national. More than 125,000 copies have been sold.

**Boyd's English Classics** . . . . . each, *1 25

MILTON'S PARADISE LOST. THOMSON'S SEASONS.
YOUNG'S NIGHT THOUGHTS. POLLOK'S COURSE OF TIME.
COWPER'S TASK, TABLE TALK, &c. LORD BACON'S ESSAYS.

This series of annotated editions of great English writers, in prose and poetry, is designed for critical reading and parsing in schools. Prof. J. R. Boyd proves himself an editor of high capacity, and the works themselves need no encomium. As auxiliary to the study of Belles Lettres, etc., these works have no equal.

**Pope's Essay on Man** . . . . . . . . . . *20

**Pope's Homer's Iliad** . . . . . . . . . . *80

The metrical translation of the great poet of antiquity, and the matchless "Essay on the Nature and State of Man," by ALEXANDER POPE, afford superior exercise in literature and parsing.

# AESTHETICS.

**Huntington's Manual of the Fine Arts** . .*1 75

A view of the rise and progress of Art in different countries, a brief account of the most eminent masters of Art, and an analysis of the principles of Art. It is complete in itself, or may precede to advantage the critical work of Lord Kames.

**Boyd's Kames' Elements of Criticism** . .*1 75

The best edition of this standard work; without the study of which none may be considered proficient in the science of the Perceptions. No other study can be pursued with so marked an effect upon the taste and refinement of the pupil.

# POLITICAL ECONOMY.

**Champlin's Lessons on Political Economy** 1 25

An improvement on previous treatises, being shorter, yet containing every thing essential, with a view of recent questions in finance, etc., which is not elsewhere found.

# CLEVELAND'S COMPENDIUMS.

## TESTIMONIALS.

*From the New Englander.*

This is the very best book of the kind we have ever examined.

*From* GEORGE B. EMERSON, Esq., *Boston.*

The Biographical Sketches are just and discriminating; the selections are admirable, and I have adopted the work as a text-book for my first class.

*From* PROF. MOSES COIT TYLER, *of the Michigan University.*

I have given your book a thorough examination, and am greatly delighted with it; and shall have great pleasure in directing the attention of my classes to a work which affords so admirable a bird's-eye view of recent "English Literature."

*From the Saturday Review.*

It acquaints the reader with the characteristic method, tone, and quality of all the chief notabilities of the period, and will give the careful student a better idea of the recent history of English Literature than nine educated Englishmen in ten possess.

*From the Methodist Quarterly Review, New York.*

This work is a transcript of the best American mind; a vehicle of the noblest American spirit. No parent who would introduce his child to a knowledge of our country's literature, and at the same time indoctrinate his heart in the purest principles, need fear to put this manual in the youthful hand.

*From* REV. C. PEIRCE, *Principal, West Newton, Mass.*

I do not believe the work is to be found from which, within the same limits, so much interesting and valuable information in regard to English writers and English literature of every age, can be obtained; and it deserves to find a place in all our high schools and academies, as well as in every private library.

*From the Independent.*

The work of selection and compilation—requiring a perfect familiarity with the whole range of English literature, a judgment clear and impartial, a taste at once delicate and severe, and a most sensitive regard to purity of thought or feeling—has been better accomplished in this than in any kindred volume with which we are acquainted.

*From the Christian Examiner.*

To form such a Compendium, good taste, fine scholarship, familiar acquaintance with English literature, unwearied industry, tact acquired by practice, an interest in the culture of the young, a regard for truth, purity, philanthropy, religion, as the highest attainment and the highest beauty,—all these were needed, and they are united in Mr. Cleveland.

---

# CHAMPLIN'S POLITICAL ECONOMY.

*From* J. L. BOTHWELL, *Prin. Public School No. 14, Albany, N.Y.*

I have examined Champlin's Political Economy with much pleasure, and shall be pleased to put it into the hands of my pupils. In quantity and quality I think it superior to anything that I have examined.

*From* PRES. N. E. COBLEIGH, *East Tennessee Wesleyan University.*

An examination of Champlin's Political Economy has satisfied me that it is the book I want. For brevity and compactness, division of the subject, and clear statement, and for appropriateness of treatment, I consider it a better text-book than any other in the market.

*From the Evening Mail, New York.*

A new interest has been imparted to the science of political economy since we have been necessitated to raise such vast sums of money for the support of the government. The time, therefore, is favorable for the introduction of works like the above. This little volume of two hundred pages is intended for beginners, for the common school and academy. It is intended as a basis upon which to rear a more elaborate superstructure. There is nothing in the principles of political economy above the comprehension of average scholars, when they are clearly set forth. This seems to have been done by President Champlin in an easy and graceful manner.

# ELOCUTION.

**Taverner Graham's Reasonable Elocution,** $1 25

Based upon the belief that true Elocution is the right interpretation of THOUGHT, and guiding the student to an intelligent appreciation, instead of a merely mechanical knowledge, of its rules.

**Zachos' Analytic Elocution** . . . . . . . 1 50

All departments of elocution—such as the analysis of the voice and the sentence, phonology, rhythm, expression, gesture, &c.—are here arranged for instruction in classes, illustrated by copious examples.

**Sherwood's Self Culture** . . . . . . . . . 1 00

Self-culture in reading, speaking, and conversation—a very valuable treatise to those who would perfect themselves in these accomplishments.

# SPEAKERS.

**Northend's Little Orator,** *60—**Child's Speaker** *60

Two little works of the same grade but different selections, containing simple and attractive pieces for children under twelve years of age.

**Northend's Young Declaimer** . . . . . . *75

**Northend's National Orator** . . . . . . . *1 25

Two volumes of Prose, Poetry, and Dialogue, adapted to intermediate and grammar classes respectively.

**Northend's Entertaining Dialogues** . . . . *1 25

Extracts eminently adapted to cultivate the dramatic faculties, as well as entertain an audience.

**Swett's Common School Speaker** . . . . *1 25

Selections from recent literature.

**Raymond's Patriotic Speaker** . . . . . . *2 00

A superb compilation of modern eloquence and poetry, with original dramatic exercises. Nearly every eminent *living* orator is represented, without distinction of place or party.

# COMPOSITION, &c.

**Brookfield's First Book in Composition** . 50

Making the cultivation of this important art feasible for the smallest child. By a new method, to induce and stimulate thought.

**Boyd's Composition and Rhetoric** . . . . 1 50

This work furnishes all the aid that is needful or can be desired in the various departments and styles of composition, both in prose and verse.

**Day's Art of Rhetoric** . . . . . . . . . . 1 25

Noted for exactness of definition, clear limitation, and philosophical development of subject; the large share of attention given to Invention, as a branch of Rhetoric, and the unequalled analysis of style

# MENTAL PHILOSOPHY.

**Mahan's Intellectual Philosophy** . . . . . $1 75

The subject exhaustively considered. The author has evinced learning, candor, and independent thinking.

**Mahan's Science of Logic** . . . . . . . . . 2 00

A profound analysis of the laws of thought. The system possesses the merit of being intelligible and self consistent. In addition to the author's carefully elaborated views, it embraces results attained by the ablest minds of Great Britain, Germany, and France, in this department.

**Boyd's Elements of Logic** . . . . . . . . . 1 25

A systematic and philosophic condensation of the subject, fortified with additions from Watts, Abercrombie, Whately, &c.

**Watts on the Mind** . . . . . . . . . . . . 50

The Improvement of the Mind, by Isaac Watts, is designed as a guide for the attainment of useful knowledge. As a text-book it is unparalleled; and the discipline it affords cannot be too highly esteemed by the educator.

# MORALS.

**Peabody's Moral Philosophy** . . . . . . . . 1 25

A short course; by the Professor of Christian Morals, Harvard University—for the Freshman Class and for High Schools.

**Alden's Text-Book of Ethics** . . . . . . . . 60

For young pupils. To aid in systematizing the ethical teachings of the Bible, and point out the coincidences between the instructions of the sacred volume and the sound conclusions of reason.

**Willard's Morals for the Young** . . . . . . 75

Lessons in conversational style to inculcate the elements of moral philosophy. The study is made attractive by narratives and engravings.

# GOVERNMENT.

**Howe's Young Citizen's Catechism** . . . . 75

Explaining the duties of District, Town, City, County, State, and United States Officers, with rules for parliamentary and commercial business—that which every future "sovereign" ought to know, and so few are taught.

**Young's Lessons in Civil Government** . . 1 25

A comprehensive view of Government, and abstract of the laws showing the rights, duties, and responsibilities of citizens.

**Mansfield's Political Manual** . . . . . . 1 25

This is a complete view of the theory and practice of the General and State Governments of the United States, designed as a text-book. The author is an esteemed and able professor of constitutional law, widely known for his sagacious utterances in matters of statecraft through the public press. Recent events teach with emphasis the vital necessity that the rising generation should comprehend the noble polity of the American government, that they may act intelligently when endowed with a voice in it.

# MODERN LANGUAGE.

**French and English Primer,** . . . . . . $ 10
**German and English Primer,** . . . . . . . 10
**Spanish and English Primer,** . . . . . . . 10

The names of common objects properly illustrated and arranged in easy lessons.

**Ledru's French Fables,** . . . . . . . . . . 75
**Ledru's French Grammar,** . . . . . . . . 1 00
**Ledru's French Reader,** . . . . . . . . . 1 00

The author's long experience has enabled him to present the most thoroughly practical text-books extant, in this branch. The system of pronunciation (by phonetic illustration) is original with this author, and will commend itself to all American teachers, as it enables their pupils to secure an absolutely correct pronunciation without the assistance of a native master. This feature is peculiarly valuable also to "self-taught" students. The directions for ascertaining the gender of French nouns—also a great stumbling-block—are peculiar to this work, and will be found remarkably competent to the end proposed. The criticism of teachers and the test of the school-room is invited to this excellent series, with confidence.

**Worman's French Echo,** . . . . . . . . . 1 25

To teach conversational French by actual practice, on an entirely new plan, which recognizes the importance of the student learning *to think* in the language which he speaks. It furnishes an extensive vocabulary of words and expressions in common use, and suffices to free the learner from the embarrassments which the peculiarities of his own tongue are likely to be to him, and to make him thoroughly familiar with the use of proper idioms.

**Worman's German Echo,** . . . . . . . . . 1 25

On the same plan. See Worman's German Series, page 42.

**Pujol's Complete French Class-Book,** . . . 2 25

Offers, in one volume, methodically arranged, a complete French course —usually embraced in series of from five to twelve books, including the bulky and expensive Lexicon. Here are Grammar, Conversation, and choice Literature—selected from the best French authors. Each branch is thoroughly handled; and the student, having diligently completed the course as prescribed, may consider himself, without further application, *au fait* in the most polite and elegant language of modern times.

**Maurice-Poitevin's Grammaire Francaise,** . 1 00

American schools are at last supplied with an American edition of this famous text-book. Many of our best institutions have for years been procuring it from abroad rather than forego the advantages it offers. The policy of putting students who have acquired some proficiency from the ordinary text-books, into a Grammar written in the vernacular, can not be too highly commended. It affords an opportunity for finish and review at once; while embodying abundant practice of its own rules.

**Joynes' French Pronunciation,** . . . . . . 30

**Willard's Historia de los Estados Unidos,** . 2 00

The History of the United States, translated by Professors TOLON and DE TORNOS, will be found a valuable, instructive, and entertaining reading-book for Spanish classes.

# Pujol's Complete French Class-Book.

## TESTIMONIALS.

*From* PROF. ELIAS PEISSNER, *Union College.*

I take great pleasure in recommending Pujol and Van Norman's French Class-Book, as there is no French grammar or class-book which can be compared with it in completeness, system, clearness, and general utility.

*From* EDWARD NORTH, *President of Hamilton College.*

I have carefully examined Pujol and Van Norman's French Class-Book, and am satisfied of its superiority, for college purposes, over any other heretofore used. We shall not fail to use it with our next class in French.

*From* A. CURTIS, *Pres't of Cincinnati Literary and Scientific Institute.*

I am confident that it may be made an instrument in conveying to the student, in from six months to a year, the art of speaking and writing the French with almost native fluency and propriety.

*From* HIRAM ORCUTT, A. M., *Prin. Glenwood and Tilden Ladies' Seminaries.*

I have used Pujol's French Grammar in my two seminaries, exclusively, for more than a year, and have no hesitation in saying that I regard it the best text-book in this department extant. And my opinion is confirmed by the testimony of Prof. F. De Launay and Mademoiselle Marindin. They assure me that the book is eminently accurate and practical, as tested in the school-room.

*From* PROF. THEO. F. DE FUMAT, *Hebrew Educational Institute, Memphis, Tenn.*

M. Pujol's French Grammar is one of the best and most practical works. The French language is chosen and elegant in style—modern and easy. It is far superior to the other French class-books in this country. The selection of the conversational part is very good; and will interest pupils; and being all completed in only one volume, it is especially desirable to have it introduced in our schools.

*From* PROF. JAMES H. WORMAN, *Bordentown Female College, N. J.*

The work is upon the same plan as the text-books for the study of French and English published in Berlin, for the study of those who have not the aid of a teacher, and these books are considered, by the first authorities, the best books. In most of our institutions, Americans teach the modern languages, and heretofore the trouble has been to give them a text-book that would dispose of the difficulties of the French pronunciation. This difficulty is successfully removed by P. and Van N., and I have every reason to believe it will soon make its way into most of our best schools.

*From* PROF. CHARLES S. DOD, *Ann Smith Academy, Lexington, Va.*

I cannot do better than to recommend "Pujol and Van Norman." For comprehensive and systematic arrangement, progressive and thorough development of all grammatical principles and idioms, with a due admixture of theoretical knowledge and practical exercise, I regard it as superior to any (other) book of the kind.

*From* A. A. FORSTER, *Prin. Pinehurst School, Toronto, C. W.*

I have great satisfaction in bearing testimony to M. Pujol's System of French Instruction, as given in his complete class-book. For clearness and comprehensiveness, adapted for all classes of pupils, I have found it superior to any other work of the kind, and have now used it for some years in my establishment with great success.

*From* PROF. OTTO FEDDER, *Maplewood Institute, Pittsfield, Mass.*

The conversational exercises will prove an immense saving of the hardest kind of labor to teachers. There is scarcely any thing more trying in the way of teaching language, than to rack your brain for short and easily intelligible bits of conversation, and to repeat them time and again with no better result than extorting at long intervals a doubting "oui," or a hesitating "non, monsieur"

☞ For further testimony of a similar character, see special circular, and current numbers of the Educational Bulletin.

# GERMAN.

## A COMPLETE COURSE IN THE GERMAN.

By JAMES H. WORMAN, A. M.

**Worman's Elementary German Grammar . $1 50**
**Worman's Complete German Grammar . 2 00**

These volumes are designed for intermediate and advanced classes respectively. Though following the same general method with "Otto" (that of 'Gaspey'), our author differs essentially in its application. He is more practical, more systematic, more accurate, and besides introduces a number of invaluable features which have never before been combined in a German grammar.

Among other things, it may be claimed for Prof. Worman that he has been *the first* to introduce in an American text-book for learning German, a system of analogy and comparison with other languages. Our best teachers are also enthusiastic about his methods of inculcating the art of speaking, of understanding the spoken language, of correct pronunciation; the sensible and convenient original classification of nouns (in four declensions), and of irregular verbs, also deserves much praise. We also note the use of heavy type to indicate etymological changes in the paradigms and, in the exercises, the parts which specially illustrate preceding rules.

**Worman's Elementary German Reader . . 1 25**
**Worman's Collegiate German Reader . . . 2 00**

The finest and most judicious compilation of classical and standard German Literature. These works embrace, progressively arranged, selections from the masterpieces of Goethe, Schiller, Korner, Seume, Uhland, Freiligrath, Heine, Schlegel, Holty, Lenau, Wieland, Herder, Lessing, Kant, Fichte, Schelling, Winkelmann, Humboldt, Ranke, Raumer, Menzel, Gervinus, &c., and contains complete Goethe's "Iphigenie," Schiller's "Jungfrau;" also, for instruction in modern conversational German, Benedix's "Eigensinn."

There are besides, Biographical Sketches of each author contributing, Notes, explanatory and philological (after the text), Grammatical References to all leading grammars, as well as the editor's own, and an adequate Vocabulary.

**Worman's German Echo . . . . . . . . . 1 25**

Consists of exercises in colloquial style entirely in the German, with an adequate vocabulary, not only of words but of idioms. The object of the system developed in this work (and its companion volume in the French) is to break up the laborious and tedious habit of *translating the thoughts*, which is the student's most effectual bar to fluent conversation, and to lead him to *think in the language in which he speaks*. As the exercises illustrate scenes in actual life, a considerable knowledge of the manners and customs of the German people is also acquired from the use of this manual.

**Worman's German Copy-Books, 3 Numbers, each 15**

On the same plan as the most approved systems for English penmanship, with progressive copies.

# Worman's German Grammars.

## TESTIMONIALS.

*From Prof.* R. W. JONES, *Petersburg Female College, Va.*

From what I have seen of the work it is almost certain *I shall introduce it* into this institution.

*From Prof.* G. CAMPBELL, *University of Minnesota.*

*A valuable addition* to our school-books, and will find many friends, and do great good.

*From Prof.* O. H P. CORPREW, *Mary Military Inst., Md.*

I am better pleased with them than any I have ever taught. I have already ordered through our booksellers.

*From Prof.* R. S. KENDALL, *Vernon Academy, Conn.*

I at once put the Elementary Grammar into the hands of a class of beginners, and have used it *with great satisfaction.*

*From Prof.* D. E. HOLMES, *Berlin Academy, Wis.*

Worman's German works are *superior.* I shall use them hereafter in my German classes.

*From Prof.* MAGNUS BUCHHOLTZ, *Hiram College, Ohio.*

I have examined the Complete Grammar, and find it *excellent.* You may rely that it will be used here.

*From Prin.* THOS. W. TOBEY, *Paducah Female Seminary, Ky.*

The Complete German Grammar is worthy of an extensive circulation. It is *admirably adapted* to the class-room. I shall use it.

*From Prof.* ALEX. ROSENSPITZ, *Houston Academy, Texas.*

Bearer will take and pay for 3 dozen copies. Mr. Worman deserves the approbation and esteem of the teacher and the thanks of the student.

*From Prof.* G. MALMENE, *Augusta Seminary, Maine.*

The Complete Grammar cannot fail to *give great satisfaction* by the simplicity of its arrangement, and by its completeness.

*From Prin.* OVAL PIRKEY, *Christian University, Mo.*

*Just such a series* as is positively necessary. I do hope the author will succeed as well in the French, &c., as he has in the German.

*From Prof.* S. D. HILLMAN, *Dickinson College, Pa.*

The class have lately commenced, and my examination thus far warrants me in saying that I regard it as *the best* grammar for instruction in the German.

*From Prin.* SILAS LIVERMORE, *Bloomfield Seminary, Mo.*

I have found a classically and scientifically educated Prussian gentleman whom I propose to make German instructor. I have shown him both your German grammars. He has expressed *his approbation* of them generally.

*From Prof.* Z. TEST, *Howland School for Young Ladies, N. Y.*

I shall introduce the books. From a cursory examination I have no hesitation in pronouncing the Complete Grammar *a decided improvement* on the text-books at present in use in this country.

*From Prof.* LEWIS KISTLER, *Northwestern University, Ill.*

Having looked through the Complete Grammar with some care I must say that you have produced *a good book*; you may be awarded with this gratification—that your grammar promotes the facility of learning the German language, and of becoming acquainted with its rich literature.

*From Pres.* J. P. ROUS, *Stockwell Collegiate Inst., Ind.*

I supplied a class with the Elementary Grammar, and it gives *complete satisfaction.* The conversational and reading exercises are well calculated to illustrate the principles, and lead the student on an easy yet thorough course. I think the Complete Grammar equally attractive.

# THE CLASSICS.

## LATIN.

**Silber's Latin Course,** . . . . . . . . . . $1 25

The book contains an Epitome of Latin Grammar, followed by Reading Exercises, with explanatory Notes and copious References to the leading Latin Grammars, and also to the Epitome which precedes the work. Then follow a Latin-English Vocabulary and Exercises in Latin Prose Composition, being thus complete in itself, and a very suitable work to put in the hands of one about to study the language.

**Searing's Virgil's Æneid,** . . . . . . . . 2 25

It contains only the first six books of the Æneid. 2. A very carefully constructed Dictionary. 3. Sufficiently copious Notes. 4. Grammatical references to four leading Grammars. 5. Numerous Illustrations of the highest order, 6. A superb Map of the Mediterranean and adjacent countries. 7. Dr. S. H. Taylor's "Questions on the Æneid." 8. A Metrical Index, and an Essay on the Poetical Style. 9. A photographic *fac simile* of an early Latin M.S. 10. The text according to Jahn, but paragraphed according to Ladewig. 11. Superior mechanical execution.

**Blair's Latin Pronunciation,** . . . . . . . 1 00

An inquiry into the proper sounds of the Language during the Classical Period. By Prof. Blair, of Hampden Sidney College, Va.

**Andrews & Stoddard's Latin Grammar,** *1 50
**Andrews' Questions on the Grammar,** . *0 15
**Andrews' Latin Exercises,** . . . . . . . . *1 25
**Andrews' Viri Romæ,** . . . . . . . . . . *1 25
**Andrews' Sallust's Jugurthine War, &c.** *1 50
**Andrews' Eclogues & Georgics of Virgil,** *1 50
**Andrews' Cæsar's Commentaries,** . . . . *1 50
**Andrews' Ovid's Metamorphoses,** . . . *1 25

## GREEK.

**Crosby's Greek Grammar,** . . . . . . . . 2 00
**Crosby's Xenophon's Anabasis,** . . . . . 1 25

**Searing's Homer's Iliad,** . . . . . . . . . —

## MYTHOLOGY.

**Dwight's Grecian and Roman Mythology.**

School edition, $1 25; University edition, *3 00

A knowledge of the fables of antiquity, thus presented in a systematic form, is as indispensable to the student of general literature as to him who would peruse intelligently the classical authors. The mythological allusions so frequent in literature are readily understood with such a Key as this.

# SEARING'S VIRGIL.

## SPECIMEN FRAGMENTS OF LETTERS.

"I adopt it gladly."—PRIN. V. DABNEY, *Loudoun School, Va.*

"I like Searing's Virgil."—PROF. BRISTOL, *Ripon College, Wis.*

"Meets my desires very thoroughly."—PROF. CLARK, *Berea College, Ohio.*

"Superior to any other edition of Virgil."—PRES. HALL, *Macon College, Mo.*

"Shall adopt it at once."—PRIN. B. P. BAKER, *Searcy Female Institute, Ark.*

"Your Virgil is a *beauty*."—PROF. W. H. DE MOTTE, *Illinois Female College.*

"After use, I regard it the best."—PRIN. G. H. BARTON, *Rome Academy, N. Y.*

"We like it better every day."—PRIN. R. K. BUEHRLE, *Allentown Academy, Pa.*

"I am delighted with your Virgil."—PRIN. W. T. LEONARD, *Pierce Academy, Mass.*

"Stands well the test of class-room."—PRIN. F. A. CHASE, *Lyons Col. Inst., Iowa.*

"I do not see how it can be improved."—PRIN. N. F. D. BROWNE, *Charl. Hall, Md.*

"The most complete that I have seen."—PRIN. A. BROWN, *Columbus High School, Ohio.*

"Our Professor of Language very highly approves."—SUPT. J. G. JAMES, *Texas Military Institute.*

"It responds to a want long felt by teachers. It is beautiful and complete."—PROF. BROOKS, *University of Minnesota.*

"The ideal edition. We want a few more classics of the same sort."—PRIN. C. F. P. BANCROFT, *Lookout Mountain Institute, Tenn.*

"I certainly have never seen an edition so complete with important requisites for a student, nor with such fine text and general mechanical execution."—PRES. J. R. PARK, *University of Deseret, Utah.*

"It is charming both in its design and execution. And, on the whole, I think it is the best thing of the kind that I have seen."—PROF. J. DE F. RICHARDS, *Pres. pro tem. of University of Alabama.*

"In beauty of execution, in judicious notes, and in an adequate vocabulary, it merits all praise. I shall recommend its introduction."—PRES. J. K. PATTERSON, *Kentucky Agricultural and Mechanical College.*

"Containing a good vocabulary and judicious notes, it will enable the industrious student to acquire an accurate knowledge of the most interesting part of Virgil's works."—PROF. J. T. DUNKLIN, *East Alabama College.*

"It wants no element of completeness. It is by far the best classical text-book with which I am acquainted. The notes are just right. They help the student when he most needs help."—PRIN. C. A. BUNKER, *Caledonia Grammar School, Vt.*

"I have examined Searing's Virgil with interest, and find that it more nearly meets the wants of students than that of any other edition with which I am acquainted. I am able to introduce it to some extent at once."—PRIN. J. EASTER, *East Genesee Conference Seminary.*

"I have been wishing to get a sight of it, and it exceeds my expectations. It is a beautiful book in every respect, and bears evidence of careful and critical study. The engravings add instruction as well as interest to the work. I shall recommend it to my classes."—PRIN. CHAS. H. CHANDLER, *Glenwood Ladies' Seminary.*

"A. S. Barnes & Co. have published an edition of the first six books of Virgil's Æneid, which is superior to its predecessors in several respects. The publishers have done a good service to the cause of classical education, and the book deserves a large circulation."—PROF. GEORGE W. COLLORD, *Brooklyn Polytechnic, N. Y.*

"My attention was called to Searing's Virgil by the fact of its containing a vocabulary which would obviate the necessity of procuring a lexicon. But use in the class-room has impressed me most favorably with the accuracy and just proportion of its notes, and the general excellence of its grammatical suggestions. The general character of the book in its paper, its typography, and its engravings is highly commendable, and the fac-simile manuscript is a valuable feature. I take great pleasure in commending the book to all who do not wish a complete edition of Virgil. It suits our short school courses admirably."—HENRY L. BOLTWOOD, *Master of Princeton High School, Ill.*

# RECORDS.

**Cole's Self-Reporting Class-Book, . . . . *$0 50**

For saving the Teacher's labor in averaging. At each opening are a full set of Tables showing any scholar's standing at a glance and entirely obviating the necessity of computation.

**Tracy's School-Record, *0 75. Pocket edition, *0 65**

For keeping a simple but exact record of Attendance, Deportment, and Scholarship. The larger edition contains also a Calendar, an extensive list of Topics for Compositions and Colloquies, Themes for Short Lectures, Suggestions to Young Teachers, etc.

**Brooks' Teacher's Register, . . . . . . . . *1 00**

Presents at one view a record of Attendance, Recitations, and Deportment for the whole term.

**Carter's Record and Roll-Book, . . . . . *1 50**

This is the most complete and convenient Record offered to the public. Besides the usual spaces for General Scholarship, Deportment, Attendance, etc., for each name and day, there is a space in red lines enclosing six minor spaces in blue for recording Recitations.

**National School Diary, . . . . . Per dozen, *1 00**

A little book of blank forms for weekly report of the standing of each scholar, from teacher to parent. A great convenience.

# REWARDS.

**National School Currency, . . . . Per set,*$1 50**

A little box containing certificates in the form of Money. The most entertaining and stimulating system of school rewards. The scholar is paid for his merits and fined for his shortcomings. Of course the most faithful are the most successful in business. In this way the use and value of money and the method of keeping accounts are also taught. One box of Currency will supply a school of fifty pupils.

# TACTICS.

**The Boy Soldier, . . . . . . . . . . . . . . 75**

Complete Infantry Tactics for Schools, with illustrations, for the use of those who would introduce this pleasing relaxation from the confining duties of the desk.

# CHARTS.

**McKenzie's Elocutionary Chart,** . . . . . . $3 50

**Baade's Reading Case,** . . . . . . . . . . . *10 00

This remarkable piece of school-room furniture is a receptacle containing a number of primary cards. By an arrangement of slides on the front, one sentence at a time is shown to the class. Twenty-eight thousand transpositions may be made, affording a variety of progressive exercises which no other piece of apparatus offers. One of its best features is, that it is so exceedingly simple as not to get out of order, while it may be operated with one finger.

**Marcy's Eureka Tablet,** . . . . . . . . . . . *1 50

A new system for the Alphabet, by which it may be taught without fail in nine lessons.

**Scofield's School Tablets,** . . . . . . . . . *8 00

On Five Cards, exhibiting Ten Surfaces. These Tablets teach Orthography, Reading, Object-Lessons, Color, Form, etc.

**Watson's Phonetic Tablets,** . . . . . . . . *8 00

Four Cards, and Eight Surfaces; teaching Pronunciation and Elocution phonetically for class exercises.

**Page's Normal Chart,** . . . . . . . . . . . . *3 75

The whole science of Elementary Sounds tabulated. By the author of Page's Theory and Practice of Teaching.

**Clark's Grammatical Chart,** . . . . . . . . . *3 75

Exhibits the whole Science of Language in one comprehensive diagram.

**Davies' Mathematical Chart,** . . . . . . . . *75

Mathematics made simple to the eye.

**Monteith's Reference Maps** (School Series), . . *20 00

Eight Numbers. Mounted on Rollers. Names all laid down in small type, so that to the pupil at a short distance they are Outline Maps, while they serve as *their own key* to the teacher.

**Willard's Chronographers,** . . . . . Each, *2 00

Historical. Four Numbers. Ancient Chronographer; English Chronographer; American Chronographer; Temple of Time (general). Dates and Events represented to the eye.

# APPARATUS.

**Harrington's Geometrical Blocks,** . . . . *$10 00

These patented blocks are *hinged*, so that each form can be dissected.

**Harrington's Fractional Blocks,** . . . . . . *8 00

**Steele's Chemical Apparatus,** . . *20 00

**Steele's Philosophical Apparatus,** (see p.28) *125 00

**Steele's Geological Cabinet,** (see p.28) . . . *40 00

**Wood's Botanical Apparatus,** (see p.30) . . *8 00

**Bock's Physiological Apparatus,** . . . . 175 00

# MUSIC.

**Jepson's Music Readers.** 3 vols. . . . Each, 75 cts.

These are not books from which children simply learn songs, parrot-like, but teach the subject progressively—the scholar learning to read music by methods similar to those employed in teaching him to read printed language. Any teacher, however ignorant of music, provided he can, upon trial, simply sound the scale, may teach it without assistance, and will end by being a good singer himself. The "Elementary Music Reader," or first volume, heretofore issued by another publisher, has attained results in the State of Connecticut, where only it has been known, entirely unprecedented in the history of teaching music. The two companion volumes carry the same method into the higher grades.

**Nash & Bristow's Cantara.** No. 1, $1.15; No. 2, $1.40

The first volume is a complete musical text-book for schools of every grade. No. 2 is a choice selection of Solos and Part Songs. The authors are Directors of Music in the public schools of New York City, in which these books are the standard of instruction.

| | |
|---|---|
| **Curtis' Little Singer,** . . . . . . . . . . . | $0 60 |
| **Curtis' School Vocalist,** . . . . . . . . . . | 1 00 |
| **Kingsley's School-Room Choir,** . . . . . . . | 60 |
| **Kingsley's Young Ladies' Harp,** . . . . . . | 1 00 |
| **Hager's Echo,** . . . . . . . . . . . . . . | 75 |
| **Perkins' Sabbath Carols** (for Sunday-Schools), . . | 35 |
| **Phillips' Singing Annual** do. do. . . | 25 |

# DEVOTION.

**Brooks' School Manual of Devotion,** . . . $0 75

This volume contains daily devotional exercises, consisting of a hymn, selections of Scripture for alternate reading by teacher and pupils, and a prayer. Its value for opening and closing school is apparent.

**Brooks' School Harmonist,** . . . . . . . . *75

Contains appropriate *tunes* for each hymn in the "Manual of Devotion" described above.

THE

# TEACHERS' LIBRARY.

**Object Lessons—Welch** . . . . . . . . . . .*$1 00

This is a complete exposition of the popular modern system of "object-teaching," for teachers of primary classes.

**Theory and Practice of Teaching—Page** . . *1 50

This volume has, without doubt, been read by two hundred thousand teachers, and its popularity remains undiminished—large editions being exhausted yearly. It was the pioneer, as it is now the patriarch of professional works for teachers.

**The Graded School—Wells** . . . . . . . . . *1 25

The proper way to organize graded schools is here illustrated. The author has availed himself of the best elements of the several systems prevalent in Boston, New York, Philadelphia, Cincinnati, St. Louis, and other cities.

**The Normal—Holbrook** . . . . . . . . . . *1 50

Carries a working school on its visit to teachers, showing the most approved methods of teaching all the common branches, including the technicalities, explanations, demonstrations, and definitions introductory and peculiar to each branch.

**The Teachers' Institute—Fowle** . . . . . . . *1 25

This is a volume of suggestions inspired by the author's experience at institutes, in the instruction of young teachers. A thousand points of interest to this class are most satisfactorily dealt with.

**Schools and Schoolmasters—Dickens** . . . *1 25

Appropriate selections from the writings of the great novelist.

**The Metric System—Davies** . . . . . . . . *1 50

Considered with reference to its general introduction, and embracing the views of John Quincy Adams and Sir John Herschel.

**The Student—The Educator—Phelps** . each,*1 50

**The Discipline of Life—Phelps** . . . . . . . *1 75

The authoress of these works is one of the most distinguished writers on education; and they cannot fail to prove a valuable addition to the School and Teachers' Libraries, being in a high degree both interesting and instructive.

**A Scientific Basis of Education—Hecker** . . *2 50

Adaptation of study and classification by temperaments.

**American Education—Mansfield . . . . . .$1 50**

A treatise on the principles and elements of education, as practiced in this country, with ideas towards distinctive republican and Christian education.

**American Institutions—De Tocqueville . .*1 50**

A valuable index to the genius of our Government.

**Universal Education—Mayhew . . . . . .*1 75**

The subject is approached with the clear, keen perception of one who has observed its necessity, and realized its feasibility and expediency alike. The redeeming and elevating power of improved common schools constitutes the inspiration of the volume.

**Higher Christian Education—Dwight . . .*1 50**

A treatise on the principles and spirit, the modes, directions, and results of all true teaching; showing that right education should appeal to every element of enthusiasm in the teacher' ature.

**Oral Training Lessons--Barnard . . . . *1 00**

The object of this very useful work is to furnish material for instructors to impart orally to their classes, in branches not usually taught in common schools, embracing all departments of Natural Science and much general knowledge.

**Lectures on Natural History—Chadbourne * 75**

Affording many themes for oral instruction in this interesting science—specially in schools where it is not pursued as a class exercise.

**Outlines of Mathematical Science—Davies *1 00**

A manual suggesting the best methods of presenting mathematical instruction on the part of the teacher, with that comprehensive view of the whole which is necessary to the intelligent treatment of a part, in science.

**Nature & Utility of Mathematics—Davies . .*1 50**

An elaborate and lucid exposition of the principles which lie at the foundation of pure mathematics, with a highly ingenious application of their results to the development of the essential idea of the different branches of the science.

**Mathematical Dictionary—Davies & Peck .*5 00**

This cyclopædia of mathematical science defines with completeness, precision, and accuracy, every technical term, thus constituting a popular treatise on each branch, and a general view of the whole subject.

**School Architecture—Barnard . . . . . .*2 25**

Attention is here called to the vital connection between a good schoolhouse and a good school, with plans and specifications for securing the former in the most economical and satisfactory manner.

## Liberal Education of Women—Orton . . *$1 50

Treats of "the demand and the method;" being a compilation of the best and most advanced thought on this subject, by the leading writers and educators in England and America. Edited by a Professor in Vassar College.

## Education Abroad—Northrop . . . . . . . *1 50

A thorough discussion of the advantages and disadvantages of sending American children to Europe to be educated; also, Papers on Legal Prevention of Illiteracy, Study and Health, Labor as an Educator, and other kindred subjects. By the Hon. Secretary of Education for Connecticut.

## The Teacher and the Parent—Northend . . *1 50

A treatise upon common-school education, designed to lead teachers to view their calling in its true light, and to stimulate them to fidelity.

## The Teachers' Assistant—Northend . . . . *1 50

A natural continuation of the author's previous work, more directly calculated for daily use in the administration of school discipline and instruction.

## School Government—Jewell . . . . . . . . *1 50

Full of advanced ideas on the subject which its title indicates. The criticisms upon current theories of punishment and schemes of administration have excited general attention and comment.

## Grammatical Diagrams—Jewell . . . . . *1 00

The diagram system of teaching grammar explained, defended, and improved. The curious in literature, the searcher for truth, those interested in new inventions, as well as the disciples of Prof. Clark, who would see their favorite theory fairly treated, all want this book. There are many who would like to be made familiar with this system before risking its use in a class. The opportunity is here afforded.

## The Complete Examiner—Stone . . . . . . . *1 25

Consists of a series of questions on every English branch of school and academic instruction, with reference to a given page or article of leading text-books where the answer may be found in full. Prepared to aid teachers in securing certificates, pupils in preparing for promotion, and teachers in selecting review questions.

## School Amusements—Root . . . . . . . . . . *1 50

To assist teachers in making the school interesting, with hints upon the management of the school-room. Rules for military and gymnastic exercises are included. Illustrated by diagrams.

## Institute Lectures—Bates . . . . . . . . . . *1 50

These lectures, originally delivered before institutes, are based upon various topics in the departments of mental and moral culture. The volume is calculated to prepare the will, awaken the inquiry, and stimulate the thought of the zealous teacher.

## Method of Teachers' Institutes—Bates . . . *75

Sets forth the best method of conducting institutes, with a detailed account of the object, organization, plan of instruction, and true theory of education on which such instruction should be based.

## History and Progress of Education . . . . *1 50

The systems of education prevailing in all nations and ages, the gradual advance to the present time, and the bearing of the past upon the present in this regard, are worthy of the careful investigation of all concerned in education.

# THE SCHOOL LIBRARY.

The two elements of instruction and entertainment were never more happily combined than in this collection of standard books. Children and adults alike will here find ample food for the mind, of the sort that is easily *digested*, while not degenerating to the level of modern romance.

## LIBRARY OF LITERATURE.

**Milton's Paradise Lost.** Boyd's Illustrated Ed., $1 60

**Young's Night Thoughts** . . . . do. . . 1 60

**Cowper's Task, Table Talk, &c.** . do. . . 1 60

**Thomson's Seasons** . . . . . . . do. . . 1 60

**Pollok's Course of Time** . . . . do. . . 1 60

These works, models of the best and purest literature, are beautifully illustrated, and notes explain all doubtful meanings.

**Lord Bacon's Essays** (Boyd's Edition) . . . 1 60

Another grand English classic, affording the highest example of purity in language and style.

**The Iliad of Homer.** Translated by POPE. . . 80

Those who are unable to read this greatest of ancient writers in the original, should not fail to avail themselves of this metrical version.

**Compendium of Eng. Literature—Cleveland,** 2 50

**English Literature of XIXth Century** do. 2 50

**Compendium of American Literature** do. 2 50

Nearly one hundred and fifty thousand volumes of Prof. CLEVELAND's inimitable compendiums have been sold. Taken together they present a complete view of literature. To the man who can afford but a few books these will supply the place of an extensive library. From commendations of the very highest authorities the following extracts will give some idea of the enthusiasm with which the works are regarded by scholars:

With the Bible and your volumes one might leave libraries without very painful regret.—The work cannot be found from which in the same limits so much interesting and valuable information may be obtained.—Good taste, fine scholarship, familiar acquaintance with literature, unwearied industry, tact acquired by practice, an interest in the culture of the young, and regard for truth, purity, philanthropy and religion are united in Mr. Cleveland.—A judgment clear and impartial, a taste at once delicate and severe.—The biographies are just and discriminating.—An admirable bird's-eye view.—Acquaints the reader with the characteristic method, tone, and quality of each writer.—Succinct, carefully written, and wonderfully comprehensive in detail, etc., etc.

**Milton's Poetical Works**—CLEVELAND . . . 2 50

This is the very best edition of the great Poet. It includes a life of the author, notes, dissertations on each poem, a faultless text, and is *the only* edition of Milton with a complete verbal Index.

## LIBRARY OF HISTORY.

**History of Europe—Alison** . . . . . . . $2 50

A reliable and standard work, which covers with clear, connected, and complete narrative, the eventful occurrences transpiring from A. D. 1789 to 1815, being mainly a history of the career of Napoleon Bonaparte.

**History of England—Berard** . . . . . . . . 1 75

Combining a history of the social life of the English people with that of the civil and military transactions of the realm.

**History of Rome—Ricord** . . . . . . . . . 1 60

Possesses all the charm of an attractive romance. The fables with which this history abounds are introduced in such away as not to deceive the inexperienced reader, while adding vastly to the interest of the work and affording a pleasing index to the genius of the Roman people. Illustrated.

**The Republic of America—Willard** . . . 2 25

**Universal History in Perspective—Willard** 2 25

From these two comparatively brief treatises the intelligent mind may obtain a comprehensive knowledge of the history of the world in both hemispheres. Mrs. Willard's reputation as an historian is wide as the land. Illustrated.

**Ecclesiastical History—Marsh** . . . . . . 2 00

A history of the Church in all ages, with a comprehensive review of all forms of religion from the creation of the world. No other source affords, in the same compass, the information here conveyed.

**History of the Ancient Hebrews—Mills** . . 1 75

The record of "God's people" from the call of Abraham to the destruction of Jerusalem; gathered from sources sacred and profane.

**The Mexican War—Mansfield** . . . . . . . 1 50

A history of its origin, and a detailed account of its victories; with official despatches, the treaty of peace, and valuable tables. Illustrated.

**Early History of Michigan—Sheldon** . . . 2 50

A work of value and deep interest to the people of the West. Compiled under the supervision of Hon. Lewis Cass. Portraits.

**History of Texas—Baker** . . . . . . . . . 1 25

A pithy and interesting resumé. Copiously illustrated. The State constitution and extracts from the speeches and writings of eminent Texans are appended.

## LIBRARY OF BIOGRAPHY.

**Life of Dr. Sam. Johnson—Boswell . . .$2 25**

This work has been before the public for seventy years, with increasing approbation. Boswell is known as "the prince of biographers."

**Henry Clay's Life and Speeches—Mallory 2 vols. . . . . . . . . . . . . . . . . 4 50**

This great American statesman commands the admiration, and his character and deeds solicit the study of every patriot.

**Life & Services of General Scott—Mansfield 1 75**

The hero of the Mexican war, who was for many years the most prominent figure in American military circles, should not be forgotten in the whirl of more recent events than those by which he signalized himself. Illustrated.

**Garibaldi's Autobiography . . . . . . . . 1 50**

The Italian patriot's record of his own life, translated and edited by his friend and admirer. A thrilling narrative of a romantic career. With portrait.

**Lives of the Signers—Dwight . . . . . . . 1 50**

The memory of the noble men who declared our country free at the peril of their own "lives, fortunes, and sacred honor," should be embalmed in every American's heart.

**Life of Sir Joshua Reynolds—Cunningham 1 50**

A candid, truthful, and appreciative memoir of the great painter, with a compilation of his discourses. The volume is a text-book for artists, as well as those who would acquire the rudiments of art. With a portrait.

**Prison Life . . . . . . . . . . . . . . . 75**

Interesting biographies of celebrated prisoners and martyrs, designed especially for the instruction and cultivation of youth.

## LIBRARY OF NATURAL SCIENCE.

**The Treasury of Knowledge** . . . . . . $1 25

A cyclopædia of ten thousand common things, embracing the widest range of subject-matter. Illustrated.

**Ganot's Popular Physics** . . . . . . . . . 1 75

The elements of natural philosophy for both student and the general reader. The original work is celebrated for the magnificent character of its illustrations, all of which are literally reproduced here.

**Principles of Chemistry—Porter** . . . . . . 2 00

A work which commends itself to the amateur in science by its extreme simplicity, and careful avoidance of unnecessary detail. Illustrated.

**Class-Book of Botany—Wood** . . . . . . 3 50

Indispensable as a work of reference. Illustrated.

**The Laws of Health—Jarvis** . . . . . . . 1 65

This is not an abstract *anatomy*, but all its teachings are directed to the best methods of preserving health, as inculcated by an intelligent knowledge of the structure and needs of the human body. Illustrated.

**Vegetable & Animal Physiology—Hamilton** 1 25

An exhaustive analysis of the conditions of life in all animate nature. Illustrated.

**Elements of Zoology—Chambers** . . . . . 1 50

A complete view of the animal kingdom as a portion of external nature. Illustrated.

**Astronography—Willard** . . . . . . . . . 1 00

The elements of astronomy in a compact and readable form. Illustrated.

**Elements of Geology—Page** . . . . . . . . 1 25

The subject presented in its two aspects of interesting and important. Illustrated.

**Lectures on Natural History—Chadbourne** 75

The subject is here considered in its relations to intellect, taste, health, and religion.

## LIBRARY OF TRAVEL.

### Life in the Sandwich Islands—Cheever . .$1 50

The "heart of the Pacific, as it was and is," shows most vividly the contrast between the depth of degradation and barbarism, and the light and liberty of civilization, so rapidly realized in these islands under the humanizing influence of the Christian religion. Illustrated.

### The Republic of Liberia—Stockwell, . . . 1 25

This volume treats of the geography, climate, soil, and productions of this interesting country on the coast of Africa, with a History of its early settlement. Our colored citizens especially, from whom the founders of the new State went forth, should read Mr. Stockwell's account of it. It is so arranged as to be available for a School Reader, and in colored schools is peculiarly appropriate as an instrument of education for the young. Liberia is likely to bear an important part in the future of their race.

### Ancient Monasteries of the East—Curzon . 1 50

The exploration of these ancient seats of learning has thrown much light upon the researches of the historian, the philologist, and the theologian, as well as the general student of antiquity. Illustrated.

### Discoveries in Babylon & Nineveh—Layard 1 75

Valuable alike for the information imparted with regard to these most interesting ruins, and the pleasant adventures and observations of the author in regions that to most men seem like Fairyland. Illustrated.

### A Run Through Europe—Benedict, . . . . 2 00

A work replete with instruction and interest.

### St. Petersburgh—Jermann . . . . . . . . 1 00

Americans are less familiar with the history and social customs of the Russian people than those of any other modern civilized nation. Opportunities such as this book affords are not, therefore, to be neglected.

### The Polar Regions—Osborn . . . . . . . . 1 25

A thrilling and intensely interesting narrative of one of the famous expeditions in search of Sir John Franklin—unsuccessful in its main object, but adding many facts to the repertoire of science.

### Thirteen Months in the Confederate Army 75

The author, a northern man conscripted into the Confederate service, and rising from the ranks by soldierly conduct to positions of responsibility, had remarkable opportunities for the acquisition of facts respecting the conduct of the Southern armies, and the policy and deeds of their leaders. He participated in many engagements, and his book is one of the most exciting narratives of adventure ever published. Mr. Stevenson takes no ground as a partizan, but views the whole subject as with the eye of a neutral—only interested in subserving the ends of history by the contribution of impartial facts. Illustrated.

## LIBRARY OF REFERENCE.

**Home Cyclopædia of Literature & Fine Arts** $3 00

A complete index to all terms employed in belles lettres, philosophy, theology, law, mythology, painting, music, sculpture, architecture, and all kindred arts.

**The Rhyming Dictionary—Walker** . . . . 1 25

A serviceable manual to composers, being a complete index of allowable rhymes.

**The Topical Lexicon—Williams** . . . . . . 1 75

The useful terms of the English language *classified by subjects* and arranged according to their affinities of meaning, with etymologies, definitions and illustrations. A very entertaining and instructive work.

**Mathematical Dictionary—Davies & Peck** . 5 00

A thorough compendium of the science, with illustrations and definitions.

## RELIGIOUS LIBRARY.

**The Service of Song—Stacy** . . . . . . . . $1 50

A treatise on Singing, in public and private devotion. Its history, office, and importance considered.

**True Success in Life—Palmer** . . . . . . . $1 50

Earnest words for the young who are just about to meet the responsibilities and temptations of mature life.

**"Remember Me"—Palmer** . . . . . . . . 1 50

Preparation for the Holy Communion.

**Chrysostom, or the Mouth of Gold—Johnson** 1 00

An entertaining dramatic sketch, by Rev. Edwin Johnson, illustrating the life and times of St. Chrysostom.

**The Memorial Pulpit—Robinson.** 2 vols., each 1 50

A series of wide-awake sermons by the popular pastor of the Memorial Presbyterian Church, New York.

**Responsive Worship—Budington** . . . . . . 60

An argument in favor of alternate Scripture reading by Pastor and Congregation.

**Lady Willoughby** . . . . . . . . . . . . . 1 00

The diary of a wife and mother. An historical romance of the seventeenth century. At once beautiful and pathetic, entertaining and instructive.

**Favorite Hymns Restored—Gage** . . . . . 1 25

Most of the standard hymns have undergone modification or abridgment by compilers, but this volume contains them exactly as written by the authors.

**Poets' Gift of Consolation** . . . . . . . . . 1 50

A beautiful selection of poems referring to the death of children.

# VALUABLE LIBRARY BOOKS.

**The Political Manual—Mansfield . . . . . $1 25**

Every American youth should be familiar with the principles of the government under which he lives, especially as the policy of this country will one day call upon him to participate in it, at least to the extent of his ballot.

**American Institutions—De Tocqueville . . 1 50**

**Democracy in America—De Tocqueville . . 2 50**

The views of this distinguished foreigner on the genius of our political institutions are of unquestionable value, as proceeding from a standpoint whence we seldom have an opportunity to hear.

**Constitutions of the United States . . . . 2 25**

Contains the Constitution of the General Government, and of the several State Governments, the Declaration of Independence, and other important documents relating to American history. Indispensable as a work of reference.

**Public Economy of the United States . . . 2 25**

A full discussion of the relations of the United States with other nations, especially the feasibility of a free-trade policy.

**Grecian and Roman Mythology—Dwight . 3 00**

The presentation, in a systematic form, of the Fables of Antiquity, affords most entertaining reading, and is valuable to all as an index to the mythological allusions so frequent in literature, as well as to students of the classics who would peruse intelligently the classical authors. Illustrated.

**General View of the Fine Arts—Huntington 1 75**

The preparation of this work was suggested by the interested inquiries of a group of young people concerning the productions and styles of the great masters of art, whose names only were familiar. This statement is sufficient index of its character.

**The Poets of Connecticut—Everest . . . . 1 75**

With the biographical sketches, this volume forms a complete history of the poetical literature of the State.

**The Son of a Genius—Hofland . . . . . . 75**

A juvenile classic which never wears out, and finds many interested readers in every generation of youth.

**Sunny Hours of Childhood . . . . . . . . 75**

Interesting and moral stories for children.

**Morals for the Young—Willard . . . . . 75**

A series of moral stories, by one of the most experienced of American educators. Illustrated.

**Improvement of the Mind—Isaac Watts . . 50**

A classical standard. No young person should grow up without having perused it

# PUBLIC WORSHIP.

**Songs for the Sanctuary,** . . . . . . . . . $2 50

By Rev. C. S. Robinson. 1344 Hymns, with Tunes. The most successful modern hymn and tune-book, for congregational singing. More than 200,000 copies have been sold. Separate editions for Presbyterian, Congregational, and Baptist Churches. Editions without Tunes, $1.75; in large type, $2.50. Abridged edition ("Songs for Christian Worship"), 859 Hymns, with Tunes, $1.50. Chapel edition. 607 Hymns, with Tunes, $1.40.

**International Singing Annual,** . . . . . . 25

**Metrical Tune Book,** . . . . . . . . . . . . 1 00

To be used with any hymn-book. By Philip Phillips.

**Baptist Praise Book,** . . . . . . . . . . . . 2 50

By Rev. Drs. Fuller, Levy, Phelps, Fish, Armitage, Winkler, Evarts, Lorimer and Manly, and J. P. Holbrook, Esq. 1311 Hymns, with Tunes. Edition without Tunes, $1.75. Chapel edition, 550 Hymns, with Tunes, $1.25.

**Plymouth Collection,** . . . . . . . . . . . . 2 50

(Congregational.) By Rev. Henry Ward Beecher. 1374 Hymns, with Tunes. Separate edition for Baptist Churches. Editions without Tunes, $1.25 and $1.75.

**Hymns of the Church,** . . . . . . . . . . . 2 75

(Undenominational.) By Rev. Drs. Thompson, Vermilye, and Eddy. 1007 Hymns, with Tunes. The use of this book is required in all congregations of the Reformed Church in America. Edition without Tunes, $1.75. Chapel edition ("Hymns of Prayer and Praise"), 320 Hymns, with Tunes, 75 cts.

**Episcopal Common Praise,** . . . . . . . . . 2 75

The Service set to appropriate Music, with Tunes for all the Hymns in the Book of Common Prayer.

**Hymnal, with Tunes,** . . . . . . . . . . . 1 25

(Episcopal.) By Hall & Whiteley. The new Hymnal, set to Music. Edition with Chants, $1.50. Edition of Hymns only ("Companion" Hymnal), 60 cts.

**Quartet and Chorus Choir,** . . . . . . . . . 3 00

By J. P. Holbrook. Containing Music for the Unadapted Hymns in Songs for the Sanctuary.

**Christian Melodies.** By Geo. B. Cheever. Hymns and Tunes. 1 00

**Mount Zion Collection.** By T. E. Perkins. For the Choir. 1 25

**Selah.** By Thos. Hastings. For the Choir. . . . . . . . . 1 25

---

**Public Worship** (Partly Responsive) . . . . $1 00

Containing complete services (not Episcopal) for five Sabbaths; for use in schools, public institutions, summer resorts, churches without a settled pastor; in short, wherever Christians desire to worship—no clergyman being present.

**The Union Prayer Book,** . . . . . . . . . 2 50

A Manual for Public and Private Worship. With those features which are objectionable to other denominations of Christians than Episcopal eliminated or modified. Contains a Service for Sunday Schools and Family Prayers.

**The Psalter,** . . . . . . . . 16mo, 60 cts.; 8vo, 90

Selections from the Psalms, for responsive reading.

# FURNITURE.

(SUPPLIED BY THE NATIONAL SCHOOL FURNITURE CO.)

## PEARD'S PATENT FOLDING DESK AND SETTEE.

This great improvement for the school-room has come already into such astonishing demand as to tax the utmost resources of the company's two factories to supply it. By a simple movement the desk-lid is folded away over the back of the settee attached in front, making a false back, and at once converting the school-room into a lecture or assembly-room. When the seat also is folded, the whole occupies *only ten inches of space*, leaving room for gymnastic exercises, marching, etc., or for the janitor to clean the room effectively.

## NATIONAL STUDY DESK AND SETTEE.

When not in use for writing, the desk-lid slides back vertically into a chamber, leaving in front an "easel," with clamps, upon which the student places his book and studies in an erect posture. As a folding-desk this offers many of the same advantages as the "Peard."

## THE GEM DESK AND SETTEE.

Fixed top, and folding seat. This is the *neatest* pattern of the Standard School Desk, and the *strongest* in use.

## THE ECONOMIC DESK AND SETTEE.

This is the *cheapest* good desk, with stationary lid and folding seat.

All descriptions of

**HIGH SCHOOL DESKS,**
**TEACHERS' DESKS,**
**BLACKBOARDS,**
**CHAIRS,**
**SCHOOL SETTEES,**
**CHURCH SETTEES,**
**PEW ENDS,**
**LECTERNS, Etc.**

Also,

## TAYLOR'S PATENT

# CLASS AND LECTURE CHAIR.

The difficulty of reconciling furniture appropriate for the Lecture-room or Church with that convenient for the Sunday-school is an old one. This article effectually remedies it. It consists simply of a plan by which chairs of a somewhat peculiar shape are connected with a coupling. The rows of chairs thus adjusted may at pleasure and with ease be spread out straight in one line, forming pews or benches; or they may be bent in an instant into a semi-circular form to accomodate classes of any size to receive instruction from teachers seated in their midst.

For further particulars, consult catalogues of the National School Furniture Co. and the Taylor Patent Chair Co., which may be obtained of A. S. Barnes & Co.

# The Peabody Correspondence.

NEW YORK, April 29, 1867.

TO THE BOARD OF TRUSTEES OF THE PEABODY EDUCATIONAL FUND:

GENTLEMEN—Having been for many years intimately connected with the educational interests of the South, we are desirous of expressing our appreciation of the noble charity which you represent. The Peabody Fund, to encourage and aid common schools in these war-desolated States, cannot fail of accomplishing a great and good work, the beneficent results of which, as they will be exhibited in the future, not only of the stricken population of the South, but of the nation at large, seem almost incalculable.

It is probable that the use of meritorious text-books will prove a most effective agency toward the thorough accomplishment of Mr. Peabody's benevolent design. As we publish many which are considered such, we have selected from our list some of the most valuable, and ask the privilege of placing them in your hands for gratuitous distribution in connection with the fund of which you have charge, among the teachers and in the schools of the destitute South.

Observing that the training of teachers (through the agency of Normal Schools and otherwise) is to be a prominent feature of your undertaking, we offer you for this purpose 5,000 volumes of the "Teachers' Library,"—a series of professional works designed for the efficient self-education of those who are in their turn to teach others—as follows:—

500 Page's Theory and Practice of Teaching.
500 Welch's Manual of Object-Lessons.
500 Davies' Outlines of Mathematical Science.
250 Holbrook's Normal Methods of Teaching.
250 Wells on Graded Schools.
250 Jewell on School Government.
250 Fowle's Teachers' Institute.
250 Bates' Method of Teachers' Institutes
250 De Tocqueville's American Instit'ns
250 Dwight's Higher Christian Educat'n.
250 History of Education.
250 Mansfield on American Education.
250 Mayhew on Universal Education.
250 Northend's Teachers' Assistant.
250 Northend's Teacher and Parent.
250 Root on School Amusements.
250 Stone's Teachers' Examiner.

In addition to these we also ask that you will accept 25,000 volumes of school-books for intermediate classes, embracing—

5,000 The National Second Reader.
5,000 Davies' Written Arithmetic.
5,000 Monteith's Second Book in Geography.
3,000 Monteith's United States History.
5,000 Beers' Penmanship.
500 First Book of Science.
500 Jarvis' Physiology and Health.
500 Peck's Ganot's Natural Philosophy.
500 Smith & Martin's Book-keeping.

Should your Board consent to undertake the distribution of these volumes, we shall hold ourselves in readiness to pack and ship the same in such quantities and to such points as you may designate.

We further propose that, should you find it advisable to use a greater quantity of our publications in the prosecution of your plans, we will donate, for the benefit of this cause, *twenty-five per cent.* of the usual wholesale price of the books needed.

Hoping that our request will meet with your approval, and that we may have the pleasure of contributing in this way to wants with which we deeply sympathize, we are, gentlemen, very respectfully yours, A. S. BARNES & CO.

BOSTON, *May* 7, 1867.

MESSRS. A. S. BARNES & CO., PUBLISHERS, NEW YORK:

GENTLEMEN—Your communication of the 29th ult., addressed to the Trustees of the Peabody Education Fund, has been handed to me by our general agent, the Rev. Dr. Sears. I shall take the greatest pleasure in laying it before the board at their earliest meeting. I am unwilling, however, to postpone its acknowledgment so long, and hasten to assure you of the high value which I place upon your gift. Five thousand volumes of your "Teachers' Library," and twenty-five thousand volumes of "School-books for intermediate classes," make up a most munificent contribution to the cause of Southern education in which we are engaged. Dr. Sears is well acquainted with the books you have so generously offered us, and unites with me in the highest appreciation of the gift. You will be glad to know, too, that your letter reached us in season to be communicated to Mr. Peabody, before he embarked for England on the 1st inst., and that he expressed the greatest gratification and gratitude on hearing what you had offered.

Believe me, gentlemen, with the highest respect and regard, your obliged and obedient servant, ROBT. C. WINTHROP, Chairman.

## GENERAL INDEX TO
# A. S. BARNES & CO.'S DESCRIPTIVE CATALOGUE

www.ingramcontent.com/pod-product-compliance
Lightning Source LLC
LaVergne TN
LVHW021251110826
845151LV00002BA/391

* 9 7 8 1 4 2 5 5 3 8 8 5 9 *